MARCO POLO

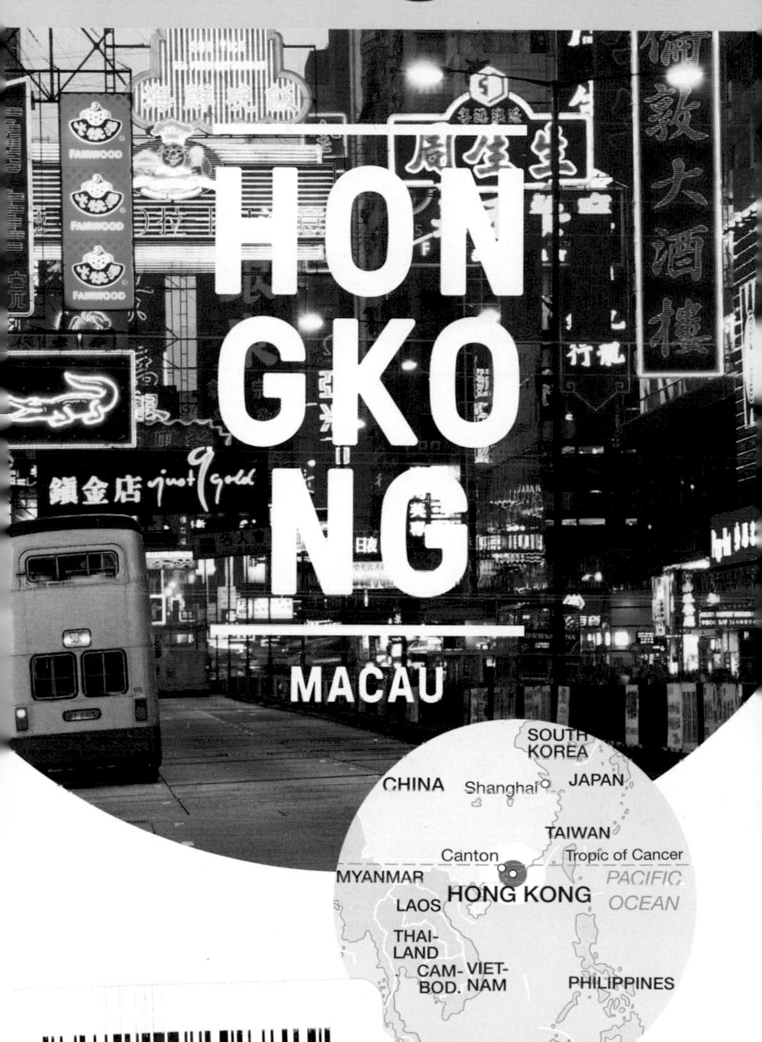

SOUTH KOREA
CHINA
Shanghai
JAPAN
TAIWAN
Canton
Tropic of Cancer
MYANMAR
HONG KONG
PACIFIC OCEAN
LAOS
THAI-LAND
CAM-BOD.
VIET-NAM
PHILIPPINES
MALAYSIA
BRUNEI

www.marco-polo.com

FREE!
THE
TOURING APP
shows you the way...
including routes and offline maps!

GET MORE OUT OF YOUR MARCO POLO GUIDE

IT'S AS SIMPLE AS THIS

1 go.marco-polo.com/hon

2 download and discover

GO!

WORKS OFFLINE!

SYMBOLS

- INSIDER TIP — Insider Tip
- ★ — Highlight
- ●●●● — Best of...
- Scenic view
- Responsible travel: for ecological or fair trade aspects
- (*) Telephone numbers that are not toll-free

PRICE CATEGORIES HOTELS

Expensive	over 1855 HK$
Moderate	1200–1855 HK$
Budget	under 1200 HK$

Prices are for a double room per night, not including breakfast

PRICE CATEGORIES RESTAURANTS

Expensive	over 370 HK$
Moderate	200–370 HK$
Budget	under 200 HK$

Prices are for one meal per person, not including drinks and expensive specialities

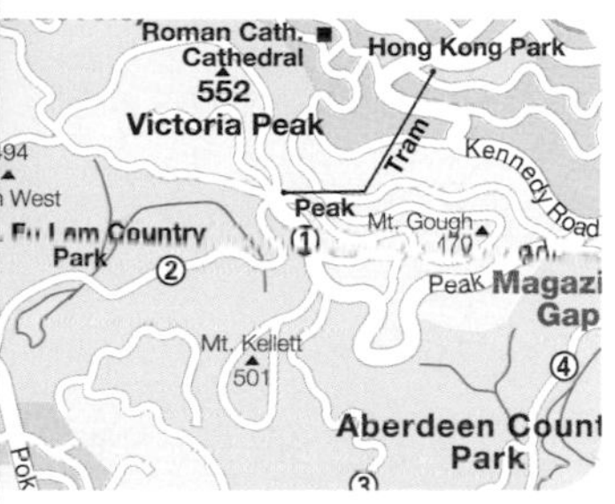

DID YOU KNOW?

MAPS IN THE GUIDEBOOK

(132 A1) Page numbers and coordinates refer to the street atlas
(0) Site/address located off the map
Coordinates are also given for places that are not marked on the street atlas
Map of surrounding area on p. 142/143, maps of Macau, Taipa/Coloane on p. 148–151
(U A1) General map on the back cover

(A–B 2–3) refers to the removable pull-out map
(a–b 2–3) refers to the additional map on the pull-out map

INSIDE FRONT COVER:
The best Highlights

INSIDE BACK COVER:
Hong Kong public transport map

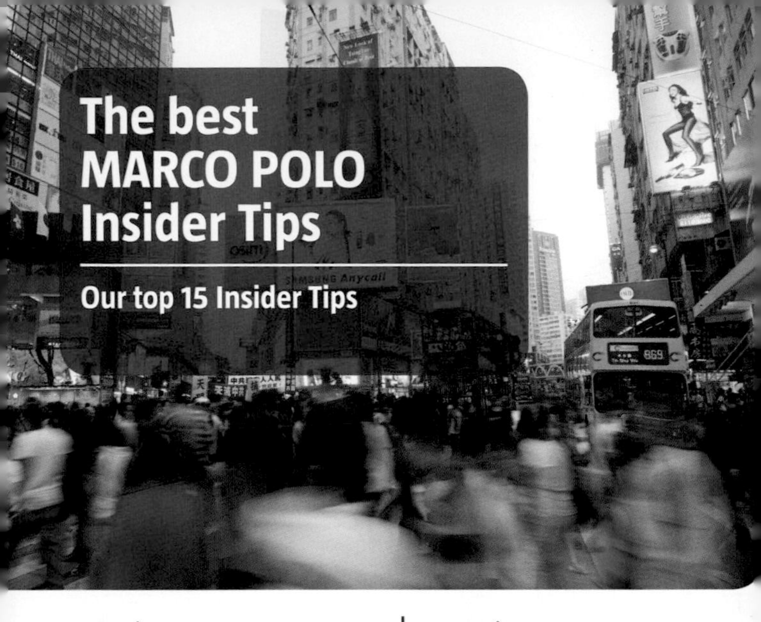

The best MARCO POLO Insider Tips

Our top 15 Insider Tips

INSIDER TIP Full, loud, tasty, fun – yam cha!
Hong Kong's joie-de-vivre is best felt over a dim sum lunch in a teahouse on Sunday – the epitome of the Hong Kong experience → **p. 55**

INSIDER TIP Enter the fray!
Shopping, dining, watching a film: the *Causeway Bay* district with its megastores, restaurants and cinemas draws in the crowds after work (photo above) → **p. 76**

INSIDER TIP Entertaining the gods
The whole island of Cheung Chau celebrates the *Bun Festival* in honour of its patron saint, the Emperor of the North. Visitors will find all sorts of things to marvel at → **p. 114**

INSIDER TIP A day at the beach
For example on one of the beaches supervised by lifeguards on car-free Lamma Island. And why not stay overnight at *Concerto Inn* right on the seafront? → **p. 87**

INSIDER TIP City lights
The highlight of any stay in Hong Kong: the panorama of the city and harbour from Peak Path is breathtaking at any time but it becomes absolutely overwhelming in the *twilight hours* → **p. 33**

INSIDER TIP Trial membership in the Jockey Club
This is possible with the *Tourist Badge*, and everybody is captivated by the atmosphere of Hong Kong's leading gambling institution – experience it at the Happy Valley racetrack → **p. 38**

INSIDER TIP Mountain paths and the roar of the surf
No skyscraper in sight, no car and not even an electricity cable: a day spent hiking to secluded *Tai Long Wan Bay* – with two wonderful beaches – shows a completely unexpected side of Hong Kong (photo right) → **p. 53**

INSIDER TIP Marvels of everyday life
That is what visitors discover wandering through the *Yau Ma Tei* district where they will discover an exotic world far removed from international consumerism → **p. 93**

INSIDER TIP Treasures from the sea and buildings on stilts
You will find both in the fishing village of *Lei Yue Mun* that can only be explored on foot but is easy to reach by underground → **p. 51**

INSIDER TIP Pilgrimage to the ship shrine
Hong Kong's boatmen receive their blessing for the coming year on the *birthday of the "Empress of Heaven" Tin Hau* → **p. 114**

INSIDER TIP Bio-dynamic view of the harbour
Vegetarian food with a panoramic view of the city: the only place to find both is in the chic, but inexpensive, Chinese restaurant *Kung Tak Lam* in a Kowloon skyscraper → **p. 58**

INSIDER TIP Feel like a colonial gent
You can do that at the afternoon *high tea* in the magnificient foyer in the famous Peninsula Hotel → **p. 43**

INSIDER TIP Are there really dragons?
Of course there are! And *flame-spewing dragons* can even be seen dancing in the evening under the full moon during the mid-autumn festival → **p. 115**

INSIDER TIP Seafood, wine and fresh air
...and don't forget a sampan cruise through the labyrinth of islands in Rocky Harbour: an excursion to *Sai Kung* will show you how relaxing Hong Kong can be → **p. 53**

INSIDER TIP What happens in Macau, stays in Macau
The bright lights of the *Cotai Strip* in Macau are most dazzling at night – spend an evening in Las Vegas style at the casino palaces → **p. 110**

BEST OF...

GREAT PLACES FOR FREE

Discover new places and save money

FOR FREE

● ***In the sculpture garden***

You have to pay to see artworks in other places but the modern sculptures in *Kowloon Park* are there for everyone to admire. There is no admission fee here, nor in any of the other parks in Hong Kong → p. 42

● ***Dip into history***

Admission to the state museums is free on Wednesdays and none is more fascinating than the *Museum of History.* Whole scenes and buildings have been built on a scale of 1:1 and even sounds and smells will transport visitors back to past times → p. 42

● ***A different view of the harbour***

Although the panorama from The Peak is incomparable, the view from the *rooftop of the IFC Mall* is easier to reach and free of charge. Here, you are much closer to the harbour with the excitement of all the shipping taking place and surrounded by the glittering atmosphere of the skyscrapers in the metropolis (photo) → p. 30

● ***More fun than a barrel of monkeys***

You can experience all that Hong Kong's *Zoological and Botanical Gardens* have to offer free of charge. The main attractions in the well cared for, shady complex with occasional views of the city's maze of skyscrapers are the elegant ibises and the orangutans → p. 36

● ***Immerse yourself in classical China***

You can do so free of charge at the Buddhist *Chi Lin Nunnery*, built in a style that dates back more than 1100 years ago, with golden effigies and the wonderful Nan Lian Garden that is part of the complex → p. 47

● ***Experience the Grand Prix***

If you missed out on seeing the Macau Grand Prix race "live", you can learn all about its history and have a thrilling driving experience in the *Grand Prix Museum* – for free → p. 103

Unique experiences

Cruise the harbour

Take the *Star Ferry* – Hong Kong's number one traditional means of transport! It lost its importance after the construction of the underground, but there is no nicer way to get from Tsim Sha Tsui to Wan Chai or Central than with the chubby boats that can travel both forwards and backwards → p. 26

City tour for 30 cents

With the *tram* – the number two traditional means of transport! No other way of getting an idea of life in Hong Kong is more comfortable, less expensive and more characteristic than from the top deck as the tram makes its way through canyons of the high buildings on Hong Kong Island → p. 26

Get to the top

With the help of the *Peak Tram* (photo)– transport institution number three! At the very latest, you will realise that it was a good idea to come to Hong Kong when you see the spectacular panorama opening up before your eyes as the tram climbs higher and higher → p. 33

Buy t-shirts, consult a fortune teller...

...or listen to operatic arias. The evening market on *Temple Street* offers this and much, much more every night. And, of course, it is also another Hong Kong institution! → p. 79

Try dim sums

One of the best places to try these Cantonese delicacies for tea is *Maxim's Palace* in City Hall where foreigners are especially welcome. The most typical day is Sunday when it is especially loud and tumultuous → p. 59

Shopping labyrinths

Go on a shopping spree at *Island Beverley* and in *Causeway Place* for the latest fashion trends. These tiny boutiques reveal Hong Kong's space problems and the city's innovative ideas to use what little land it has → p. 69

One-armed bandits and baroque paintings

Macau, the Las Vegas of the East, offers this strange combination in its craziest casino-hotel-theatre-shopping mall: *The Venetian* on Cotai → p. 103

BEST OF...

AND IF IT RAINS?

Activities to brighten your day

RAIN

● ***Stay dry in Central***

How can you get around in the *Central District* without getting wet even though don't have an umbrella? Covered pedestrian bridges make it possible for you to walk for miles and you are even under cover on the Central Escalator → **p. 28**

● ***Explore new design***

The *PMQ* design centre is a mixed-use venue with studios and shops which attracts urban trend setters and provides a stage for Hong Kong's creative scene → **p. 34**

● ***Eleven floors of window shopping***

Or could there be twelve? In any case, the shopping delights under a roof in *Times Square* stretch from several floors below ground level to the 9th floor above. And, if you're hungry, you won't have to go outside to have a bite to eat either (photo) → **p. 67**

● ***Pretend to be a millionaire***

Do it in the lobby of the venerable *Mandarin Oriental*. Relaxing over a cup of English tea is the perfect way to while away a rainy afternoon. You can people watch, read a bit and enjoy the luxurious surroundings without it costing the earth → **p. 83**

● ***Stroll through Macau's history***

Macau is proud of its history and you will be able to experience its essence at *Macau Museum* – much of it on a 1:1 scale! There is more than enough to keep you busy for at least two rainy hours → **p. 106**

● ***Dreaming***

At least that's what the name of the *City of Dreams* in Macau promises. Here you can dream about winning in the casino and spending the money in the luxury shops – and why not finish off by visiting "The House of Dancing Water" Show? → **p. 103**

RELAX AND CHILL OUT

Take it easy and spoil yourself

● ***Be kneaded***
There are many places offering foot massages in Hong Kong but *Iyara* has much more to make you feel good – going as far as treatments lasting for hours – and that in an amazingly central location near the Central Escalator → **p. 39**

● ***Time for tea***
The Cantonese-Hong Kong tea culture can be best experienced at a tasting session in the *Lock Cha Tea House.* The friendly atmosphere and a light snack will help you enjoy your relaxing rest → **p. 73**

● ***Lie on the divan...***
... prop your head up and, gently swaying, let the panorama of Hong Kong's skyscrapers drift past you for an hour. You will find a tour on the junk *Aqua Luna* one of the most peaceful ways to see the city and the harbour → **p. 125**

● ***Sofas, cocktails, shisha***
Hidden in the courtyard terrace of the Mira hotel, *Vibes* is an open-air lounge with sofas, cocktails and shishas to unwind in style or dance away the night after a hard day at work → **p. 79**

● ***Laze on the beach***
There are many possibilities to do this in Hong Kong. *Repulse Bay* is the easiest beach to reach. There is nothing lovelier than lying on one of the pontoons being gently rocked by the waves. And then: just close your eyes, feel the water and sun caressing your skin and imagine you are in the South Seas (photo) → **p. 48**

● ***Dreaming to music***
The romantic *Jardim de Lou Lim Ieoc* invites visitors to lie back on one of its benches and enjoy a few minutes of peace listening to its sounds of crickets or amateur musicians playing in the pavilion → **p. 105**

INTRODUCTION

DISCOVER HONG KONG!

There is no doubt about it. Hong Kong is a synonym for the fascination of the Far East. Everybody has a certain picture in their mind. On the one hand, one expects an ***extremely modern**, international metropolis* whose economic dynamism manifests itself in a forest of skyscrapers and where the wealthy are chauffeured around in Rolls Royces. On the other hand, visitors hope to experience the exotic atmosphere of China, the enigmatic, the unfamiliar. And, you would not be really far off there either. This Chinese metropolis with 155 years of British tradition is both cosmopolitan and fascinatingly different. Here, the Chinese has been moulded by ***the British***, striving for profit has been amalgamated with traditional Chinese values and the liberal economic atmosphere and work discipline go hand in hand with culture and pleasure. The only thing you should forget is the cliché about the city being a stronghold of criminality and secret societies. Things in Hong Kong are much more orderly than in many large European cities. The first time you visit Hong Kong, you will find coming to grips with the city somewhat challenging. The pushing and shoving on the streets, the smell of exhaust fumes from cars in the canyons between high buildings, the noise of the swarms of buses, cement mixers and pneumatic drills reverberating off the ***façades of the high-rises*** in

Photo: View from the Peak

this incessantly hectic city. Some visitors are even happy to leave after only two days of shopping and a single city tour.

Of course, they won't have missed out on palaces or romantic ruins, famous museums or charming squares. Hong Kong's records are much more sober: Asia's second-largest financial metropolis (after Tokyo), the *highest shop rentals in the world,* the underground with the world's largest transport volume per kilometre, the globe's fourth-largest container port and some of the highest skyscrapers on earth. But the truth is: Hong Kong itself is a unique attraction with its *contrasting mountains and water,* its skyscrapers and its culinary delights. It almost seems to be a miracle that this capitalist eldorado on the doorstep of the Chinese giant can function at all – on a problematic piece of land suitable for just about anything but being the site of a metropolis with a population of several millions.

Records appear rather sober – Hong Kong itself is the attraction

At the beginning, this location south of the Tropic of Cancer was missing all the prerequisites for such a success story. When the British occupied the island as one of the *spoils of war in 1841,* they planned to establish a military base and not a large city. It soon became clear that there was a serious lack of building space and land in the

Time for a shopping spree: at the Times Square Shopping centre

surrounding area that could sustain a rapidly growing town. At the time, Viscount Palmerston – speaking at Westminster – said that Hong Kong was just "a barren island with hardly a house upon it". And that is why the British expanded their booty twice: in 1860 to include the *Kowloon Peninsula* – ceded by China "for eternity", just like the island – and, in 1898, the neighbouring *section of the mainland and additional islands,* the "New Territories" as they are still called today. With them, Hong Kong grew tenfold – restricted to 99 years.

From the outset, Hong Kong's main *raison d'être* was as a place to do business, and many Chinese knew how to profit from that; they left their homeland that was reeling from one crisis to the next and started to settle in Hong Kong soon after its foundation. A great *flood of migrants* took place during the Civil War and the advancement of the Communists (1947–49). Soon, the slopes of the hills were covered with gigantic settlements for poor people. The most pressing task was to create social housing in order to prevent the colony from falling into chaos – but where could space be found for that? Efforts to create *new land* on embankments had already begun in the 19th century; Queen's Road, the first to be built along the shore, is now up to 650 m/2000 ft from the water. Entire bays have disappeared and mountains moved, and Hong Kong is still expanding several square miles every year. Above all, new towns had to be built in the rural *New Territories* where almost half of Hong Kong's 7.3 million inhabitants live today.

"A barren island with hardly a house upon it"

Outsiders might not find these *skyscraper settlements* particularly attractive but there is no alternative, especially not for those living there, many of whom experienced – at first hand – life in the slums that have now disappeared. The European luxury cars you will see on the parking levels in many of these skyscraper complexes is proof that the people living there are often amazingly *wealthy*. On the other hand, the "housing cages" frequently talked about in Europe, that elderly unemployed people are squeezed into, are only a peripheral phenomenon. The art of coping with a *lack of space* is, however, something that almost everybody in everybody in Hong Kong has to come to terms, with the exception of the extremely wealthy who live in villas.

The second major challenge facing Hong Kong was its traffic problem. The Territory consists of 263 islands and even the large section on the mainland is broken up by peninsulas, mountains and deep bays. Things improved considerably after 1980 with the introduction of the *underground and many tunnels*. The latest megaprojects include an underground high-speed train to China and a series of linked bridges and tunnels crossing the sea channel to Macau.

The third problem was the lack of drinking water; it even had to be rationed in years when the rainfall was poor. Today, the supply is guaranteed by two *gigantic reservoirs that have been wrested from the sea,* as well as water pipes from China. The fourth problem was the easiest one to solve: unemployment. There was plenty of experience in making money. In addition, Hong Kong had taken over Shanghai's function as the Chinese *trade, production and finance centre* in 1949 and developed into China's almost sole door to the outside world – a lucrative source of revenue for the capitalistic enclave. However, in the 1990s, almost all of the industry moved back across the border into China and now many of the people of Hong Kong commute to work in Shenzhen.

Today, the territory is a place of incredible contrasts. *Cutting-edge technology and Chinese traditions,* metropolis and secluded mountains, noise and tranquillity – all of this tightly packed together. Offerings of oranges and incense are made to the God of Doors, the Earth and Prosperity in a small metal shrine next to the entrance of a sophisticated nightclub with hi-tech equipment. Fashionably dressed office workers with their smartphones go to the cemetery to tend to the graves of their ancestors and a subtropical jungle, where colourful butterflies flutter around during the day and crickets chirp at night, starts immediately behind the last 25-storey skyscraper. The most dominant feeling however is one of the *city's dynamism* and its talent for being able to realise ideas and plans in no time. The latest fashions can be found on the shelves here long before they have even been unpacked in Europe. But the times when Hong Kongers worked from the early hours of the morning until late at night and their only pleasure was an occasional evening playing mahjong have now gone. The city has developed into a *pleasure metropolis* – especially for gourmets. It is absolutely normal to go out to eat and consumers indulge themselves in the gigantic shopping malls. But the passion with which two traditional vices are cultivated has remained unbroken: horse racing and gambling in neighbouring Macau.

Fashionably dressed office workers tend to the graves of their ancestors

Macau! A visit to the *oldest European outpost in the Far East* is normally a part of any trip to Hong Kong. The small territory, which was returned to China in 1999 – a good two years after Hong Kong – is in no way just a miniature version of its formerly British counterpart at the mouth of the Pearl River. Even though today the gigantic gambling casinos attract most tourists to Macau and have made it famous as *Asia's Las Vegas,* there are many more testimonies to its centuries-long past as a Portuguese colony here than through the much shorter British presence in Hong Kong.

Many visitors feel that both cities have become completely westernised; but this impression fades away if you look closer. Of course, many British elements have been preserved since Hong Kong's "return" in 1997: the currency, bilingualism, the judicial system, visa-free entry and the border to the new mother, and old father, coun-

Embedded in Chinese tradition: morning gymnastics in Victoria Park

try. Thoroughfares such as Queen's Road and Prince Edward Road have also kept their old names. But only a minority speaks more-or-less good English. The skyscrapers are "homemade", constructed with the help of traditional bamboo scaffolding. And family solidarity is still of the utmost importance. The city and people living in it are modern and enthusiastic about the latest technology but it would be a mistake to think that everything that is not old-Chinese is western.

The panorama from The Peak is Hong Kong's greatest marvel

As you wander through the labyrinth of skyscrapers, you will be amazed at the high level of social order. The spotless underground is absolutely safe and there are no signs of graffiti. Travel out to the ***islands***, hike over the ***hills,*** explore the ***beaches.*** Relish the seafood and all of the other delicacies the local restaurants have to offer. The first two days in Hong Kong are always terrible. Stay for seven days and you will want to extend for another week. If you really only have half a day, travel to The Peak. The ***magnificent panorama*** will show you what the city and people living there have had to – and have – achieve(d). That is the real Hong Kong miracle. You can buy silk blouses when you get home.

WHAT'S HOT

1 The beer revolution

Craft beer Hong Kong has fallen in love with craft beer. Microbreweries have finally unshackled themselves from beer purity laws and are adding new, unorthodox ingredients to create a variety of refreshing tastes, appealing to the most adamant beer purists. Hong Kong is now home to around ten such microbreweries, and even satellite towns or the car-free Lamma Island have "tapped" into this craze. Well-known names include *Young Master Ales, Moonzen* and *Mak's* and local bars also serve a selection of craft beers on tap.

2 Young and wild

Fashion Hong Kong is crazy about the latest fashion trends. That makes competitions for up-and-coming designers, such as the "Young Designers Contest" at the *Hong Kong Fashion Week (www.hktdc.com),* so important. Talents including *Mountain Yam (www.facebook.com/112mountainyam) (photo)* and Mim Mak with his label *Hang (www.hangggggg.com)* were discovered here. A new popular forum for young designers is the *Centrestage* show *(www.centrestage.com.hk).*

3 Shisha temples

Smoking waterpipes could be the city's latest countertrend to smoking which is virtually out in Hong Kong and no longer permitted even in the city's parks. Ever since Istanbul emerged as a popular destination for tourists from the Far East, these splendid oriental inhalation apparatuses can be seen outside many Hong Kong bars and not just in the pub district Lan Kwai Fong. Although this fun does not come cheap, the aromas drifting from the bars are intoxicating and shisha bar guests usually end up smoking more than just one.

There are lots of new things to discover in Hong Kong. A few of the most interesting are listed below

Design capital

4

Creative power Hong Kong is rapidly establishing itself as a design metropolis and not just in terms of fashion. This creative movement was originally sparked by the Jockey Club, who financed the build of the *Jockey Club Creative Arts Centre (www.jccac.org.hk)* in Shek Kip Mei from its horserace betting takings. Towering even higher is the design faculty of the *Polytechnic University* in *Innovation Tower (Chatham Road South)*, a spectacular design by Zaha Hadid. These buildings are the result of non-profit organisations, the private industry and politics joining creative forces. This collaborative spirit is also evident in *G.O.D. (Goods of Desire)*, a pioneer of lifestyle design and retail brand producing items which range from furniture to mouse pads.

Quinoa superfood

5

Eco food Like elsewhere in the world, healthy eating is the latest culinary trend to hit Hong Kong and the gluten-free, South American pseudocereal quinoa is a must-have ingredient of restaurants claiming to specialise in healthy food. The vegetables served with it may also have been organically grown in Hong Kong. To make the most of the limited space available in the New Territories, cereals and vegetables are cultivated in hydroponic greenhouses using the latest scientific methods. *Farm Direct (www.farmdirect.hk)*, the leading supplier, sells its fresh products in its own farm stores. Hobby gardeners are also getting involved: at *Fruitful Organic Farm (Kam Sheung Road | Yuen Long | www.flowerworld hk.com)* you can rent your own allotment space. A list of organic stores, retailers and restaurants in Hong Kong can be found at *www.greenqueen.com.hk*.

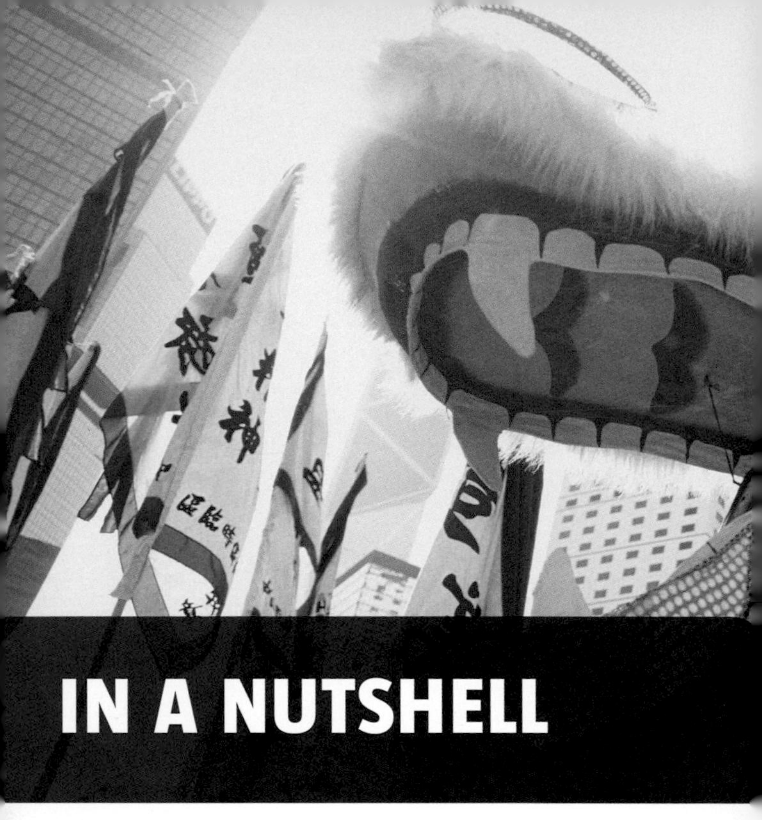

IN A NUTSHELL

BAUHINIA, THE BEAUTIFUL

Have you ever noticed Hong Kong's red-and-white flag? Its ornament is the city flower, the blossom of the bauhinia tree. And yes, it truly is beautiful. It flowers in pink and violet hues in the winter, from November to March, and can be admired on promenades and squares. There is even a golden version: the gigantic object next to the Convention and Exhibition Centre came as a gift of the Chinese government.

COUNTRY PARKS

It is hard to believe if you do not know Hong Kong well: there is so much green land that it is possible to go on mountain hikes lasting for days. This is due to the *24 Country Parks*, landscape conservation areas that were established after 1976 to protect the city's water reserves. They are spread over Hong Kong Island, Lantau and the mainland, cover 40 per cent of the land area and consist of partly wooded, partly grassy, hilly terrain. Hikers will be pleased to find well-marked paths, camping sites, shelters, barbecue areas, information boards and visitors' centres that provide details on the flora and fauna. Four main trails lead to the most beautiful places; some sections can be reached by bus. You might come across snakes so make sure you wear sturdy shoes!
Further information is available under *www.gov.hk/en/residents/culture/trail* as well as *www.afcd.gov.hk/eindex.*

 Photo: Dance of the dragon at the Chinese New Year celebrations

Patron Saint and opium: Some background information on what to expect in the Special Administrative Area of Hong Kong

html; the best maps can be obtained from *www.landsd.gov.hk/mapping/en/digital_map/mapprod.htm*.

HELL MONEY AND FENG SHUI

Will I pass my final exams? Will I find the perfect partner for life? Will my new job be a success? In search of answers to these life-important dilemmas, Hongkongers head directly to their local temple taking along a gift of fruit or lamp oil and after burning some incense, they consult an oracle or fortune-teller. The Gods are willing to help anyone who is prepared to offer a small (or not so small) donation. Deceased relatives, such as grandparents, are also believed to offer their advice from beyond the grave. Visitors will regularly make paper gifts, such as model houses, and then burn them in order to send their essence to their dead relatives with the aim of keeping them happy and comfortable. The same is done with "hell money", or joss paper, burned as an offering to ancestors in order to escape punishment for any misdeeds. You will get an impression of how Hongkongers worship their ancestors in the memorial halls where places for ancestral tablets can be purchased, such as in the Man Mo temple. You should walk anticlockwise around the temple and not forget to leave a small donation when you leave. The mini shrines, which can be found on door steps and in many shops, are evidence of the nation's popular beliefs and rituals and show a traditional side to this buzzing, ultra-modern metropolis.

This brings us neatly to the subject of Feng Shui, "wind and water". Supposedly, feng shui masters have a lot to say when a new high-rise or family home is to be placed and designed in such a way as to collect favorable influences and fend off the evil ones that bring poverty and sickness. However, building takes place everywhere it's allowed – as high as possible, feng shui or not. No feng shui master has ever prevented a building being constructed. A good image always takes first place.

GAMBLING AND HORSE RACING

Every lotto player knows the thrill of challenging Fortuna, the goddess of luck. She is unknown in Hong Kong but this has no effect on the passion people feel about the possibility of making loads of money with just a small wager. There are two legal ways to do this in Hong Kong: to bet at the racetrack or play mahjong. Mahjong is usually played at home with four people taking part. There are special mahjong tables of just the right size with a drawer for each player to keep his winnings and bets; mahjong without the added attraction of winning would be "kids' stuff". Things are a bit more serious in the mahjong salons. But even there, the bets are not very high; if they were, winnings would be taxed.

THE COLD TRAP

There is no restaurant owner who wants to have a reputation for skimping on air-conditioning of all things. You'll always arrive dripping in sweat which will feel like an icy shower down your back after 15 mins. By the third day at the latest you'll have a streaming cold. So always take a cardigan or sweatshirt with you!

Win or place? Suspense at the Happy Valley Racetrack

The popularity of horse racing can only really be explained by the fact that you can bet. The never-ending flow of income has made the Hong Kong Jockey Club a financially potent charitable institution. But, Macau is the place to go if you want to really live your passion for gambling to the utmost. This former Portuguese overseas province has developed into the world's largest heaven on earth for gamblers – mainly due to the nouveau riche from the mainland, many of them government officials made wealthy through corruption.

LUNAR CALENDAR

Most of China's traditional festivities are based on the moon calendar with a 354 or 355-day year. It is actually a moon-and-sun calendar because every 33 to 35 months an intercalary month is added at the beginning of the year to adapt it to the solar year. The Chinese lunar year always begins with the first full moon after 21 January. As a rule, there is more activity in the temples at new moon and full moon than at other times. That is when offerings of money are also burned in red metal buckets on the roadside.

COMMUNICATION PROBLEMS

Walking through the streets of Hong Kong, it is evident that the city's population comprises 94 percent ethnic Chinese (from a total of 7.3 million inhabitants) yet the majority of them speak Cantonese – a dialect not understood by other Chinese. Nowhere else is this South Chinese dialect spoken as widely as it is in Hong Kong – even the popular newspapers are written in dialect. Cantonese is the official language of Hong Kong and Macau and announcements in the bus or on the underground are made in Cantonese first. Some think that the dialect sounds slightly similar to Dutch. By the way English is the second official language and most young people speak it well.

tion of war and the first Opium War began. With the Nanking Peace treaty in 1842, China was forced to open four additional ports to overseas trade and cede the island of Hong Kong to the Brit-

Asking the fortune-teller in Man Mo Temple whether things are on the up

ish Crown "in perpetuity". 18 years later, in the second Opium War, Kowloon (as far as Boundary Street) was added, followed in 1898 by the lease of the New Territories.

OPIUM WAR

If the British had not been so fond of tea 200 years ago, Hong Kong would probably not exist today. Tea came from China but trade was a one-way street: the Middle Kingdom did not buy anything from the British until the latter came up with the idea of drug smuggling. The business of trafficking with Indian opium flourished. More and more Chinese became addicted and more silver left China than came in through exporting tea.

The Emperor sent an incorruptible official to Canton: Lin Zexu. In 1839, he had all of the opium stored in Canton destroyed. Great Britain considered this a declara-

ORACLES AND FORTUNE TELLING

The simplest and cheapest form of an oracle can often be seen in temples: the person seeking advice holds two kidney-shaped pieces of wood in his or her hand, moves them up and down in front of the altar and silently implores the appropriate god before throwing them onto the ground. Depending on whether their round or flat side lies on the bottom,

this can mean "yes", "no" or "maybe". The stick oracle is the appropriate form for more complicated matters. A box with numbered sticks is shaken until one falls out; the temple's fortune teller then looks up the number in a book and interprets the saying in keeping with the concern the believer has.
Physiognomers, who tell the future from a person's face and chiromancers who do the same by looking at the lines on your palms often work together with a temple. Trained birds are also used as oracles; they pull a saying out of a heap of papers.

THE FATE OF TYCOONS

The Japanese word "taikun" literally means "Great Lord" or "Supreme Commander" and is used to mean a wealthy business magnate. Hong Kong is famous for its tycoons who hit the tabloid press headlines in Hong Kong as often as the Royal Family in the UK. Born in 1928, Lee Ka-shing is one such magnate and is one of the world's leading property investors and developers with an estimated net worth of 30 billion dollars. He came to Hong Kong during the war as a refugee and, due to his father's death, was forced to work when he was just twelve years old in a factory which made watch straps. The start of his business career was funded by an uncle and Li himself is known for his modest lifestyle, donating hundreds of millions of dollars to charitable organisations.
Nina Wang has a different story to tell and would deserve an honorary medal from Hong Kong's tabloid press if she were still alive today. She married into money and her husband was kidnapped twice. The first time he was released after the ransom was paid, but the second time he was not recovered. Once he was declared legally dead, she took over his business and built it into a successful company. Nicknamed "Little Sweetie" by the press, she was noted for her short height (just 152 cm/60 in), her two pigtails and her love of wearing miniskirts until her death in 2007. After her lover was named as the sole beneficiary in her will after her death, the tabloid press again had a field day – just like her lawyers who cashed in on the lengthy court battle over her estate which ensued. The name of this remarkable woman lives on in the 318 m/1043 ft high Nina Towers, a skyscraper she planned and developed herself.

A "FRAGRANT HARBOUR"?

When the British first came to Hong Kong, they bunkered fresh water at a dock near Aberdeen where agarwood, one of the raw materials used for making incense, was traded. When asked the name of the place, the local sailors answered in their dialect: "Hong Kong", incense harbour. However, the British thought that this was the name of the entire island and wrongly translated the *hong* (Cantonese *höng*, Standard Chinese *xiang*) which can mean both "fragrance" and "incense" with *fragrant*. This misunderstanding was only cleared up a good 140 years later but still stubbornly persists.

SIGHTSEEING

> **CITY WHERE TO START?**
> **Statue Square (137 E3)** *(C11)*: the central point in the Central District marked by the Old Supreme Court Building, the HSBC building and the elegant Mandarin Oriental Hotel. The tram stops at the south end; four underground lines converge here and with the Prince's Building on the west side, a network of footbridges begins, providing access to a large part of Central leading northwards to the tower of the International Finance Centre with its shopping mall and view of the harbour and onwards to the ferry terminals.

Don't worry about the heat, rain and the ubiquitous stench! You will not have to walk very far to discover the real Hong Kong – the modern city as well as the traditional districts such as Yau Ma Tei and Sheung Wan.

The parks provide peaceful areas to catch your breath, the shopping centres cool air and the museums will broaden your horizons. Those who want to experience the city sitting down instead of sweating can take the nostalgic ● *tram* (136–137 C–F 1–3, 138–139 A–F 2–4) *(A–H 10–12)* has connected the districts in the north of the island with each other since 1904, and the chubby boats of the ● *Star Ferry Line* (134 B6, 137 E–F 1–2) *(C–D 9–10)* have chugged their way between Tsim Sha and Central since 1898.

Photo: Wong Tai Sin Temple

Between The Peak and the harbour: palatial banks and temples blackened with incense – and much more waiting to be discovered

A visit to a museum is not merely a good idea when it's raining. Although they are not world-famous, many of them are well worth a visit. Generous benefactors have donated wonderful artistic treasures and the exemplary methods of presentation make a foreign culture accessible to visitors to these government-run institutions. And a new vibrant cultural quarter is currently under construction in the West Kowloon Cultural District *(www.westkowloon.hk/en).* The permanent exhibitions at the Museum of Art, Museum of History and other museums can be visited free of charge. You can find a list of others, including the Medicine, Police and Railway Museums at *www.discoverhongkong.com* (under Things to Do / Culture & Heritage).
It is easy to reach more distant locations on the speedy, air-conditioned trains operated by the MTR underground as well as the Kowloon-Canton railway. However, the crowning highlight is always the cable car trip to The Peak.

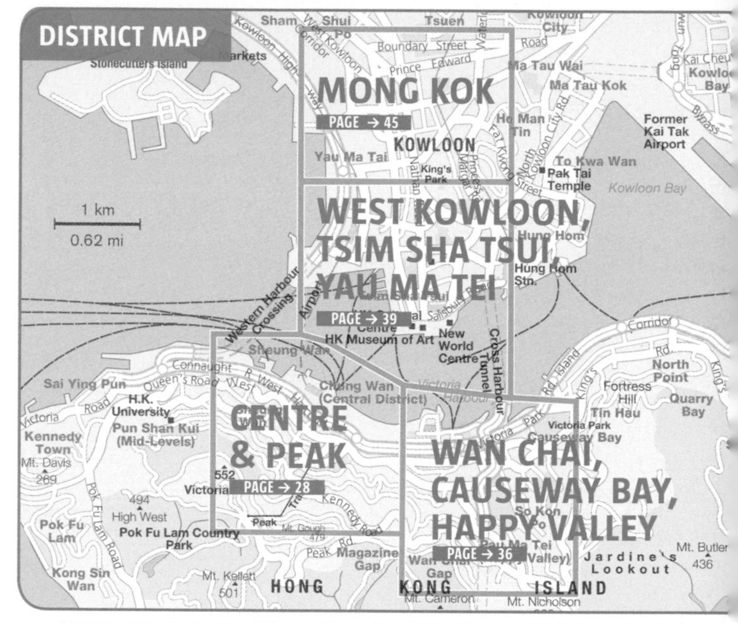

The map shows the location of the most interesting districts. There is a detailed map of each district on which each of the sights described is numbered.

CENTRE & PEAK (中環, 山頂)

This is the nucleus of the former Crown Colony; this is where the British flag was raised for the first time.

And this is where the city, which was named Victoria at the time, was built along and above Queen's Road (both named after Queen Victoria); it was the forerunner of today's Central District that, together with the neighbouring Admiralty District to the east, forms the heart of Hong Kong's commercial life. Visitors reach some of the oldest, most colourful and most densely populated districts to the west and east; as you proceed upwards, things become greener, more elegant and much more expensive.

● *Central District:* Here, you can walk for miles over bridges and wander through buildings without ever going down to street level. Hong Kong's "front room", overshadowed by the Hong Kong Bank, is *Statue Square* (137 E3) (*🕮 C11*). This is where Filipino maids living in the city organise a gigantic picnic every Sunday. The oldest section of Central with the *Central Market* (137 D2) (*🕮 C11*), which is currently being revamped, is on the west side of the square; from here the almost 880 m/2890ft-long *Central Escalator* whisks people up to the Mid-levels residential area. Since the 1970s, earth has been filled into the area north of Connaught Road to create building land. The

420 m/1378ft-high tower of the *International Finance Centre* towers up like an enormous exclamation mark. The *City Hall*, with rooms for all kinds of events, is located on what was once the shoreline on Edinburgh Place to the north-east of the square. The *Admiralty* office district (formerly naval parade grounds) with the Bank of China Tower follows on the eastern side. Central is dominated by The Peak, the villa district with Hong Kong's main attraction: the panoramic view of the harbour and city.

Sheung Wan is to the west of Central (136 C2) (*🕮 B10–11*). In spite of the encroaching office buildings, a feeling for Hong Kong's exotic flair has survived here. The highlights are listed in the Discovery Tour No. 4.

The most comfortable place to get an impression of life in the north of the island (reaching to the east far beyond Causeway Bay) is from the top of the tram. The double-decker carriages, which also serve as mobile advertisement hoardings, are considered attractions in their own right. You will have no trouble getting one of the best seats at the front of the upper deck if you catch the tram at a terminus such as the one at Western Market. The lines to Shau Kei Wan and Kennedy Town are the longest; the ones to Happy Valley end in a drab branch line.

1 CENTRAL HARBOURFRONT (中環海濱) ★ (137 E–F 2–3) (*🕮 C–D11*)

Situated to the east of Star Ferry Pier, this island has been undergoing a complete revamp since 2013 with a waterfront park and promenade offering visitors and locals more open space to breathe. The promenade extends to a large recreational space in the west which is dominated by the recently opened Ferris wheel *(Observation Wheel | daily 11am–11pm | HK$ 100 for a 20-minute ride)* which will be around until the end of 2017. Designed in the shape of an enormous archway, the striking *Central Government Offices* are also part of this

MARCO POLO HIGHLIGHTS

★ Hong Kong Park
Oasis of greenery in the skyscraper jungle → p. 30

★ Peak Trail
Breathtaking panorama of the city → p. 33

★ Museum of Art
Cultural treasures from China and modern art from Hong Kong → p. 42

★ Museum of History
A revelation for museum-haters → p. 42

★ Central Harbourfront
Hong Kong's friendly new face → p. 29

★ Mong Kok
The city's market place – even with pedestrian precincts → p. 45

★ Ocean Park
A trip in a gondola and a dolphin show with a view of the ocean in Hong Kong's best amusement park → p. 47

★ Stanley
Hong Kong's southernmost district attracts visitors with its clothes market, promenade, bars and restaurants → p. 48

★ Wong Tai Sin Temple
Offerings and fortune tellers → p. 49

★ Lantau and Po Lin Monastery
Long beaches and a giant Buddha on Hong Kong's largest island → p. 50

landmark project and are situated 600 m/2000 ft further east, an area which is also home to the Legislative Council. The waterfront park is the perfect place to unwind and relax in the right weather and visitors are invited to walk on the lawn. *MTR Central, Admiralty*

2 CENTRAL POLICE STATION (前中區警署) (137 D3) (*B–C11*)

The former main police station (complete with prison) forms the largest ensemble of colonial-style buildings to have been preserved in Hong Kong. They were built between 1864 and 1925. Until 2018, with the historic buildings being preserved, a smart new centre with restaurants and art galleries is being built. *Hollywood Rd. | 荷李活道 | corner Arbuthnot Rd. | MTR Central*

3 EXCHANGE SQUARE AND IFC MALL (交易廣場 AND 國際金融中心商場) (137 D–E2) (*C11*)

This is a vast and very glamourous crowd puller in the Central District. The *IFC Mall* not only lures you with luxury shops, restaurants and a huge hall with check-in counters for the airport, but also the glorious INSIDER TIP rooftop gardens with free views over Hong Kong's harbour. Walk between towers 1 and 2 to the Oval Atrium on the banks of the harbour and take the escalators up to level 3 (harbour view) and 4 (gastronomy, rooftop garden). You can take a break on both levels to enjoy the panorama without having to order anything in the restaurant. Once you have seen enough of the waterfront, turn to face the mountains: there is often a hive of activity behind the silver mirrored glass façade of the pink-coloured granite marble building; this is *Exchange Square,* one of the world's largest stock exchanges. *MTR Central*

4 HONG KONG PARK (香港公園) ★ (137 E3–4) (*C–D 12–13*)

Visitors to Hong Kong's loveliest park can wander in the shade of old trees to the Tropics and Desert glasshouses, and go into a gigantic aviary with a zigzag walk

The heart of the financial hub: Exchange Square

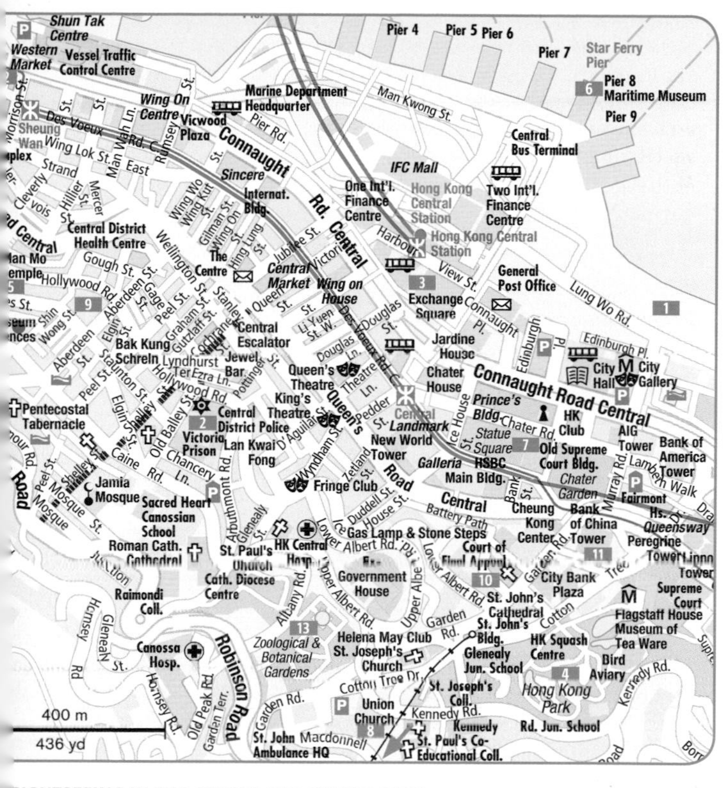

SIGHTSEEING IN THE CENTRE AND ON THE PEAK

1 Central Harbourfront
2 Central Police Station
3 Exchange Square and IFC Mall
4 Hong Kong Park
5 Man Mo Temple
6 Maritime Museum
7 Old Supreme Court Building
8 Peak
9 PMQ
10 St. John's Cathedral
11 Statue Square and Financial District
12 Western Market
13 Zoological and Botanical Gardens

through the treetops where 150 different species of Southeast Asian birds fly around over their heads. Newlyweds pose for photos near the registry office on the western edge of the 25 acre park. To the east, escalators glide up to the *Pacific Place* Shopping Centre. Hong Kong's most charming museum, the *Museum of Tea Ware* in the city's oldest colonial building *Flagstaff House*, shows all kinds of historical articles associated with tea and many other curios. In addition, large colour photos, historical illustrations and texts give an insight into the development of Chinese tea culture. The architecture of the *K.S. Lo Gallery* – a small collection of porcelain and seals provided by the donor Lo – only a few yards away, was adapted to match

Flagstaff House. *Both museums Wed–Mon 10am–6pm | admission free | 19 Cotton Tree Drive 紅棉路 19 | MTR Admiralty | C1 exit, access to park over the bridge into the Pacific Place shopping centre, continue up the escalators and at the top turn right*

He informs the ten judges of hell (seen on the left behind the entrance) about how the deceased behaved during his or her lifetime. It's always a good idea to light some incense to put him in the right mood. Many women head straight

Hong Kong Park: visitors' walkway in the treetops of the free-flight aviary

to the centre hall where they share all their worries, from marital woes to problems with their children, with the Buddhist Goddess of Mercy, Guanyin. You can also seek the advice of fortune-tellers who beckon you in here and in the room on the right, which also serves as an ancestral temple.

A space for a "spirit tablet" with the name of the deceased in the back room (hidden behind a transverse "spirit wall") can cost as much as HK$ 180,000! Proceeds go to a hospital. *Daily 8am–6pm | 124–126 Hollywood Rd. 荷李活道 124–126 | MTR Sheung Wan*

5 MAN MO TEMPLE (文武廟) (136 C2) (*M B11*)

Dwarfed by neighbouring skyscrapers, this temple is a hive of activity. Aside from the crowds of tourists descending from the city's excursion buses, the temple is a popular place of worship for Hong Kong citizens who come to light incense and share their worries with the Gods. Two ornately decorated patrons tower over the altar in the main hall (far left); one stands for the God of Literature (Cantonese: man) and one of War (mo) who give the temple its name. The God of Justice, Bao Gong, stands on the far left with his counterpart, the God of the City, in the right-hand shrine.

6 MARITIME MUSEUM (海事博物館) (137 E2) (*C11*)

Housed in the closed-down Pier 8 building, the maritime museum exhibits ship models, original artefacts, reproductions and audio-visual media to detail maritime history in the Far East and show what the Hong Kong harbour was like in the 19th century. *Mon–Fri 9.30am–5.30pm, Sat, Sun 10am–7pm | admission 30 $ | www.hkmaritimemuseum.org | MTR Central*

7 OLD SUPREME COURT BUILDING (舊最高法院大樓) (137 E3) (*C11–12*)

Built between 1899 and 1910, this domed building housed the former Supreme Court until 1983. After serving several other purposes, it has accommodated the Hong Kong Court of Final Appeal since 2015. The building is the only remaining example of neo-classical colonial architecture in the city. Before the invention of air-conditioning, the two-storey Ionic column passageways kept the interior cool in summer and allowed the windows to be left open when it rained. Blindfolded and holding a scale in one hand and a sword in the other, Lady Justice stands on the west gable. *Statue Square | 皇后像廣場 | MTR Central*

8 PEAK (山頂) (136 A–C 3–5) (*A–B 12–13*)

This is a once in a lifetime experience with a view to literally take your breath away. And if you climb up on foot, it won't cost you a penny. Peak is the name of the whole area around the highest elevation on the island, 552 m/1811 ft above sea level (136 B4) (*A12*). In the 19th century, when tropical diseases were a problem in Hong Kong, the colonialists thought that The Peak was the only area on the island where one had a good chance of surviving the summer. Chinese were not permitted to live here until 1945. A trip in the old cable car, the Peak Tram, is an absolute must. You arrive at *Peak Tower* (136 C5) (*B13*) at the top, a complex of shops, restaurants, terraces and many other temptations.

It is a good idea however to ignore Peak Tower and turn right into narrow Lugard Road after you leave the exit. Only people who take this 800 yard walk to the INSIDER TIP escarpment (136 B–C3) (*A12*) will experience the panorama in all its glory. The INSIDER TIP view at twilight is absolutely breathtaking. You will need around 50 minutes, without a break, for the entire ★ *Peak Trail* (no gradients). It is hardly worth climbing all the way to the top, but don't miss out on taking a break at the *Peak Lookout* (see p. 63).

If you want a good walk, you should come back during the daytime and explore the amazing *Central Green Trail*. Go past Peak Tower towards the east *(Findlay Road)*. When you reach a junction, stay on the downhill side *(Severn Road)* until you reach *Hospital Path* (137 D5) (*C13*) signposted where you turn off to the left. When you reach the end, go a little way to the right. At the end of the car park you will see a sign with information on the trail that leads down along Chatham Path through subtropical vegetation – it frequently lightens to provide wonderful views of another jungle, the city's skyscrapers. Turn right where the trail intersects with another. The route crosses the Peak Tram track twice, goes down Clovelly Path, Brewin Park and Tramway Path until it ends at the lower terminal. *Duration: 1–1½ hours; be careful: the path is dangerously slippery when wet!*

● *Peak Tram*: Two air-conditioned double carriages, each pulled by a 1500

The Old Supreme Court Building - the last colonial landmark on Statue Square

m/1-mile-long cable, run between the lower terminal on Garden Road (137 E3–4) (*C12*) and the top station at an altitude of 400 m/1312ft and overcome a difference in height of 367 m/1200ft. There is absolutely no need to feel nervous; since it started operating in 1888 there has never been an accident. *Peak Tram 32 HK$, return 45 HK$ | Don't buy the expensive Sky Pass!*

9 INSIDER TIP PMQ (元創方) ● (136 C2) (*B11*)

The city's new designer headquarters housed in the former Police Married Quarters. This mixed-use venue showcases the latest trends from the city's arts and design scene in workshops and stores on a total of seven floors across two buildings. This centre captures the essence of fun in art and visitors have a good selection of eateries to choose from. The garden on top of the new middle wing, which connects the two blocks, is a good place to take a break at no extra cost. Do not visit the PMQ in the morning because most of the stores are closed. *Aberdeen St./corner of Staunton St. | 鴨巴甸街/士丹頓街 | www.pmq.org.hk*

10 ST. JOHN'S CATHEDRAL (聖約翰座堂) (137 E3) (*C12*)

The main Anglican church in Hong Kong was consecrated in 1849 and extended between 1869 and 1872. The Japanese occupying forces used the building as a casino in 1944/45 after which the interior decoration and windows had to be virtually completely renewed. Today, the Gothic Revival building almost disappears between all the skyscrapers. *4–8 Garden Rd. | 花園道 4–8 | MTR Central*

11 STATUE SQUARE AND FINANCIAL DISTRICT (皇后像廣場 AND 國際金融中心) (137 E2–3) (*C11–12*)

A leisurely square with benches, fountains and flowerbeds yet it is not the main attraction at the heart of the metropolis. Nowhere else on the planet can you find such a concentration of financial institutions with the arteries of the financial world pulsating behind their façades. It's exciting to gaze up and compare how the various international star architects have incorporated the theme of finance into their designs. The best viewpoint over the square is on the bridge over a pool of water in the south of the square (facing uphill).

Stand with your back facing the harbour and straight in front of you stands the *Hong Kong and Shanghai Banking Corporation (HSBC)*, the most traditional of the three central banks in Hong Kong (with the bronze lions Stephen and Stitt guarding the entrance of the building). Towering over the south end of the square, this landmark building seems to say: "This bank is open to everyone!" as almost the entire ground floor lobby has been kept open as a public space. You can see directly into the heart of the building, its main hall, through a giant horizontal window. By means of an adjustable „light scoop" on the south façade, mirrors are used to reflect natural sunlight into the building. Comprising tiered bridges and suspended floors, the entire construction was designed by Norman Foster and the project proved to be extremely costly. Although at only 179 m/587 ft, the building is not particularly high, it was the world's most expensive skyscraper on completion in 1985. Immediately to the left is the old building of the Bank of China, a relic from a bygone era. Further left, the silver tower is the *Cheung Kong Centre* of the tycoon Li Kashing who could be looking down on the square in his bathrobe. He uses the 62nd floor not only as his office; it also contains a private swimming pool and garden. Continuing left, one of Hong Kong's most noticeable skyscrapers is set back from the square, the *Bank of China Tower* with its distinctive vertical shafts which reflect as a giant X onto the building's mirrored façade. Many Hong Kong citizens were initially appalled by the building's design from the Chinese-born American architect IM Pei because it ignored the rules of Feng-shui, its sharp edges resembled spears threatening the neighbouring buildings and the two rooftop antennas looked like incense sticks. If you take a closer look at the tower, its fortress-like base with its battlements resembles a medieval castle and seems to be sending out the warning "Hands off our money!".

Now turn right around and gaze high up to see Tower 2 of the *International Finance Centre (IFC)*, an exquisitely-designed 420m/1378ft high masterpiece from the architect César Pelli. Home to Hong Kong's monetary authorities, the construction extols the power of money. Now you are here, the building on your left overshadowed by the IFC tower is the elegant *Mandarin Oriental* Hotel (see p. 83) and the old colonial-style domed building behind you is the *Old Supreme Court Building* (see p. 33).

LOW BUDGET

Tram: You can travel as far as you want for a mere HK$ 2.30.

Star Ferry: Take a cruise across the harbour between Tsim Sha Tsui (Kowloon) and Central on the lower deck of the ferries for only HK$ 2 on weekdays.

Museums: admission to the major state-run museums is free, albeit only on Wednesdays in the Science Museum.

The name *Statue Square* is reference to the statue of Queen Victoria. However look as hard as you might, you will not find the old lady: the monument was taken to Japan to be melted down during World War II. *MTR Central*

12 WESTERN MARKET (西港城) (136 C2) (*B10–11*)

This brick building, constructed in 1906, once housed a food market. After this moved to a larger, more modern site in 1988, the building was declared a historic monument. Cloth and souvenir dealers moved in. *Daily 10am–5pm | MTR Sheung Wan*

13 ZOOLOGICAL AND BOTANICAL GARDENS (動植物公園) ● (137 D3–4) (*C12*)

The garden is not very big but worth a visit. The scarlet ibises, flamingos and rare species of peacock are some of the main attractions. Visitors are also attracted by the orangutans and gibbons. The complex was founded in 1864 and a rest in the shade of the old trees is bliss. Early in the morning, many Hong Kongers come here to shadow box. *Daily 6am–10pm | admission free | Garden Rd. | 花園道 | MTR Central*

WAN CHAI, CAUSEWAY BAY, HAPPY VALLEY (灣仔, 銅鑼灣, 跑馬地)

Wan Chai, with its famous red-light district around Jaffe Road and Lockhart Road, in the centre of the north coast is a fine example of the give and take between old residential and new commercial buildings.

The *Convention and Exhibition Centre*, with its elegantly curved roof stretching out into the harbour, is the architectural highlight of this district. It is connected to two luxury hotels including the spectacular *Grand Hyatt* with the tower of the *Central Plaza* (138 A4) (*E12*) soaring up behind

Sweeping elegance on the harbour in Wan Chai: the Convention and Exhibition Centre

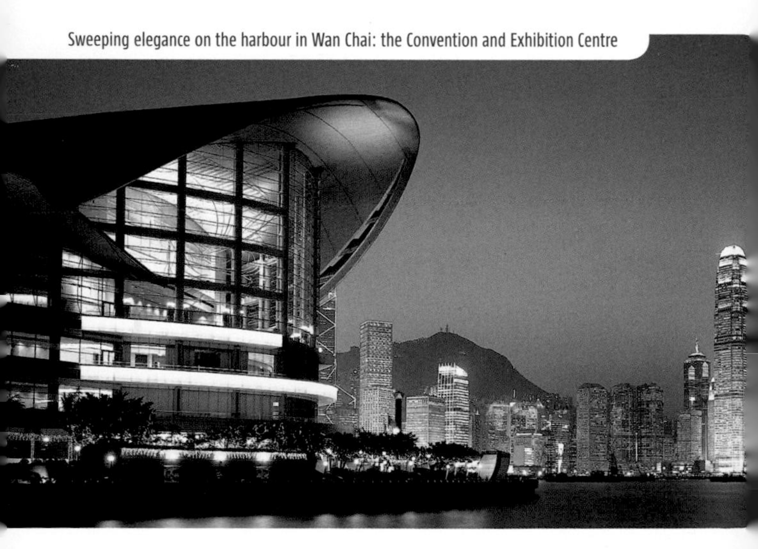

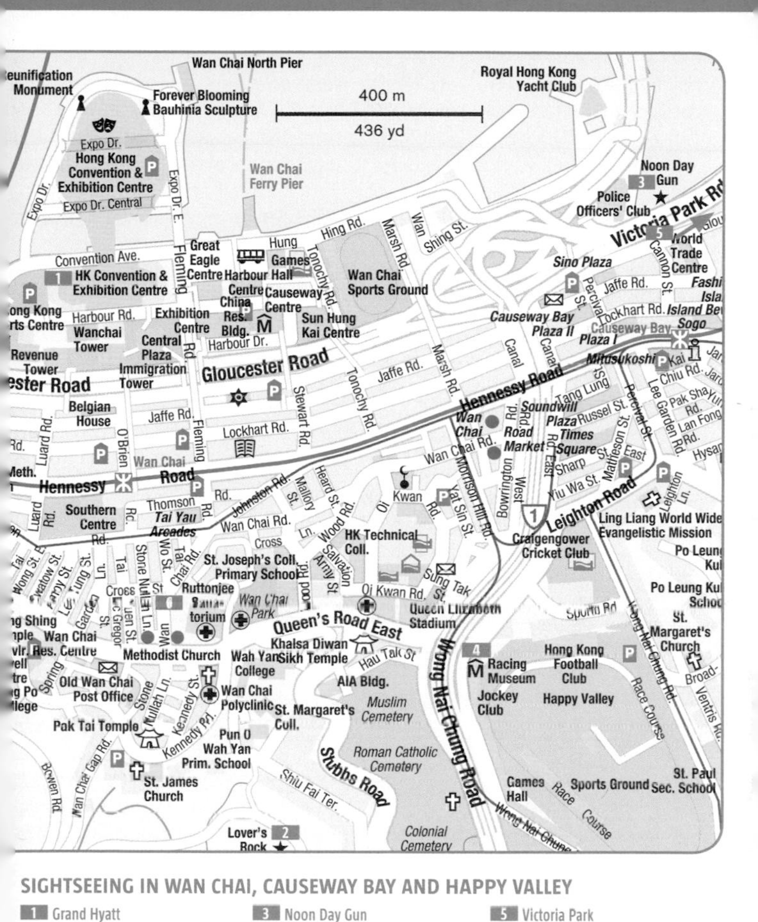

SIGHTSEEING IN WAN CHAI, CAUSEWAY BAY AND HAPPY VALLEY

1 Grand Hyatt
2 Lover's Rock
3 Noon Day Gun
4 Racing Museum
5 Victoria Park
6 Wan Chai Market

it. To the west, the *Academy for Performing Arts* and the *Arts Centre* have created two lively cultural centres (138 A4) (*🕮 E12*). The oldest section of Wan Chai – south of Johnston Road, which used to be directly on the waterfront – is currently undergoing extensive redevelopment. Luckily, the picturesque *Wan Chai Market* has not been affected so far.

With its palatial shopping centres (including *Times Square* mall and the gigantic *Sogo* department store) (138 C4) (*🕮 G–H 11–12*), cinemas, restaurants and a couple of pedestrian precincts, *Causeway Bay* to the east acts as one of the city's main recreational magnets and a paradise for shoppers. This is the place to get the real feel of Hong Kong especially in the evening. If you need fresh air, you can find it in neighbouring Victoria Park. *Happy Valley* further inland is dominated by Hong Kong's oldest racetrack. If you want to experience the Hong Kong passion for gambling at its best, don't miss out on a visit to Happy Valley or the second racetrack in Sha Tin. The INSIDER TIP *Tourist Badge (see entertainment.hkjc.com/entertainment/English/tourist-corner)*, which you can purchase for HK$ 130 at the grandstand entrance for Jockey Club members if you show your passport, will even make it possible to enter their elegant boxes (minimum age 18 years; please note: strict dress code!).

As is the case all over the north of the island, the tram is ideal for visitors who want to see what is going on. Some cars turn around at the corner of Victoria Park. More on trams under "Central & Peak".

Gold and marble splendour in the foyer of the Grand Hyatt

1 GRAND HYATT (君悅酒店) (138 A3) (*E11–12*)

Even after one-and-a-half centuries of British rule, "understatement" is one word that has remained foreign in Hong Kong and the more than amply dimensioned Art Deco foyer in this hotel is one of the plushest examples of all. A golden oval sky hovers above an elegantly curved black marble staircase. *1 Harbour Rd.| 港灣道 1 | MTR Wan Chai*

2 INSIDER TIP LOVER'S ROCK (姻緣石) (138 B5) (*E13*)

This 9 m/30 ft-high, lavishly decorated monolith rises out of the jungle on a mountain slope above Wan Chai. Its phallic shape attracts women looking for Mr Right or hoping to have male children to come here and make sacrifices. The wonderful view and the hike along shady pedestrianised Bowen Road (with a keep-fit trail) are two other good reasons for a visit. *Above Bowen Rd. | 寶雲道 | to the east of Wan Chai Gap Rd. | bus 15 from City Hall to Bowen Rd.*

3 NOON DAY GUN (午炮) (138 C3) (*G11*)

Every day in front of the Excelsior Hotel, at noon precisely, a shot is fired from the shining replica of a cannon with which the Jardine trading house used to greet its ships coming into port from the shore. If you want to witness this charming little ceremony – a lovingly cultivated leftover from colonial days – take the tunnel beneath the urban motorway that starts next to the underground car park of the hotel at the World Trade Center. *MTR Causeway Bay*

4 RACING MUSEUM (賽馬博物館) (138 C5) (*F13*)

Documents, models, films and interactive monitors in the beautiful rooms with a panoramic view of the Happy Valley Racetrack give an impression of the history of horse racing in Hong Kong since its beginnings in 1846. *Daily noon–7pm, 10am–9pm on race days | admission free | Wong Nai Chung Rd. | 黃泥涌道 | 2/F, northern end of the grandstand building | tel. information 29 66 80 65*

5 VICTORIA PARK (維多利亞公園) (139 D3) (*G–H11*)

The '"green lung" of Causeway Bay was once an ocean inlet. It is an ideal place for jogging or shadow boxing in the morning. The benches, footpaths and an area of gravel for foot massages are delightful at any time. *MTR Causeway Bay*

6 WAN CHAI MARKET (灣仔街市) (138 B4–5) (*E12*)

A colourful market, mainly selling all kinds of food, is held every day in the oldest residential area in Wan Chai – a perfect place to take in the atmosphere. *Tai Yuen St. | 太原街 | Cross St. | 交加街 | and neighbourhood | MTR Wan Chai*

WEST KOWLOON, TSIM SHA TSUI, YAU MA TEI (西九龍, 尖沙咀, 油麻地)

Kowloon: "Nine Dragons" is the name of the peninsula opposite the island – or more precisely, the area as far as Boundary Street (132–133 A–E5) (*D–G4*) **which formed the northern border of the Crown Colony after 1860.**

Today, Kowloon is considered to be the entire area south of the Lion Rock hills

TIME TO CHILL

Podium Garden (135 D5–6) (*F9*)

If you go over the wide bridge at the east end of the Avenue of Stars that leads to this square, a garden on the roof of the bus terminal, you can sit and relax under elegant awnings, and watch what's going on in the harbour without having to consume anything at all. *MTR Central, Hong Kong*

Iyara ● (137 D2) (*B11*)

The second level of relaxation: here, next to the Central Escalator, you can have an affordable half-hour foot massage as well as – more expensive – beauty treatments or even a 4-hour "Ultimate Half-day Escape". *26 Cochrane St. | tel. 25 23 87 00 | www.iyaradayspa.com | MTR Central*

Spa in the Four Seasons Hotel (137 D2) (*C11*)

The third level of relaxation: this 21,500ft² feel-good oasis in the luxury hotel near the IFC complex will make a dent in your budget but the list of treatments reads like pure poetry. There is no better way to be pampered. *8 Finance St | tel. 31 96 89 00 | www.fourseasons.com/hongkong/spa | MTR Central, Hong Kong*

and consists of the southern section of the peninsula with two districts.

Tsim Sha Tsui: Tourism, with its hotels, bars and thousands of shops, is concentrated in the southernmost section of Kowloon. There is a never-ending row of shopping emporiums on the western shore from the *China Hong Kong City* (with its ferry terminal) (134 B–C5) (*🕮 D–E8*) to the *Ocean Terminal* (134 B6) (*🕮 D9*) where the cruise ships dock. At the southern tip, the *Clock Tower* rises up next to the Star Ferry landing stage – it is all that is left of the former railway station – with the *Cultural Centre* in a prime location behind it. The harbour promenade – as the *Avenue of Stars*, it pays homage to Hong Kong's most famous film actors and actresses – offers magnificent panoramic views. The main southwest axis of Kowloon, the more than 3.5 km/2¼ miles-long *Nathan Road* (132 B5–6, 134 C1–6) (*🕮 E4–9*), starts next to the time-honoured *Peninsula Hotel*.

Yau Ma Tei: The top locations in this interesting district are the *Tin Hau Temple* with its shady forecourt, the *jade market* and the *night market on Temple Street*; Discovery Tour No. 2 takes you to all of them.

You can shorten the distances between the sights in Kowloon by taking the underground or one of the numerous buses that travel under and along Nathan Rd. Kowloon Park is a pleasant place to relax.

1 HONG KONG CULTURAL CENTRE (香港文化中心) (134 C6) (*🕮 E9*)

The southern tip of Kowloon has been dominated by the salmon-pink tiled Cultural Centre since 1989. With its concert hall (2100 seats), theatre (1750 seats), studio theatre, a gigantic foyer and the Museum of Art it demonstrates the city's cultural ambitions. Many people made fun of the architecture ("ski slope") and it is at least strange that the almost windowless building ignores the exquisite view. *10 Salisbury Rd. | 梳士巴利道 | MTR Tsim Sha Tsui*

The Nathan Road cuts through Kowloon from Victoria Harbour to Boundary Street

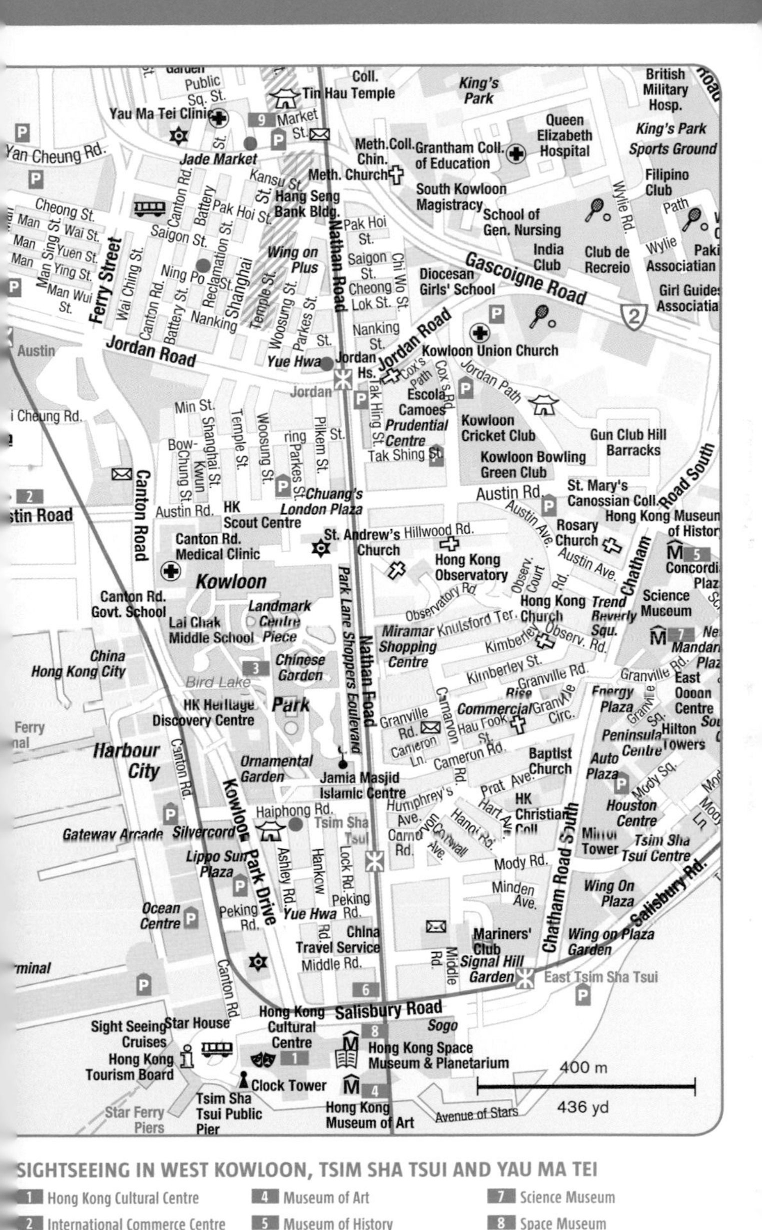

SIGHTSEEING IN WEST KOWLOON, TSIM SHA TSUI AND YAU MA TEI

- 1 Hong Kong Cultural Centre
- 2 International Commerce Centre
- 3 Kowloon Park
- 4 Museum of Art
- 5 Museum of History
- 6 Peninsula Hotel
- 7 Science Museum
- 8 Space Museum
- 9 Tin Hau Temple

2 INTERNATIONAL COMMERCE CENTER (環球貿易廣場) **(134 A–B4)** *(𝔐 C8)*

Hong Kong's new super skyscraper (484 m/ 1588 ft high) stands at the entrance to the western harbour tunnel. The Ritz Carlton Hotel occupies the top 15 floors. The building also caters to the general public: INSIDER TIP *Sky 100 (Sun–Thu 10am–9pm, Fri until 10pm, Sat until 11.30pm | admission HK$ 168, online HK$ 151 | www.sky100.com.hk)*, at a height of 393 m/1300 ft, has an observation platform with a panoramic view – and it is almost as high as The Peak. *MTR Kowloon*

Calligraphy in the Museum of Art: fine examples of "analogue" handwriting!

3 KOWLOON PARK (九龍公園) ● **(134 C5)** *(𝔐 E8–9)*

The most interesting section of Kowloon's "green lung" is the Sculpture Garden with contemporary works by local sculptors. Children will probably prefer the aviaries. There is also a swimming pool in the north of the park. The *Heritage Discovery Centre* in the south holds exhibitions on Hong Kong's cultural heritage and also has a café. *Park daily 6.30am–midnight | Haiphong Rd. | 海防道 | MTR Tsim Sha Tsui*

4 MUSEUM OF ART (香港藝術館) ★ **(134 C6)** *(𝔐 E9)*

This building, opened in 1991 on the southern tip of Kowloon, does not seem very inviting at first sight but it is a demonstration of the cultural ambitions the city had at the time. Wealthy collectors donated a large number of masterpieces of classical Chinese art to the Museum. These mainly consist of ink paintings and calligraphy, but also sculptures, lacquer ware, jade, bronzes, ceramics and textiles. Part of the 62,000ft² exhibition area is used to show interesting works of art by contemporary Hong Kong artists. *Closed due to renovations at the time of going to print; re-opening planned for 2018 | admission HK$ 10, Wed free | MTR Tsim Sha Tsui*

5 MUSEUM OF HISTORY (香港歷史博物館) ★ ● **(135 D4)** *(𝔐 F8)*

This is one of the world's finest history museums. Visitors find it hard to tear themselves away from the great variety of subjects dealt with and the sophisticated presentation. Where the natural environment is explained, visitors see original-sized jungle trees and hear animals calling; in the cultural-history section, entire houses and theatre stages have been reconstructed, wall-sized photos of old Hong Kong merge with real objects on a scale of one-to-one – for example, a picture of the harbour blends in with a replica of a junk – and the historical chemist's shop even smells like one! Interactive media, multilingual slide shows and historical film material make the journey through the past, known as "The Hong Kong Story", complete. *Mon, Wed–Fri 10am–6pm, Sat/Sun 10am–7pm | admission free | MTR Hung Hom*

6 PENINSULA HOTEL (半島酒店) (134 C6) (*F9*)

This grandiose luxury hotel is the most impressive architectural example of former colonial greatness. The opening of the hotel in 1928 was a milestone in Kowloon's development. In spite of the location in what was at the time an unattractive suburb, the hotel profited from the neighbouring railway station and the fantastic view of the island – although this is now obstructed. The best time to take in the atmosphere of the foyer with its magnificent golden plasterwork is in the afternoon at INSIDER TIP *high tea*. *Salisbury Rd. | 梳士巴利道 | MTR Tsim Sha Tsui*

7 SCIENCE MUSEUM (香港科學館) (135 D4–5) (*F8*)

The largest museum building in Hong Kong is devoted to science and technology. Many new educational ideas have been implemented here with great skill with most objects being hands-on exhibits. There is a room for special exhibitions on the ground floor and an introduction to the "World of Mirrors". The protection of the environment and endangered species, as well as life sciences, are also dealt with. There is a *Children's Zone* for the youngest visitors; cildren and teenagers will also have a great time in the computer section on the first floor – where the entrance is located. One level up, communications, transport ("Betsy", Hong Kong's first commercial airliner, is an eye-catcher on the ceiling), and food and household technology are dealt with. On the third floor is the energy efficiency display. The museum is particularly proud of its 20 m/66ft-high "Energy Machine" in the atrium where rolling balls trigger all kinds of move-

FOR BOOKWORMS AND FILM BUFFS

Noble House – Written by James Clavell, probably the most famous novel about Hong Kong deals with intrigues for economic power (1981)

The World of Suzie Wong – Richard Mason wrote the book about the beauty from the Wan Chai red-light district who became world famous through the film adaptation with William Holden and Nancy Kwan (1960, director Richard Quine).

Love is a Many-Splendored Thing – The western/oriental love story by Han Suyin (1952) is set in the difficult post-war years in Hong Kong.

Chungking Express – A genuine Hong Kong film that made it into the cinemas of the west. It tells two love stories set in the city's police milieu (1994, directed by Wong Kar Wei).

ments and sound effects. *Mon–Wed, Fri 10am–7pm, Sat/Sun 10am–9pm | admission HK$ 20, Wed free | 2 Science Museum Rd. | 科學館道 2 | MTR Hung Hom*

8 SPACE MUSEUM (香港太空館) (134 C6) (*Ⅲ E9*)

This museum makes astronomy, solar engineering and space travel easy to understand and it will especially appeal to children and teenagers. The main attraction is the Planetarium. *Mon, Wed–Fri 1pm–9pm, Sat/Sun 10am–9pm | admission HK$ 10, Wed free, Planetarium from HK$ 24 | Salisbury Rd. | 梳士巴利道 | MTR Tsim Sha Tsui*

9 TIN HAU TEMPLE (天后廟) (134 C3) (*Ⅲ E7*)

The chaos of big city life is swept away as soon as you enter the square in front of the temple. Old men can be seen playing chess while others are reading the newspaper or enjoying the view through the ancient trees which shade the square. The pace of life slows down further when you enter this sanctuary of tranquillity. Its atrium is filled with a permanent cloud of grey and white smoke from the spirals of incense below which stay lit for up to a week. Four of the five halls (the fifth hall on the far right is reserved for an exhibition) are home to splendidly dressed gods and deities in their extravagantly adorned shrines. The main figure in the centre hall is the girl-like patron saint of seafarers, Tin Hau, otherwise known as the "Empress of Heaven", referring to her power to settle storms, calm waters and rescue sailors aided by the frightening figures in front of her. Gifts for the dead are often prepared in the adjacent rooms: you can sometimes see entire houses made of paper and bamboo decorated with interior furnishings. In one of the ovens between the buildings, these gifts are then burnt as offerings to the deceased who are pictured on the photos lining the shelves around the temple. *Daily 8am–6pm | 10 Public Square St. | 眾坊街 10 | MTR Yau Ma Tei*

An idyllic spot in the big city: the bird market in Mong Kok

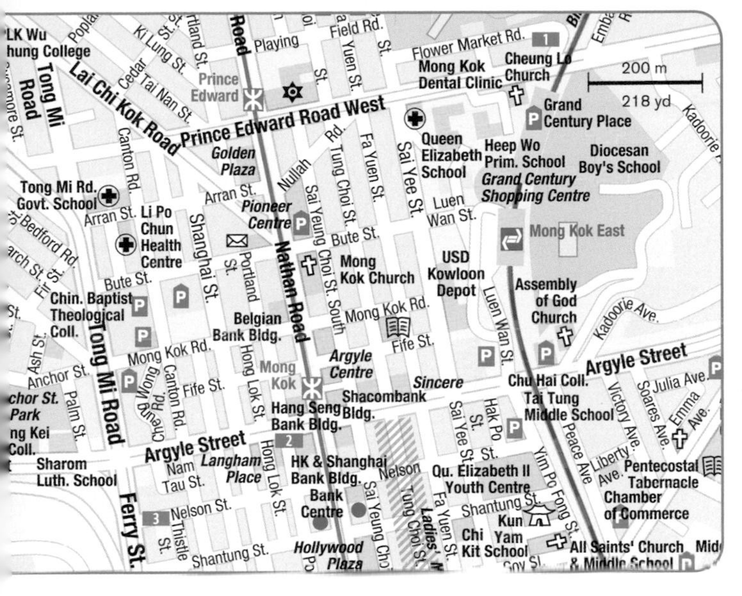

SIGHTSEEING IN MONG KOK

1 Flower and bird market
2 Langham Place
3 Food market

MONG KOK (旺角)

★ This extremely densely populated district of the city delights its visitors with its large variety of street markets and other shopping possibilities.

Some sections of the streets in Mong Kok have even been turned into pedestrian precincts – something very rare in Hong Kong. The *markets for food, flowers and birds* are described below; see "Shopping" for information on the market on *Fa Yuen Street* and the *Ladies' Market.* The market where ornamental fish are sold on *Tung Choi Street* near Bute Street (132 B6) (*D–E5*) is an attractive place to go for a stroll and get a glimpse of everyday life.

1 FLOWER AND BIRD MARKET (花墟, 園圃街雀鳥花園) (132 B–C5) (*E4*)

These are actually two separate markets but you have to pass the flower market on your way to the bird market. The Yuen Po Street Bird Garden, to give it its proper name, was specifically established here – with small houses and a lot of green, it is an idyllic, photogenic location and it is closed to traffic! The flower market is more or less just a block of houses (on the south side of Flower Market Road) with countless flower and plant shops. *MTR Prince Edward, Mong Kok East*

2 LANGHAM PLACE (朗豪坊) (134 C1) (*E5*)

Its architecture makes Hong Kong's futuristic shoppers' paradise the most spectacular of all – 9 storeys high, with a winter garden glazed on two sides and no right angles. *Portland St./corner of Argyle St. | 砵蘭街/亞皆老街 | MTR Mong Kok*

Full steam ahead: sampan tours are the hit in the harbour at Aberdeen

3 FOOD MARKET (旺角街市)
(134 B1) *(🕮 D5)*

All the ingredients needed for Cantonese cooking are sold every day on the corner of Argyle Street and Canton Road and in intersecting Nelson Street. Vegetables and dried mushrooms, fruit and meat, as well as fish, mussels, toads and crabs that are all still alive. The market is at its liveliest in the morning. *MTR Mong Kok*

MORE SIGHTS

ABERDEEN (香港仔)
(140 A–C 2–4) *(🕮 B–D 16–17)*

This skyscraper settlement in the southwest of the island is still described as a "fishing village" in some brochures – what a misrepresentation!

Harbour: The formerly famous junk town no longer looks like it did in countless films. Nobody lives permanently on the water here anymore but the more than 100 motorised junks remaining at least create a touch of the exotic atmosphere of the Far East. The free ferry trip to the gigantic floating restaurant *Jumbo* will give you some idea of this. This monument to Chinese kitsch, laden down with gold, is anchored on the other side of the bridge to Ap Lei Chau opposite the exclusive Yacht Club. It serves good dim sums. If you feel like taking a sampan trip, bargain with the ladies who approach you on the promenade with their cries of "Sampan, sampan!" (around HK$m60 per person for 20 minutes). *Bus 70 from Exchange Square to the terminus, then to the west and cross over the pedestrian bridge; the ferries to the restaurant leave from the promenade a few yards to the right*

Cemetery: Ancestors deserve the very best which is why Cantonese graves always enjoy prime locations – although they usually get built up after a while in Hong Kong. The large *Aberdeen Chinese Permanent Cemetery* (140 A2–3) (*B16–17*) is probably the closest you will come to experiencing the original. A visit is especially worthwhile at the Ching Ming and "double nine" – held on the 9th day of the 9th month in the Chinese calendar – festivals when offerings are made at the graves. *Entrance over a flight of steps on the slope*

CHI LIN NUNNERY (志蓮淨苑) ●
(U D1) (*0*)

The newest of Hong Kong's temple convents was completed in 2000. It is also the most representative because it was built as a classical Chinese wooden construction in the massive, but simple style of the Tang period. The mostly gilded pictures show that it is still possible to create impressive Buddhist works of art. *Daily 9am–4.30pm*

Visitors reach the superbly cultivated *Nan Lian Garden (daily 7am–9pm | admission free | www.nanliangarden.org)* opposite the convent over a bridge. The 9 acres make it the largest example of Chinese garden art in Hong Kong. It also has an exquisite vegetarian restaurant. *At the east end of Fung Tak Rd.| 鳳德道 | MTR Diamond Hill, exit C2*

LION ROCK (獅子山) (143 D3) (*0*)

This conspicuous 495 m/1624 ft-high peak in the shape of a lion's head is more of an eyecatcher than a hiking destination. It gave its name to the entire range of hills that borders Kowloon to the north.

OCEAN PARK (海洋公園) ★
(141 E–F 3–4, D–E 5–6) (*E–F 17–20*)

Hong Kong's most delightful leisure park is a mixture of an amusement park, zoo and circus in a fantastic location with a view over the South China Sea. The 217-acre complex is divided into two sections: *Waterfront* near the entrance and *Summit*

FIT IN THE CITY

At *Victoria Park* **(139 D3)** (**G–H11**) there is a jogging track with keep-fit apparatus as well as a section where you can walk over loose round stones to massage your feet. *Bowen Road* is Hong Kong's most beautiful jogging stretch: above Happy Valley and Wan Chai a traffic-free road takes you through leafy scenery – with occasional views of the forest of skyscrapers; keep-fit apparatus can also be found at various points on the route. Recommendation: go up over Wan Chai Gap **(138 A–B 5–6)** (***E 13***) and then run to the east to the end of Stubbs Road and, from there, take any bus back into town.

Shadow boxing: Masters of Tai chi guan, the proper name of this form of Chinese gymnastics, go to the nearest park soon after 6am. Others gather in front of the *Museum of Art* **(134 C6)** (***E9***) on Mon, Wed and Fri at 7.30am: that is where William and Pandora hold training sessions for a small fee.

higher up. The two are connected by a 1.5 km/1-mile cable railway as well as the *Ocean Express*, an underground cable car that simulates an underwater voyage. Maritime themes set the tone, but the range of attractions is much wider.
Waterfront is more for young visitors with children's merry-go-rounds, games of skill and trained sea lions – this is also where Hong Kong's three panda bears are at home, and South-East Asian birds and otters live in a free flight hall. The *Aqua City*, an aquarium 3-floors deep with 5000 fish of 400 species, is the pride of the park. Ocean Park is also involved in protecting endangered species; part of the proceeds flow into a foundation.
Visitors learn to about nature in the *Summit* region too, where there is a magnificent **INSIDER TIP** jellyfish aquarium and an open-air enclosure in the form of an artificial rocky coast for seals, complete with waves, at *Pacific Pier*. A looping track and other rides provide plenty of thrills nearby. Escalators glide down to the lower level with the *Raging River* rapids ride. *Mon–Sat 10am–6pm, Sun 10am–7pm, longer opening times until max. 10 pm in the summer | admission HK$ 385 | for information on possible changes and performance times, see www.oceanpark.com.hk/html/en/plan-your-visit/calendar | MTR Ocean Park*

REPULSE BAY (淺水灣) ● (U D5) (*ꟾ 0*)

Hong Kong's most popular beach for swimming is always overcrowded during the summer months. Swimming out to one of the pontoons and being gently rocked by the waves is a wonderful way to relax. There are many restaurants and a wonderfully kitschy Tin Hau temple at the southern end. *Buses 6, 6X from Exchange Square*

STANLEY (赤柱) ★ (U D6) (*ꟾ 0*)

Stanley is Hong Kong's southernmost area. Most visitors go to the large clothes

New start in Stanley: an excellent waterfront location for the restaurant in Murray House

market in the centre. Other attractions include the Promenade with ☀ *Murray House* that was originally built in 1844 in Central District and then demolished for the construction of the Bank of China Tower in 1982. It was moved here and now houses several restaurants where you can dine with sea views. There's also an old *Tin Hau temple* nearby as well as a long beach for swimming with various possibilities for water sports. *Buses 6, 6X from Exchange Square*

VICTORIA HARBOUR (維多利亞港)
(U C3) *(🕮 A–H 6–11)*

This is really the heart of Hong Kong, one of the most beautiful natural harbours in the world – today one of world's largest container ports. Kwai Chung in the northwest of Kowloon is the loading centre. The *Star Ferry Company* and *Watertours* organise daily tours.

WONG TAI SIN TEMPLE
(黃大仙祠) ★ (133 F2) *(🕮 H1–2)*

Hong Kong's largest and busiest temple complex: Every year more than 3 million faithful make offerings to a miracle-working saint here. The complex also has a 2-storey building with rooms for 160 fortune tellers and several shops selling devotional objects. The main hall with its double roof – closed to the public – was consecrated in 1973, most of the other buildings in 1982. This is where you will be able to experience Hong Kong's syncretism; Confucius, Lao Tse and Buddha are also worshipped here. A clinic is part of the temple complex; like the temple, it belongs to the Sik Sik Yuen charity organisation and is financed through donations made by the faithful. *Daily 7am–5.30pm | MTR Wong Tai Sin, exits A and B*

FURTHER AFIELD

CHEUNG CHAU (長洲)
(142 B–C5) *(🕮 0)*

Translated, Cheung Chau means "Long Land" and it is the largest and liveliest of all the traditional settlements in Hong Kong. The narrow streets are lined with 2-storey houses clustered together. With the exception of a few mini-pickups, there are no cars. There are still some junks in the harbour although there has been a great decline in fishing. The quay is lined with fish restaurants and kiosks where holiday flats can be booked; it is also possible to rent bikes.

If you turn to the left coming from the landing place, you reach a large square (with a sports ground in front of it) with the religious centre of the community, the *Pak Tai Temple* from 1783, where the patron saint, the Emperor of the Northern Heaven, is honoured. He is thanked every year during the famous Bun Festival. You can then head south (parallel to the quay) along narrow Pak She Street with many small shops.

Turn to the left when you come to the former market square (Tung Wan Road) and walk past a revered tree until you reach the beach. There is a prehistoric scratch drawing preserved on a rock ledge below the Warwick Hotel at the southern end. It is the most accessible example of this type of rock picture in the Hong Kong territory; most of them were discovered near the shore in recent decades. Nothing is known about their age or who drew them (probably not Chinese) and they show animal forms stylised to geometrical patterns.

Go up Cheung Chau Sports Road above the hotel and take Fa Peng Road to Peak Road and turn left. Follow this about 2.2

km/1½ mile to the west to *Care Village* in the southwest and take the sampan ferry from there back to the main settlement. If you also intend to go swimming, half a day will not be enough for Cheung Chau and a full day is never too long. *Ferries from Central, Pier 5, approx. twice an hour, travelling time 60 mins (30 by express ferry)*

AIRPORT AND TSING MA BRIDGE (國際機場 AND 青馬大橋)

(142 A4) *(🗺 0)*

Although the airport is located outside the city, your arrival by plane is in true Hong Kong style. The *airport's* runway stands where water once was off the coast of Hong Kong. The old airport was relocated due to the city's notorious lack of space and is now on an off-shore island, a largely reclaimed area which is 5km long and 3km wide. The airport's accessibility proved equally as challenging as the construction itself, something you will notice when you drive along the motorway into the city (you see far more if you take the bus rather than the airport railway) passing by an area where remote wilderness once stood. The airport is connected to the city centre by three enormous bridges, all of which offer superb views. With a main span of 1377 m/4518 ft, the *Tsing Ma Bridge* is the longest suspension bridge in the world which carries road and rail traffic. A bus ride into the city is the perfect introduction to this city of superlatives. Remember to take a seat on the right side of the bus!

LAMMA ISLAND 南丫島

(142–143 C–D5) *(🗺 0)*

Beaches, hills and fish restaurants: Hong Kong's third largest island, Lamma, as well as all the other small islands, is car-free. Day-trippers come for a swim – there are two pleasant beaches: *Hung Shing Yeh* in the north and **INSIDER TIP** *Lo So Shing* in the centre – and to eat. There is a row of fish restaurants along the harbour front in the village of Sok Kwu Wan; the best is the *Rainbow (Moderate)*. You can rent rooms in Yung Shue Wan, the peaceful second village. Here, you can also enjoy your meal on a terrace near the water. It will take you around 90 minutes to walk across reforested hills from one village to the other. *Ferries from Central, Pier 4, every half to two hours, travelling time 30–50 mins.*

LANTAU AND PO LIN MONASTERY (大嶼山 AND 寶蓮寺) ★

(142 A–B 4–5) *(🗺 0)*

You should explore Hong Kong's largest island *Lantau* by bus or taxi; there are enough attractions for a full day. A new era opened up for Lantau when the airport was built; with it came new roads and railway tracks, followed by a satellite city and, in 2005, Disneyland. However, parts of the islands have remained almost deserted.

Hong Kong's largest religious building, *Po Lin Monastery*, is located at an altitude of 460 m/1500ft on the Ngong Ping Plateau. The Buddhist "Monastery of the Precious Lotus" was consecrated in 1927 and the main hall, inspired by Peking's palace architecture, in 1970. The monastery has prospered as a destination for outings. Visitors, including many from foreign countries, have streamed to the monastery since the world's largest open-air bronze Buddha (22 m/72 ft high, 34 m/112 ft with the stone base) was erected there in 1993. In 2006, *Ngong Ping 360* started operating. This includes a 5.7 km/3½-mile-long cable car (travelling time: 25 min. from the MTR terminus Tung Chung to the Buddha) as well as Ngong Ping Village at the top with shops, restaurants and a multimedia show "Walking with Buddha" that describes the life of Gauta-

ma Buddha. Ttip: take the cable car up and walk or take the bus down.
The fishing village *Tai O* at the western end of the island mainly consists of wooden houses covered with sheet metal on stilts. Mudskipper fish jump around and mangroves grow in some places. Lantau's loveliest beaches *Pui O* and *Cheung Sha* are at the centre of the south coast. Some forts from the 17th century, built to protect the area from pirates, are historically important; the largest can be visited at the southern end of *Tung Chung*.
The 70 km/43½ mile *Lantau Trail* starts at Mui Wo in the northeast and leads, in twelve stages, over the hills to the southwest cape and back again along the coast. The third stage is spectacular but quite steep; it goes over the barren *Lantau Peak* (934 m/3064 ft) to Po Lin Monastery. Easier routes: from the monastery to the south through the forest to the road or to the northeast as far as Tung Chung. *Ferries from Central, Pier 6, to Mui Wo every 30–50 mins., travelling time 1 hour; from Mui Wo with bus no. 2 to Ngong Ping (monastery), with no. 1 to Tai O and with 3M to Tung Chung; also MTR Tung Chung*

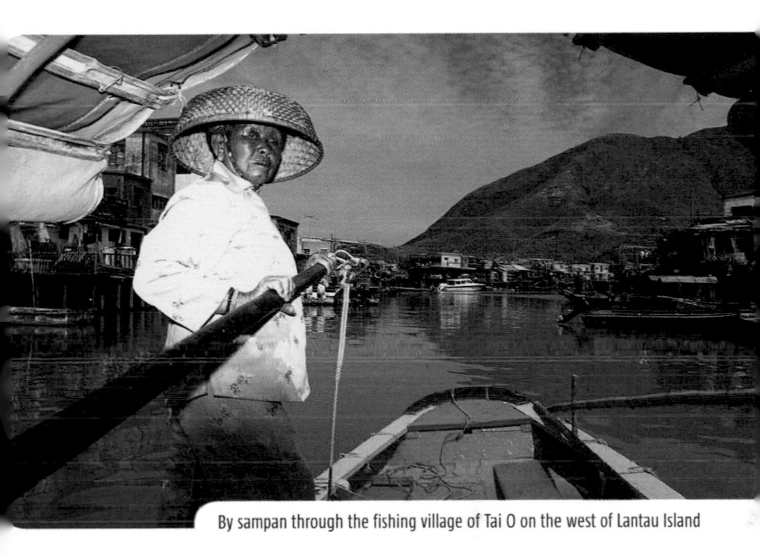
By sampan through the fishing village of Tai O on the west of Lantau Island

INSIDER TIP LEI YUE MUN (鯉魚門) (U E3) (*0*)

A stroll through a village that is easy to reach. The fishing settlement of Lei Yue Mun consists of one single long street. It is lined with fish restaurants and fishmongers selling the greatest variety of seafood available anywhere in Hong Kong. Many houses float above the water on stilts. Follow the double-bend to the right and then left and after about 500 m you will reach some large rocks and the village temple in honour of the "Empress of Heaven" Tin Hau. *MTR Kwun Tong line or Tseung Kwan O line to Yan Tong, exit A2, then walk 600 m; the village begins at the junk port.*

INSIDER TIP MAI PO NATURE RESERVE (米埔) (142 B–C 1–2) (*0*)

The fish and shrimp pools, mud flats and Hong Kong's last large belt of mangroves in the Mai Po Nature Reserve in the amphibian northwest of the New Territories provide plenty of nourishment and shelter for silver herons, ibises, kingfishers and another 250 species of birds. Many migratory birds spend the winter here. The *World Wide Fund for Nature (WWF) (only Sat, Sun | 1 Tramway Path | tel. 25 26 10 11 | www.wwf.org.hk/en/getinvolved/go maipo)* has established an information centre and observation sites in the reserve. Visits only as part of a guided tour.

NEW TERRITORIES (新界)

Although they actually include all the areas that are not part of Kowloon or Hong Kong Island, people think of them as the mainland beyond the range of hills that forms the boundary to the north and east of Kowloon. This is the site of gigantic satellite towns as well as still virtually impassable terrain with Hong Kong's highest elevation *Tai Mo Shan* (957 m/3140 ft). Two excellent tours give a fine overview of the main sights *(duration around 5 hours each | HK$ 490)*; they can be booked at *Gray Line Tours (tel. 23 68 71 11 | www.grayline.com.hk)*. The "Heritage Tour" includes a visit to an old clan village, typical of how the New Territories used to be, complete with ancestral temple, to the residence of an imperial official, to the market temple in *Tai Po* and the trees that are worshiped as being holy. "Land Between" offers a colourful selection with a temple monastery, the heron reserve *Luk Keng* and fish farms. You will see a great deal of the landscape, as well as two or three satellite towns, on both tours.
Mountain hiking: The *MacLehose Trail* runs from east to west over 100 km/62miles divided into 10 stages. The most picturesque sections (stages 1 and 2) takes hikers along the Sai Kung Peninsula. The 75 km747 mile *Wilson Trail* crosses the New Territories from north to south.

SAI KUNG PENINSULA AND TAP MUN (西貢半島 AND 塔門) (143 E–F 2–3) *(🕮 0)*

The rugged, almost deserted peninsula lies far to the east and is the best destination for a not-too-strenuous day-long walk. Take the 8.30am ferry from Ma Liu Shui Pier (143 D2–3) *(🕮 0) (MTR University Station, exit B, walk to the left and follow the signs to "Pier" or "Landing Steps")*. The sea journey takes you along the mountainous shore of Tolo Harbour to *Tap Mun Island* with its old fishing and

SPOTLIGHT ON SPORTS

Horse racing in Hong Kong: Races have been held in *Happy Valley* **(138 C5)** ***(🕮 F–G13)*** since 1846 and now usually take place on Wed evening. The *Sha Tin* **(143 D3)** ***(🕮 0)*** track was added in 1978: it is used at weekends. Where in other places, mostly upper class people watch the races, here they are popular with everyone – because of the gambling. On average, almost 50,000 spectators come to each event. The racing season lasts from mid Sept to early June. *www.hkjc.com/english/index.asp.*
Horse racing in Macau: The *Taipa* racetrack **(150 A–B2)** ***(🕮 a–b8)*** *(tel. 28 82 08 68)*, opened in 1991, holds 15,000 spectators. Most races take place at weekends. Entrance to the lower levels is free.

farming village. You can spend an hour there until the ferry comes back for the return journey or travel two stations further to *Chek Keng* and take the trail over the saddle of the mountain to the southeast. The reward for the 3.5 km/2¼ mile walk is INSIDER TIP *Tai Long Wan* the "Bay of Big Waves" with Hong Kong's two most fabulous beaches; there are simple restaurants in the nearby village.

Then it's back to Chek Keng; this time not to the pier but to the left and another 3.5 km/2¼ miles to the next bay *Wong Shek*. A bus to INSIDER TIP *Sai Kung* (143 E3) *(🕮 0)*. The small village is worth a visit even without the hike due to its tranquil atmosphere and its many sea-view restaurants serving fish such as *Chuen Kee* (see p. 57). Boat tours also depart from Sai Kung which sail through the pretty labyrinth of islands around Port Shelter and Rocky Harbour. You will find several boat tour operators along the harbour. During summer, ferries also shuttle passengers over to the idyllic beaches on nearby islands. Some of the islands and coastline are now part of a Unesco Geopark and special tours are organised for those interested in geology. Towering above entire sections of coast, the basalt columns have become a landmark attraction. Visit the *Geopark Volcano Discovery Centre (daily 9.30am–4.30pm | free admission)* at the Sai Kung bus terminal for more information. The more adventurous can hire their own sampan for HK$ 250 an hour. *Bus 92 and minibuses from MTR Choi Hung*

Excursion to Sha Tin: pagoda in the Temple of the 10,000 Buddhas

SHA TIN (沙田) (143 D3) *(🕮 0)*

There are two interesting destinations near the train station in this gigantic satellite town. In addition to temporary exhibitions, the *Heritage Museum (from the station exit A, then to the right, down the escalator, through the bus station and follow the road on the right; around 10 mins)* has a fantastic section devoted to the history and culture of the New Territories. The *Temple of 10,000 Buddhas (cross the railway, follow the street on the right past the Grand Central Plaza complex, turn left onto Pak Tau Street, then right to Sheung Wo Che Street and follow the footpath up the valley)* has occupied its site in the mountains since 1957. The path through the wood is lined with life-sized figures – some of them gold-plated – of the 500 Luohan (enlightened Buddhist monks). The interior walls of the main hall are covered with shelves with 12,800 small gilded statues of Buddha. There are many other figures, usually brightly coloured, in the forecourt, as well as a pagoda.

FOOD & DRINK

Hong Kong is a paradise for gourmets where going out to eat is part of everyday life.

And that has led to an opulent range of restaurants ranging from those for ordinary people to extremely elegant, from Chinese to European. Most Hong Kongers are Cantonese and their cooking is unquestionably the queen of all regional cuisines of China. Backbiters from other parts of the country say that the Cantonese would eat anything on four legs except a table and everything that swims, with the exception of ships, and – as long is it wasn't a plane – anything that flies. And, admittedly, chickens' feet and jellyfish might not be everyone's favourite titbit. But, the Cantonese mastery in using even the most unusual ingredients has led to the fascinating variety of dishes and Hong Kong's cooks are continuously adding new creations.

First and foremost – everything has to be fresh! Chickens are usually only slaughtered when they are bought; seafood swims in an aquarium or pond until guests order it. This is to ensure that the natural flavours can be experienced to the full. And is also the result of the way food is cooked – rapid searing or steaming – and a reasonable, even frugal, use of spices.

What should you order? Of course, seafood is the first choice. Pork and chicken are always good too. Roast duck is another delicious dish; you dunk it in sweet plum sauce. There are also excel-

 Photo: Dim Sums

Gourmet restaurants and cookhouses: every day you will be able to experience new culinary highlights – and not only Chinese cuisine

lent vegetarian dishes which frequently offer amazing imitations of meat and fish for those who prefer to let animals stay alive.

However, the *dim sums* are the real highlight. It is not actually a dish but the edible part of *yam cha*, Cantonese tea culture. Small delicacies are served along with tea in the teahouses and restaurants from early in the morning to the afternoon – small dumplings filled with shrimps or pork, ribs in plum sauce, fried balls filled with lotus-seed paste and dozens of other kinds of "heart's delights" – which is what *dim sum* means. In some restaurants, buffet trolleys are pushed through the rows of tables; in others, guests order by marking their choice on special order forms. Very few experiences in Hong Kong are more impressive and authentic than going to a INSIDER TIP Sunday lunchtime *yam cha* (tea drinking session) when whole families descend on the – often gigantic and lavishly decorated – teahouses where the noise they make brings the roof down.

The other regional cuisines of China also profit from the great variety of excellent products and high culinary standard of Hong Kong and often taste at least as good here as they do in their region of origin: Peking cooking is famous for the ber of guests is ordered and a selection is made from the various categories – duck, chicken, pork, shrimps, fish and so on – as well as a soup. The huge choice of seafood also makes it possible for you to put together a purely maritime meal.

A Chinese meal – the more diners, the greater the variety of dishes

Peking Duck, fire pot and noodle dishes, East Chinese cooking from Shanghai and Hangzhou prefers more substantial food (sometime flavoured with tea leaves), while extremely spicy dishes are typical of Szechuan cuisine. And the hearty dishes from Chaozhou are not to be overlooked. Birds' nests are famous – but very expensive. Another thing you will not forget is the strong, bitter Chaozhou digestive tea that is drunk out of tiny cups.

You should be in a group to really enjoy a meal in a Chinese restaurant. The number of delights increases with the number of diners, nobody just orders "his or her" meal, everybody shares everything on the table. One person takes charge of ordering. Usually, one more dish than the num-

Most of the better restaurants have an English menu and you will often find a waiter who can help you in others – if they are not too busy. It is a good idea to book in advance in most restaurants. Tea is the perfect beverage to accompany a Cantonese meal – especially the non-fermented green or semi-fermented Wulong tea (leaves are brewed twice). There is usually only a limited choice of wine in Chinese restaurants. Beer is a better idea, especially to go with the heavier dishes from other regions. Freshly-pressed fruit juices from fruit stands as well as chilled soya milk (sold as "Vitasoy") are ideal refreshments when out and about. The cuisine of other countries plays a major role in Hong Kong's culinary variety

Curry fans will find what they are looking for in the Indian and Indonesian restaurants, aficionados of chilli will feel at home with the Koreans and Thais, and lovers of fresh products and raw fish can choose from the many Japanese restaurants. Eating in a European restaurant in Hong Kong is not only something those suffering from homesickness do; many chefs have been inspired by the wealth of different local products and cooking techniques. But the prices are often similar to those in expensive restaurants at home. The breakfast served in large hotels is first-rate but unreasonably expensive. A more economical alternative is to have café au lait, croissants, etc. in one of the branches of *Délifrance*, e.g. *New Mandarin Plaza | 14 Science Museum Rd.* (135 D5) *(𝔐 F8)* and *1/F, Worldwide Plaza | Pedder St.* (137 D–E3) *(𝔐 C11)*. If you need a cup of tea to get you going in the morning, you should start your day with dim sums in a teahouse, e.g. from 7.30am at *Jade Garden* (138 C4) *(𝔐 G12) (Causeway Plaza II | Percival St./corner of Lockhart Rd., entrance Lockhart Rd.)*. Some special restaurants are devoted entirely to sweet temptations; a heavenly one is **INSIDER TIP** *Honeymoon Dessert*, e.g. *Shop 3001-D3, Gateway Arcade | Canton Rd.* (134 C5) *(𝔐 E9)* and *Western Market* (136 C2) *(𝔐 B10–11)*.

CHINESE CUISINE

The prices are for à la carte meals, without expensive specialities such as abalone and swallows' nests.

BO INNOVATION (廚魔)

(138 A4) *(𝔐 E12)*

Molecular cooking in Chinese. Some people find it too experimental but you can be sure of entering new culinary territory. The "Wall Street Journal" even wrote an article about it when it opened. But be prepared for the prices: from 1025 HKD. *60 Johnston Rd. | 莊士敦道 60 | entrance Ship Street | tel. 28 50 83 71 | www.boinnovation.com | MTR Wan Chai |* *Expensive*

CHUEN KEE (全記海鮮菜館) ★

(143 E3) *(𝔐 0)*

Fish and seafood fresh from the pool. You can even sit outside and watch the boats bobbing up and down in the harbour. The restaurant caters to foreign guests and has a supply of cooled white wine. *Sai Kung | 53 Hoi Pong St. | 海傍街 | Harbour Promenade, south end beyond the ceremonial gate | tel. 27 91 11 95 | bus 92 from MTR Diamond Hill |* *Moderate–Expensive*

MARCO POLO HIGHLIGHTS

★ Chuen Kee
Seafood fresh from the pool with a view of the harbour and a glass of wine → **p. 57**

★ Din Tai Fung
The dumpling king: not very cosy, but oh so good! → **p. 58**

★ Yung Kee
The epitome of Hong Kong tea house and food culture → **p. 61**

★ Peak Lookout
Hong Kong's most beautiful restaurant in an old colonial building → **p. 62**

★ Penthouse
Paella with Hong Kong flair, pasta with panorama → **p. 63**

CRYSTAL JADE (翡翠拉麵小籠包) (134 B–C5) *(D–E9)*
A trendy interpretation of home-style Shanghai cuisine. If you are lucky, you can enjoy a view of the harbour here. There are delicious dumplings and the servings of noodles are more than satisfying. You can pass the time waiting for a free table – at the entrance you have to enter the number of guests and draw a number – window shopping. *Shop 3328, Gateway Arcade Harbour City 海港城港威商場 | tel. 26 22 26 99 | MTR Tsim Sha Tsui | other branches | Budget*

DIN TAI FUNG (鼎泰豐) ★
You will almost certainly have to queue up if you want to enjoy the delicious dumplings and other small dishes from Shanghai and Taiwan served here. There is even a card giving instructions on how to eat the famous, delicate *xiaolongbao* that not only contain a solid filling but also hot broth. *68 Yee Wo St. | 怡和街 | tel. 31 60 89 98 | MTR Causeway Bay |* (139 D4) *(G12); 3/F, 30 Canton Rd. | 廣東道 30 | tel. 27 30 69 28* (134 C5) *(E9) | Budget*

INSIDER TIP KUNG TAK LAM (功德林) (134 C5) *(E9)*
Vegetarian Shanghai cuisine in a modern environment with a view of the harbour. The organic ingredients come from the restaurant's own garden. An ideal place for dim sums at lunchtime. *1 Peking Rd. | 北京道 1 | 7th floor | tel. 23 12 78 00 | MTR Tsim Sha Tsui | Budget*

INSIDER TIP LUK YU (陸羽茶室) (137 D3) *(C11)*
A journey into the past. The multi-storey tea house restaurant, named after

FAVOURITE EATERIES

Hot and intimate
We are talking about the restaurant of course. *Da Ping Huo (大平伙)* **(136 C2)** ***(B11)*** is special because of its size – there are just six tables – and its authentically hot Sichuan cuisine. The cool interior design is also appealing with contemporary paintings and black and white photos. The five-course lunch menu served in small portions is a real bargain particularly for those travelling alone. *49 Hollywood Rd. | 荷李活道 49 | entrance in Graham St. | tel. 25 59 13 17 | MTR Sheung Wan | Moderate*

Social gathering
As its name suggests, the *Social Place (唐宮小聚)* **(137 D2)** ***(B11)*** is more for larger gatherings than intimate twosomes despite the large number of tables for two in the restaurant. While office workers come for delicious dim sums for lunch, groups of "east-meets-west" friends come for dinner. Everyone comes to enjoy the modern Cantonese cooking from innovative recipes and serving small portions for you to try a bit of everything. "Eggs ain't that simple" is a fun dish with a Sichuan chicken served to the table accompanied by a raw egg cut in two. Try the egg; the yolk inside is not what it seems to be. One more piece of advice: never bite into the Sichuan pepper twigs, just licking them can be enough. *2/F The L.Place | 139 Queen's Rd. Central | 皇后大道中 139 | tel. 35 68 96 66 | MTR Sheung Wan | Moderate*

Maxim's Palace – a high-end Cantonese-style tea house

the patron saint of tea, opened in 1933 and, with its original decoration and stern waiters who are almost as old, is a living monument. It is best in the morning *(from 7am)* or at lunchtime for tea and dim sums *(then Moderate)*. *24–26 Stanley St. | 士丹利街24–26 | tel. 25 23 54 64 | MTR Central | evenings: Expensive*

MANCHU CHINA RESTAURANT (滿漢居) (137 D3) *(B11)*
This cheerful little restaurant serves cooking from Northern China including jiaozi dumplings Peking style and various sweet-and-sour dishes. *Evenings only | 33 Elgin St. | 伊利近街 33 | tel. 22 44 39 98 | Moderate*

MAXIM'S PALACE (美心皇宮) ●
(137 E3) *(D11)*
The fact that the view of the harbour is now usually one of building sites has not effected the popularity of this typical teahouse and its unique atmosphere in any way. The ladies pushing the trolleys with dim sums can usually even speak a little English, which makes it easy to get a taste of classic Cantonese teahouse culture. *Dim sum daily 11am–3pm, Sun from 9am | 2/F City Hall | 5–7 Edinburgh Place | 愛丁堡廣場 5–7| tel. 25 21 13 03 | MTR Central | Moderate*

INSIDER TIP NANHAI NO. 1 (南海一號) (134 C5) *(E9)*
Cantonese restaurant located on the 30th floor. The best seats are at the tables for two next to the window and in the second row, offering mesmerising views over Victoria Harbour and the islands. There is a minimum price of HK$ 500 per head– but the experience is worth it. *iSquare | 63 Nathan Rd. | 彌敦道 63 | tel. 24 87 36 88 | MTR Tsim Sha Tsui | Expensive*

PEKING GARDEN (北京樓)
(137 E3) *(C11)*
Peking Duck is this restaurant's speciality but you can also order Beggar's Chicken and dishes from other regions of China. The INSIDER TIP Noodle Show (at

LOCAL SPECIALITIES

DIM SUM

Most dim sum menus are only in Chinese but you will often find a waiter or waitress who can help you with your order.

CHINESE MEALS AND INGREDIENTS

Abalone – adhesive foot of a sea snail, fresh or dried
Beggar's chicken – A whole chicken is coated with clay and then roasted in its own juices
Bird's nest – Swallows' nests served as a soup or dessert
Congee – Rice soup, either plain or with vegetables or meat
Double sauteed pork – pork, cooked twice
Fish ball – Fish and shrimp meat rolled into white balls and served in broth
Garoupa – Grouper (fish such as sea bass)
Hainan chicken – Chicken in ginger marinade, served on rice
Hairy crab – A delicay in autumn and winter, served boiled
Hot pot – Meat, fish and vegetable fondue
Lo Hon vegetable – various vegetables (Buddhist meal during fasting periods)
Peking duck – Duck, marinated and roasted in the oven; the crispy skin is the best part
Wonton – A noodle-dough dumpling stuffed with shrimp meat, served in broth (photo right)
Yangchow fried rice – Fried rice with chicken, egg, peas, shrimp, mushrooms and other ingredients

about 8pm every evening) is great fun – spaghetti stretching by hand! *Alexandra House | 16–20 Chater Rd. | 遮打道 16–20 | tel. 25 26 64 56 | MTR Central, in exit H; branch without noodle show: Star House | 3 Salisbury Rd. | 梳士巴利道 3 | tel. 27 35 82 11* (134 C6) *(▯ E9)* | *Moderate*

TIM'S KITCHEN (桃花源)
(136 C2) *(▯ B11)*
This restaurant redefines the traditional tea house; a modest size instead o[f] one large room and a subtle Chinese interior design instead of the overpowe[r]ing red and gold. The chef reinterpret[s]

traditional Cantonese fare and adds his own innovative recipes. The finest culinary creations are served in a relaxed, laid-back setting. It also has an English translation of its dim sum menu for tourists. The last dim sum order is at 2.30pm. *84–90 Bonham Strand | 文咸東街 84–90 | tel. 25 43 59 19 | MTR Sheung Wan |* Moderate

YÈ SHANGHAI (夜上海)
(134 C5) (*Ⓜ E9*)
Specialities from the Lower Yangtze region are served in a nostalgic 1930s interior. Its culinary delights have earned this restaurant one Michelin star. *Marco Polo Hotel | 3 Canton Rd. | 廣東道 3 | tel. 23 76 33 22 | MTR Tsim Sha Tsui |* Moderate

YUNG KEE (鏞記) ★
(137 D3) (*Ⓜ C11*)
The three-storey high, gold-coloured façade is a proud reminder of Hong Kong's nouveau riche tradition. Established in 1942, this is an exclusive eatery where large groups of people come to dine. Waiters can often be seen carrying around the large round table tops for twelve people to sit around. The menu includes all the Cantonese favourites. Charcoal-grilled goose is the house speciality available when you order the menu for two people. Also very good for dim sums on Sunday (from 11am). *32–40 Wellington St. | 威靈頓街 32–40 | tel. 25 22 16 24 | www.yungkee.com.hk | MTR Central |* Expensive

INTERNATIONAL CUISINE

BÊP
(137 D3) (*Ⓜ B11*)
Take the Central Escalator and you will find yourself in Vietnam when you reach the top. But be warned: expect to queue for the delicious Pho noodle soup, diverse salad rolls and other classics especially at peak times as SoHo is one of Hong Kong's trendiest districts. Ease the pain of waiting by ordering yourself a cucumber and mint lem on soda. A Vietnamese baguette is the ideal snack for in between. *9–11 Staunton St. | 士丹頓街 9–11 | access via a side lane of Shelley St. | tel. 25 22 75 33 |* Expensive

Chopping, frying, steaming: classical Cantonese cooking is celebrated in the restaurant Yung Kee

CAPRICE
(137 D2) (*C11*)
The French haute cuisine in the culinary flagship Four Season's Hotel vies with the view of the open kitchen and the panorama of Victoria Harbour. Three Michelin stars. From 120 euros. *8 Finance St. | 金融街 8 | tel. 31 96 88 60 | MTR Central |* Expensive

INSIDER TIP **COLETTE'S (藝穗會餐廳)**
(137 D3) (*C12*)
Gastronomic delights on the top floor of the Fringe Club where a vegetarian gourmet lunch buffet is served at 12 noon. The spacious rooftop terrace is the restaurant's best feature. Get there before 2pm otherwise you will have to satisfy yourself with the leftovers. *2 Lower Albert Rd. | 下亞厘畢道 2 | MTR Central |* Budget

GAYLORD (爵樂印度餐廳)
(134 C5) (*E9*)
Hong Kong's best known Indian has been delighting his guests since 1972. Vegetarian meals available, elegant atmosphere, live music in the evenings. *23–25 Ashley Rd. | 亞士厘道 23–25 | tel. 23 76 10 01 | MTR Tsim Sha Tsui |* Moderate

GREYHOUND CAFÉ
(134 B–C6) (*E9*)
Italian meets Thai at this restaurant which has a wide range of dishes at decent prices. The desserts and alcohol-free fruit juice cocktails are particularly worth trying. *G/F, Ocean Terminal, Harbour City | 海港城海運大廈 | tel. 23 83 66 00 | MTR Tsim Sha Tsui |* Budget

INSIDER TIP **MANA!**
(137 D2) (*C11*)
"Fast slow food" is the advertising slogan for this organic vegetarian-vegan snack bar. Although tiny – there is just one large table which is shared with other guests – it offers an outdoor seating area (in a tiny gap between the skyscrapers or on the street in front of the eatery). The food is delicious and you get ample portions. You pay in advance at the counter. *92 Wellington St. | 威靈頓街 92 | MTR Central |* Budget

PEAK LOOKOUT (太平山餐廳) ★
(136 C5) (*B13*)
The most beautiful restaurant in Hong Kong lies hidden in luxuriant green-

LOW BUDGET

Peoples' kitchen: Noodle soup, rice soup or Yangzhou fried rice will satisfy you for less than HK$ 80. A good address is *Tsim Chai Kee* **(137 D2)** **(*B–C11*)** *(98 Wellington St. | Shop B* – the best of many similar establishments on the same street; it can be recognised by its large windows.

Lunch: A good tip in all price categories – you will even be able to afford the gourmet restaurants from Monday to Friday but be there before 1pm; that is when the lunch break begins and it gets very crowded.

Cooked Deli **(134 B5)** **(*E9*)** *(Harbour City, Gateway 3001):* A cookhouse with a view of the harbour in an air-conditioned shopping emporium – choose your meal, note the number, pay at the cash desk and then order.

ery opposite Peak Tower. It dazzles its guests with its varied Pan-Asian cooking and – above all – the incomparable atmosphere of an old colonial building with veranda and shady garden. *121 Peak Rd. | 山頂道 121 | tel. 28 49 10 00 |* *Expensive*

Yummy: feasting on Asian-Western delicacies at the Peak Lookout

PENTHOUSE ★
(138 C3) (*G12*)
A fantastic Hong Kong panorama, fine-tasting dishes from Italy and Spain and a clever mixture of table service and a buffet for salads and desserts. The terrace one floor above is the restaurant's trademark. *30/F, Soundwin Plaza | 1–29 Tang Lung St. | 登龍街 1–29 | tel. 29 70 08 28 | www.penthouse-dining.com | MTR Causeway Bay | set menu Moderate, à la carte Expensive*

PIZZA EXPRESS
(138 A4) (*D–E12*)
Chic, modern restaurant with open kitchen in a trendy area. One recommendation is the vegetarian INSIDER TIP Trifolata prepared with truffle oil; it is good enough to make a Neapolitan pizza baker envious. Many other dishes too. Several branches. *23 Wing Fung St. | 永豐街 23 | Star Street block | tel. 35 28 05 41 | www.pizzaexpress.com.hk | MTR Admiralty | Budget–Moderate*

XENRI NO TSUKI (千里之月)
(139 D4) (*G12*)
This restaurant is nowhere near being inexpensive, but if you want to try the best the Japanese kitchen has to offer, you will pay less here than in other places. Our tip: sit at the bar and watch how the cook creates his works of art. In this hidden restaurant, eating is a real feast for the eyes. *6/F, Jardine Centre | 50 Jardine's Bazaar | 渣甸街 50 | tel. 25 76 18 80 | MTR Causeway Bay | Expensive*

SHOPPING

> **CITY** **WHERE TO START?**
> People with only one day in Hong Kong and not looking for anything in particular will probably be perfectly happy with a shopping spree in **Stanley (U D6)** ***(🗺 O)***. Causeway Bay and Mong Kok are the districts where you will find the largest range of items in a small area. Luxury goods are concentrated in Central. Avoid the shops in Tsim Sha Tsui near Nathan Road: they are often expensive, dubious tourist traps. **Temple Street night market (134 C3)** ***(🗺 E7)*** is a good address in the cheap to middle-price range.

Of course, Hong Kong is *the* place to shop! But the exorbitant shop rents don't give the dealers much leeway. Thus, not every purchase is a real bargain.

Clothes, bags, accessories and household goods are cheap if you buy them at street markets. Brand names from Europe are only a little cheaper (and sometimes more expensive) than at home and are only sold if they have prestige value in Hong Kong. Alcohol and tobacco are very expensive. There are special discounts on many goods throughout the year and there are no set sales times. Only buy high-quality items in specialist shops or from authorised dealers and, best of all, from those with the seal of quality of the Hong Kong Tourism Board

Photo: The Pacific Place shopping centre

Almost unlimited shopping: the shoppers' paradise has become more expensive, but you may still need that extra suitcase when you leave

(HKTB) – a golden Q with a Chinese symbol inside it: proven quality; knowledge of the article, advice, honesty, etc. You can find a list of these companies, sorted by type of goods sold and district, under *www.discoverhongkong.com/eng/jsp/shopping/search-index.jsp*, from the HKTB visitors' centres or on their hotline: *tel. 25 08 12 34*.

If you intend to buy electrical items (cameras, video or hi-fi equipment, etc.), it is a good idea to know exactly the brand and model you want because the advice given often leaves much to be desired. You can ask the company representatives in Hong Kong for information on recommended sales prices. The HKTB will help you find the right addresses.

Department stores and supermarkets have fixed prices and the same applies to reduced articles. However, discounts are often given in camera and hi-fi shops, if you buy jewellery, watches or similar articles, as well as at street markets; it is simply a matter of your skill at bartering. If you are offered much more than a

Shop till you drop – the enormous Times Square, a paradise for serious shopaholics

10% discount on high-quality goods, you should assume that the dealer is trying to cheat you. There is usually no discount granted if you pay with your credit card. If you do not intend to pay in cash, it is a good idea to say so early on.
Make sure that you are given a globally valid guarantee as well as operating instructions in English if you buy any appliances. Some things are sold cheaper because the guarantee is only valid in Hong Kong; take this into consideration when comparing prices. Do not pay any deposit unless it is only a small amount in one of the shops with the Q sign. However, a first instalment of at least 50 percent is expected for commissioned work (tailors, opticians, etc).
Today, Hong Kong is a better place for buying typical Chinese articles than cut-rate goods. It is more expensive than in China itself, but you will usually get the top export quality. Jade is a classic buy (see "Jewellery"). Discovery Tour No. 2 will show you where to buy household goods from steaming baskets to kitchen cleavers; Tour No. 4 will take you to bric-a-brac and art (see "Art, antiques & bric-a-brac").

SPECTACLES & CONTACT LENSES

Optical 88 has branches throughout the city. If you want something exceptionally chic, go to *Eye'n-I* (137 D3) (*🕮 C11*) *(30 Queen's Rd. Central | MTR Central)*. But the real sensation when it comes to price and variety is INSIDER TIP *New Fei Optical* (132 B6) (*🕮 D5*) *(7–9 Mong Kok Rd. | www.newfei.com.hk/en | MTR Mong Kok, exit 2)* in Mong Kok.

BOOKS

SWINDON BOOK CO. (134 C5) (*🕮 E9*)
Best English bookshop in the city with a wide selection of literature on China and Hong Kong. *13–15 Lock Rd. | 樂道 13–15 | MTR Tsim Sha Tsui*

COMPUTERS

Even if you're just looking for a memory card, the labyrinths of tiny shops inside the city's electronic centres, full to bursting with the latest electronic products and older, discount items are an experience in themselves. New models from Chinese manufacturers are usually sold here before they are available in Europe. A central location is the *Wanchai Computer Centre* (138 B4) (*D E12*) *(130 Hennessy Rd. | MTR Wan Chai)*. A similar address, if not larger and generally cheaper, is the INSIDER TIP *Golden Computer Arcade* (132 A4) (*D D3*) *(146–152 Fuk Wa St. | MTR Sham Shui Po, exit D)*.

SHOPPING CENTRES

Air-conditioned consumer temples selling rows on rows of European and American fashion brands: while they are not to everyone's liking, often branded as sterile eyesores, Hongkongers love their stylish, modern shopping centres. They bring their entire family at the weekend even if just to enjoy a round of window-shopping. Whatever your opinion, they can provide decent refuge from the tropical Hong Kong rain showers. One of the best addresses is the ★ *IFC Mall* (137 D–E2) (*D C11*) *(MTR Central, Hong Kong)*; a spacious, centrally located shopping mall with a wide range of shops and restaurants, not all of them expensively priced. The ★ ● *Times Square* (138 C4) (*D G12*) *(MTR Causeway Bay)* with its gigantic atrium and lots of food outlets above and below its eleven floors is an impressive sight. Another favourite is *Pacific Place* (137 F3–4) (*D D12*) *(MTR Admiralty)*.

Shopaholics in Kowloon should head to the labyrinthine complexes *Ocean Terminal, Ocean Centre* and *Gateway Arcade* that join together to form *Harbour City* (134 B–C 5–6) (*D D–E9*). It takes hours to just walk past all the shop fronts there. *Langham Place* (134 C1) (*D E5*) *(MTR Mong Kok) is* worth a visit if only to admire the spectacular architecture.

MARCO POLO HIGHLIGHTS

★ IFC Mall
Spacious, varied and in a prime location – the shopping magnet in Central → p. 67

★ Times Square
11 floors of shopping and tasty food to recharge your batteries → p. 67

★ Shanghai Tang
Clothes, material, boxes, bags: Chinese nostalgia → p. 68

★ Granville Road
Clothing bargains in Tsim Sha Tsui → p. 69

★ Hollywood Road and Cat Street
A treasure trove of bric-a-brac and old objects → p. 70

★ Chinese Arts and Crafts
A splendid selection of Chinese craftsmanship → p. 71

★ Stanley Market
For bargain hunters: inexpensive leisure apparel – and much more → p. 71

★ Temple Street
Heaven to rummage around in: Hong Kong's popular night market → p. 72

ELECTRONIC & OPTICAL EQUIPMENT, CAMERAS

It is hardly worth buying a camera in Hong Kong these days. If you need to replace something, it's best if you go straight to INSIDER TIP *Sai Yeung Choi Street* (134 C1) (*E5–6*) (*MTR Mong Kok*) south of Nelson Street: there you will find several electronic and camera shops selling current goods at low fixed prices.

The *Fortress* and *Broadway* technology markets also sell hi-fi and video equipment as well as cameras at reasonable prices. There are branches in all the shopping centres including on the 3rd floor of *Ocean Centre* (134 C5) (*E9*) and on the 7th and 8th floors of *Times Square* (138 C4) (*f G12*). Make sure the goods that get packed are those you paid for and don't forget to check that any video equipment is compatible with the standards back home

DEPARTMENT STORES & SPECIALIST SHOPS

GOODS OF DESIRE (GOD)

G.O.D. was and still is a quintessential Hong Kong lifestyle brand. Whether bags, umbrellas, slippers, household goods - all the store's items are creative and fun and have a distinct Hong Kong flair, making them perfect as souvenirs. *PMQ (ground floor, south wing) | 35 Aberdeen St. | 鴨巴甸街 35* (136 C2) (*B11*) *| and other branches | www.god.com.hk*

INSIDER TIP HORIZON PLAZA (新海怡廣場) (140 A5) (*B18*)

Warehouse sales on 28 floors! Shopping enthusiasts can easily spend a whole day here and discover some pretty far-out items. You can buy top fashion inexpensively at *Joyce (21st floor), Armani (22nd floor)* and *Lane Crawford (25th floor);* it is also worth making the long journey for toys and home accessories. You can recover from shopping in the *Tree Café (28th floor). Ap Lei Chau | 2 Lee Wing St. | 利榮街 2 | MTR South Horizons, exit C*

MUJI (無印良品)

The epitome of minimalism and part of the Hong Kong way of life. It is no surprise that this chain has 16 stores spread across the city. Japanese design sets the trend in Hong Kong and Muji offers the latest, non-traditional products direct from Japan. Its department-store assortment ranges from shirts to files and champagne glasses to crackers. *3rd floor, Lee Theatre Plaza | 99 Percival St. | 波斯富街 99* (138 C4) (*G12*) *| MTR Causeway Bay; also Shop 415, Ocean Centre | Canton Rd. | 廣東道* (134 C5) (*E9*) *and other branches | www.muji.com.hk*

SHANGHAI TANG (上海灘) ★

(137 D3) (*C12*)

The cheekily colourful Chinese contrast to Muji , but a lot more elegant and with prices to match. On offer: classical Chinese women's clothing, as well as fabrics and boxes, cushions and bags, and all kings of odds and ends. *Duddell St. | 都爹利街 1 | MTR Central | and other branches | www.shanghaitang.com*

SOGO (崇光百貨)

Hong Kong's largest Japanese department store: fashion, delicatessen, household goods, cosmetics and much more – mostly in the mid-to-high price category. *555 Hennessy Rd.| 軒尼詩道 555* (138–139 C–D4) (*G12*) *| MTR Causeway Bay; 20 Nathan Road | 彌敦道 20* (134 C6) (*E9*) *| MTR East Tsim Sha Tsui*

YUE HWA CHINESE PRODUCTS (裕华国货) (134 C4) (*E7*)
Here you will find almost all the mid-priced consumer articles China considers fit for export – from silk cheongsams, massage chairs and Chinese medicines to arts and crafts. International branded articles are also sold. *301–309 Nathan Rd.| 彌敦道 301–309 | MTR Jordan*

CLOTHING & ACCESSORIES

Leisure and sports clothes are attractively priced. High-quality clothing is usually more expensive than in Europe but you will occasionally come across massively reduced items. Most of the haute couture boutiques are concentrated in the luxury hotels and shopping centres. The Sogo department store carries a wider range of good-quality clothing in all price categories. ★ *Granville Road* as well as its side streets between Carnavon Road and Chatham Road (134–135 C–D5) (*E–F8*) is a magnet for shoppers looking for young fashion, as well as sport and leisure time apparel. Look for *Maple, Cotton On, 6ixty8ight, Monki* and especially the mini arcade *G-Square (46 Granville Rd.)* with several small boutiques, among them INSIDER TIP *Laanaa* for chic lingerie; the brand was created by model and film star Chrissie Chau who has big plans for it. This is where it all started!
Stanley Market (U D6) (*0*): In the centre of this old place in the island's south, you'll find lots of shops and stalls selling clothing – jeans, silk blouses, jumpers, sports and leisure wear. Be aware of fake brand names and imitations!

INSIDER TIP **ISLAND BEVERLEY, CAUSEWAY PLACE (金百利商場, 銅鑼灣地帶)** ● (139 D4) (*G12*)
Labyrinths of small boutiques – trendy gear for young people in quintessential Hong Kong style. It offers an impressive selection of young women's fashion; both addresses are great if you're looking for unusual shoes and handbags. You can

Need an emergency second suitcase after all your shopping? Sogo is the place to go

even buy a custom-made pair of shoes bespoke to your own design at *Prestige (Shop 816, UG/F, Island Beverley)*. *Mini-me (Shop 133, 1/F, Island Beverley)*are an original store which manufactures personalized hand-made caricature dolls for you to create your own three-dimensional portrait. One floor above is *Shop No. 226* which sells crazy jigsaw puzzles. Even crazier is *Favour Shop (Shop 134, 1/F, Causeway Place)*, the ultimate bric-a-brac shop, offering artificial flowers under glass jars and miniature models of festively laid tables – everything is hand-made, even the coffee set with cake or dim sums. *Carol's Workshop (Shop 220, 2/F, Causeway Place)*) one floor above sells thousands of comic strip mobile phone cases, with everything from Superman to Hello Kitty. Note: the stores only open from midday. *Island Beverly: 1 Great George St. | 記利佐治街 1 | entrance: East Point Rd. | www.islandbeverley.com.hk; Causeway Place: 2–10 Great George St. | 記利佐治街 2–10 | www.causewayplace.hk | MTR Causeway Bay*

LADIES' MARKET (女人街)

(134 C1) *(E5–6)*

You will not find a great selection of clothes in European sizes (for women and men) at the many stands but there are also accessories and children's wear. Nothing very high-class, but mostly dirt cheap. *Afternoon and evening | Tung Choi St. | 通菜街 | south of Argyle St. | MTR Mong Kok*

LANE CRAWFORD (連卡佛)

Elegant department stores with international fashions (also jewellery), decorative ceramics and fine household goods. *Podium 3 International Finance Centre (IFC)* (137 E2) *(C11) | MTR Central, Hong Kong; Pacific Place | 88 Queensway | 金鐘道 88 |* (137 F3–4) *(D12) | MTR Admiralty*

SUITCASES & BAGS

Gigantic selection. Good buys in the Chinese department stores and even better (and cheaper) ones at the *Temple Street Market* (134 C3) *(E7)* and *Ladies' Market* on Tung Choi Street (134 C1) *(E5–6)*.

ART, ANTIQUES & BRIC-A-BRAC

Beware of imitations! A certificate of authenticity is not necessarily authentic and even serious merchants get taken in sometimes. In spite of all that, you are more likely to get the real thing if you buy in shops with tidy window displays where the individual articles are shown to their advantage. However, it is also possible to find something you like on the cluttered shelves at the flea market – even if it turns out to be an honest fake. But in that case, it won't have to cost a fortune. Modern art from China is very popular at the moment making it well-worth visiting Hong Kong's galleries!

HOLLYWOOD ROAD AND CAT STREET (荷李活道 AND 摩羅上街) ★

The area where the antique and art dealers do business stretches from the upper end of Wyndham Street (137 E3) *(C11)* to Possession Street (136 C2) *(B11)*. The spectrum of treasures ranges from porcelain and jade, Buddhist statues, carpets and furniture to ink paintings, lacquer goods and modern art (the latter especially on Wyndham Street). You will have most fun rummaging around on *Upper Lascar Row* (136 C2) *(B11) (MTR Sheung Wan)* that is also known as Cat Street. No matter whether Chinese arts and crafts, used household goods or memorabilia from the Mao period, there is always something to discover there. But remember that you

Stanley and its colourful market are right in the south of Hong Kong Island

will have to bargain. Discovery Tour No. 4 takes you to the two streets.

MOUNTAIN FOLKCRAFT
(137 D3) (*🕮 C11*)
Half sunken in the cellar, this delightful, tiny store specialises in traditional folk craft mainly from China. The two old ladies who run the store have some real gems, yet prices remain affordable. *12 Wo On Lane | 和安里 12 | www.mountainfolkcraft.com | MTR Central*

YAN GALLERY (仁畫廊)
(137 D3) (*🕮 B11*)
A busy modern-art gallery. *1/F, 1 Hollywood Rd. | 荷李活道 1 | MTR Central*

ARTS AND CRAFTS

China's low wages and traditional craftsmanship provide a rich offer of lacquer ware, porcelain, carvings, embroidery, jade jewellery and other exotic goods from the Far East. However, it is frequently rather difficult to recognise the real refinements and elegance of old Chinese art.

CHINESE ARTS AND CRAFTS (中藝) ★
The extensive range of goods makes this gigantic shop Hong Kong's leading place to purchase non-antique arts and crafts from China. It may be that most articles could be bought for less money elsewhere – especially in China itself – but here, there is the widest of choices and the quality is first rate. *China Hong Kong City (access from outside) | Canton Rd. | 廣東道* (134 B5) (*🕮 D8*)*; Causeway Centre | 28 Harbour Rd. | 港灣道 28* (138 B4) (*🕮 E–F12*)

MARKETS

STANLEY MARKET (赤柱市場) ★
(U D6) (*🕮 0*)
Mainly Europeans and Americans like this market – and for good reason: There's a broad range of goods from the Far East, the prices are low, the atmosphere is ex-

otic. The market in the south of the island is mainly a source of clothing but there are also many bargains for jewellery, toys, table linen, pictures and pretty arts and crafts. Be aware that the shops close already between 5.30 and 6pm. *During the day | buses 6, 6X from Exchange Square*

TEMPLE STREET (廟街) ★
(134 C3) (*🕮 E7*)
Hong Kong's popular night market is a real attraction. Especially in the southern section, shoppers find an exceptional range of goods close together: clothing, bags, sunglasses, toys, watches, new and used electronic appliances. The market continues to the north of Tin Hau Temple. You can eat just like people did years ago in one of the many traditional street cookhouses or daipadongs. Don't forget to walk around the multi-storey car park south of the temple: that is where you will find fortune tellers and amateur musicians giving their all to Cantonese opera. *Daily 6pm to around 11pm | MTR Jordan*

LOW BUDGET

Apliu Street flea market **(132 A4)** ***(🕮 C–D 3–4)*** *(daily from noon | MTR Sham Shui Po:* A lot of old odds and ends, but dirt cheap prices for brand-new small articles such as pocket torches, nail clippers, magnifying glasses, toy cars, binoculars...

Fa Yuen Street **(132 B5–6)** ***(🕮 E5)*** *(During the day | between Prince Edward Rd. and Mong Kok Rd. | MTR Prince Edward, Mong Kok East)*: Low prices and the atmosphere of 20 years ago: household goods, toys, underwear, knitwear, children's clothes, stockings, bags, towels, fruit, artificial flowers...

The Lanes **(137 D2)** ***(🕮 C11)*** *(During the day | Li Yuen St. East & West | MTR Central)*: Two tiny streets that you would hardly expect to find in Central – stands with clothing, shoes, costume jewellery, bags, material and other bits and pieces at low prices – as long as you know how to barter.

MUSIC

Be careful about buying cheap CDs at street markets: they are usually bad pirate pressings.

HMV
You will find just about everything your heart desires in Hong Kong's largest music shop. *Shop UG06, lower level, iSquare | 63 Nathan Rd. | 彌敦道 63* (134 C5) *(🕮 E9) | MTR Tsim Sha Tsui and other branches*

JEWELLERY

Going by the number of jewellers in the city, it seems buying jewellery is more a necessity than eating and drinking in Hong Kong. Tourists from China especially have a particular preference for gold and have sent prices spiralling. Chinese taste has led to its own very special designs: jade is a timeless favourite in China but also tends to be expensive. *Chinese Arts and Crafts (China Hong Kong City | Canton Rd.* (134 B5) *(🕮 D8); Causeway Centre | 28 Harbour Rd.* (138 B4) *(🕮 E–F12) offers information on offers and prices.*
Antique Chinese jewellery is particularly beautiful and is available in best quality at *C. Y. Tse* (137 E3) *(🕮 C11) (Shop 229 in the Prince's Building | 10 Chater Rd./Statue Square | MTR Central)*.

JADE MARKET (玉器市場)
(134 C3) (E7)
More than 400 small dealers offer a kaleidoscope of Chinese jade jewellery in the shadow of the urban motorway. Don't let them palm anything off on you if you are not an expert. *Daily 10am–6pm | Kansu St./corner of Reclamation St. | 甘肅街/新填地街*

INSIDER TIP **WING KUT STREET (永吉街)** (137 D2) (B11)
An entire street full of rhinestones and false pearls; but genuine, very beautiful jade jewellery is sold on the upper floor of *house no. 6–12*. Apart from that, the street also works as a small Ladies' Market. *MTR Sheung Wan*

TAILORS

The goods you get from cheap tailors are usually just a waste of money especially if they have to be made within 24 hours. Quality has its price in Hong Kong, too. Place your order at least five days before you plan to leave so that there will be time for two fittings and choose a nearby tailor. The tailors in the shopping arcades of the large hotels are accustomed to clients from abroad and have a fine selection of fabrics and fashionable cuts. Both men and women will be well catered to at *Mandarin Tailor* (137 D3) (C11) *(Room 604 | Takshing House | 20 Des Voeux Rd. | www.mandarintailor.com | MTR Central)*.

MATERIAL

You will find a wide range of material, including silk, at *Yue Hwa* (134 C4) (E7) *(301–309 Nathan Rd. | MTR Jordan)*. Another possibility is at the *Western Market* (136 C2) (B10–11) *(323 Des Voeux Rd. Central | MTR Sheung Wan)* but you will have to bargain there.

TEA & TEA SETS

The ● INSIDER TIP *Lok Cha Tea House* (137 E3) (D12) *(K. S. Lo Gallery (in the Museum of Tea Ware) | Hong Kong Park)* is a particularly charming place to taste and buy teas – perfect for a short break; they even serve vegetarian dim sums. More tea sets next door in the shop of the tea museum.
The *Fook Ming Tong Tea Shop* (134 B5) (E9) *(3316, Gateway Arcade, Harbour City)* is another lovely place that caters especially to foreign guests.

CARPETS

CHINESE CARPET CENTRE (珍藝行地毯) (135 D5) (F9)
This is the place to find a large selection of fine, elegant Chinese carpets. *Houston Centre | 63 Mody Rd.| 麼地道 63 | MTR East Tsim Sha Tsui*

TAI PING CARPETS LTD (太平地毯)
(137 E3) (C11)
Chinese carpets with modern designs. The traditional company's showrooms are small but a visit is always worthwhile. *213 Prince's Building | 太子大廈 | 10 Chater Rd./Statue Square | 遮打道 10/皇后像廣場 | MTR Central*

WATCHES

You will find a gigantic selection of watches ranging from exclusive Swiss brands and fashion watches to imitation Rolexes. You should always buy brand names from an authorised dealer. Another possibility is from one of the many branches of *City Chain (www.citychain.com)* spread throughout Hong Kong. Table or wall clocks can be purchased in the city's department stores.

ENTERTAINMENT

> **CITY WHERE TO START?**
> The ideal place to be dazzled by the neon glare of the harbour at night is at the south tip of **Kowloon (134 C6)** ***(E9)*** and the best time is at 8pm to see the laser show. The bar district **Lan Kwai Fong (137 D3)** ***(C11–12)*** is another must on the Hong Kong side. It's not far from there with the Central Escalator to the restaurants and bars in **SoHo (137 D3)** ***(B11)***. The **Temple Street night market (134 C3)** ***(E7)*** is more exotic and is easy to reach by underground from the Central Station.

Nightlife in large harbour cities is usually seen as being a bit seedy – this is also true for Hong Kong.

Single male travellers do sometimes get taken in by touts but the truth about Hong Kong at night is that, although things here might be a bit more colourful, they are also extremely civilised and relaxed. Visitors will soon feel at home whether it is at a classic concert or over a glass of beer in an Irish pub. Only when it comes to karaoke do Chinese cliques – with their love of singing – tend to keep themselves to themselves.

The public in ★ *Lan Kwai Fong*, the synonym for nightlife in Hong Kong, comes from all walks of life. The upper end of D'Aguilar Street is closed to traffic at night and this and Wyndham Street near-

Photo: Felix in the Peninsula Hotel

Bars, jazz and open-air opera: no matter whether it is Chinese music or a nightclub, you'll be certain to find something you like

by is where tourists find a lively mixture of bars, pubs and the more elegant restaurants (137 D3) (*📖 C11–12*).

The second hotspot is *Soho* "South of Hollywood Road". There are many international restaurants – some of them are also bars – here on both sides of the Central Escalator near Staunton Street and Shelley Street (137 D3) (*📖 B11*). An alternative off-scene has developed on the western fringe along INSIDER TIP *Peel Street*. The third hub is the most famous: the *Wan Chai* area (138 A4) (*📖 E12*) that is not even half as disreputable as its reputation would have you believe.

Car-free INSIDER TIP *Knutsford Terrace* (134–135 C–D4) (*📖 E8*) in Tsim Sha Tsui is a small-scale version of Lan Kwai Fong. The panorama of the harbour at night seen from the south of Kowloon near the *Cultural Centre* (134 C6) (*📖 E9*) never fails to impress. The absolute highlight is the ★ *Symphony of Lights* that takes place every evening at around 8pm. Laser projectors on 67 skyscrapers on both sides of the harbour transform it into a theatre of

Do as the locals do: meet up for dinner in Causeway Bay

light accompanied by music on the promenade and opposite the Convention & Exhibition Centre, and it is made even more exciting on certain days by fireworks displays. Or, you can join the Hong Kongers: their idea of after-work fun is to flock to department stores and boutiques, cinemas and restaurants, in INSIDER TIP *Causeway Bay* or meet for a tête-à-tête in neighbouring Victoria Park. Go for a stroll and take in the atmosphere of Hong Kong; nowhere else is it more typical. (138–139 C–D 3–4) *(🕮 F–G 11–12)*
If you feel that the evening might get to be a bit boozy, it is a good idea to take your credit cards out of your wallet and pay cash for your drinks as you order them. But careful: alcohol is very expensive!

BARS & PUBS

Besides the above-mentioned hot spots of Lan Kwai Fong, SoHo and Knutsford Terrace, there are two other smaller and far quieter districts which are also popular for nights out: the lakeside block on *Davis Street* (142 C4) *(🕮 0)* in Kennedy Town around the city's western tram terminal and the area between Ship Street and Amoy Street (with the new *Lee Tung Avenue*) in Wan Chai (138 A4–5) *(🕮 E12)*. You'll meet lots of Hong Kong expats in both districts yet tourists do not venture so far.
If live music is more your thing, head to Jaffe Road! Several bars along *Fenwick Road* (138 A4) *(🕮 E12)* have their own Filipino bands playing in the evenings from 10pm onwards, including *Dusk till Dawn* (with a large dancefloor) and the old favourite *The Wanch,* both of which are located on the same side of the road (house numbers 76 and 54).

AMOY (138 A5) *(🕮 E12)*
Small and cosy neighbourhood bar with a pleasant outdoor seating area. An added bonus is you can order something to eat in the tiny Thai snack bar *(Budget)* next door and eat it in Amoy. *1 Amoy St.* 廈門街

AQUA SPIRIT (134 C5–6) (*E9*)
The bar to end all bars, with all of Hong Kong at your feet. What a panorama! Something else will also make you stare in wonder – the prices in the right column of the list of beverages. Everything here is unforgettable. *1 Peking Rd. | 北京道 1 | 30th floor | MTR Tsim Sha Tsui*

BLOOP SHISHA LOUNGE
(137 D3) (*C11*)
Smoke water pipes while gazing over the Hong Kong skyline from the 21st floor. Inside the bar, its 8m/26ft long aquarium with real sharks will catch your eye and dancefloor parties are organised on special nights. *21/F, Ho Lee Commercial Building | 38–44 D'Aquilar St. |德己立街 38–44 | www.bloop.com.hk*

CASTRO'S (134 C5) (*E9*)
Cuban pub with diverse clientele and great atmosphere – loud and raucous fun. Smokers sit at the open windows blowing their clouds of smoke outside. *16 Ashley Rd. | 亞士厘道 16 | upper floor | entrance Ichang St. | MTR Tsim Sha Tsui*

COLETTE'S (藝穗會餐廳)
(137 D3) (*C12*)
Looking for something quieter? Then the rooftop garden on the Fringe Club is the place the go. *Colette's* serves tapas and drinks in the evenings. It also offers indoor seating. *2 Lower Albert Rd. | 下亞厘畢道 2 | MTR Central*

FELIX ★ (134 C6) (*E9*)
A different galaxy. This way-out creation designed by Philippe Starck calls itself a restaurant but the glass-floored bars and the breathtaking views at twilight are much more fantastic than the expensive food. Green mini-discotheque *Crazy Box*. Another highlight: the WCs. *The Peninsula | Salisbury Rd. | 梳士巴利道 | entrance from the western shopping arcade | MTR Tsim Sha Tsui*

INSIDER TIP LE MOMENT
(137 D2) (*B11*)
Proprietor Bobby has an amazing memory and will probably still remember you after visiting his pub a year ago. He'll ask you what type of wine you prefer and then bring a selection of bottles to your table. You can also eat in his cool wine bar while immortalising your name on its graffiti wall. *55 Peel St. | 卑利街 55*

INSIDER TIP NED KELLY'S LAST STAND
(134 C5) (*E9*)
A classic on the Hong Kong night scene since 1972. A jazz venue with free admission. *11A Ashley Rd. | 亞士厘道 11A | MTR Tsim Sha Tsui*

ORANGE PEEL (137 D3) (*C11*)
Jazz, R&B and other music genres are played live on stage in this music bar. Monday is jam session with free admission. *Closed Sun | 2/F, Ho Lee Commer-*

MARCO POLO HIGHLIGHTS

★ Lan Kwai Fong
Bar and restaurant district with a special flair → p. 74

★ Symphony of Lights
The curtain goes up on the world's largest *son et lumière* show! → p. 75

★ Felix
From a different galaxy: Philippe Starck's cabinet → p. 77

★ Temple Street
Music at the night market → p. 79

cial Building | 38–44 D'Aguilar St. | 德己立街 38–44 | orangepeelhk.com

INSIDER TIP **PEEL FRESCO MUSIC LOUNGE** (137 D2–3) *(B11)*
SoHo's music club. Real aficionados play jazz, funk, etc. here. Reasonable prices. *49 Peel St. | 卑利街 49*

Stylish night clubbing venue in the city

TIPPING POINT
(137 D3) *(C11)*
Craft beer fresh from the tap in this microbrewery. Shiny bronze tanks decorate the ground-floor guestroom. Beers from other local breweries are available as are British and European specialities including fish and chips. Its "afternoon combo" (3pm–6pm) which includes a pint of home-made beer served with a sandwich or "all day breakfast" is a great deal for just HK$ 30. *79 Wyndham St. | 雲咸街 79 | MTR Central*

INSIDER TIP **WOOLOOMOOLOO**
(138 B4) *(F12)*
The panorama of the Hong Kong cityscape from the 32nd floor terrace will take your breath away. The beer does not come cheap but you are guaranteed no end of fun especially at sunset. The rooftop bar is accessed from the steakhouse with the same name one floor below. *Daily from 3pm | 256 Hennessy Rd. | 軒尼詩道 256 | entrance in Johnston Rd. | MTR Wan Cha*

NIGHTCLUBS & DISCOTHEQUES

Be warned: if you are not fashionably dressed you won't make it through the door!

DRAGON-I
(137 D3) *(C12)*
When the night club opened in 2002, it became the city's mecca for the rich, famous and beautiful. Normal folk have a chance of entry if they get there earlier in the evening. Don't order a cocktail unless you want to watch the city's most expensive ice cube melting in front of your eyes. *60 Wyndham St. | 雲咸街 60 | uphill via steps | www.dragon-i.com.hk | MTR Central*

ESCAPE ON FENWICK
(138 A4) *(E12)*
700 m²/2300 ft² underground disco in Wan Chai, often hosts live Filipino bands. A special event is the Sunday afternoon disco where all ladies receive two free drinks. *64 Jaffe Rd. | 謝斐道 64 | www.escape.com.hk | MTR Wan Chai*

VIBES ● (134 C5) (*E8*)
The elegant Mira Hotel has a green oasis in its courtyard where you can unwind in style with a cocktail and shisha on the sofas or dance the night away. Oriental belly dancing on Thursdays. Minimum price per head HK$ 200. *5/F, The Mira | 118 Nathan Rd. | 彌敦道 118*

THEATER, CONCERTS & BALLET

Hong Kong presents a wide range of noteworthy international cultural events at a variety of venues. However, it is often very difficult for local performers to assert themselves in the face of international guest stars. There are several orchestras, a ballet company and many small, (amateur) groups.

ARTS CENTRE (藝術中心)
(138 A4) (*E12*)
The complex organises a highly varied assortment of theatre, cinema, exhibitions and concerts and plays a major role in Hong Kong's cultural life. *2 Harbour Rd. | 港灣道 2 | tel. 25 82 02 00 | MTR Wan Chai*

CITY HALL (大會堂)
(137 E3) (*D11*)
The City Hall acts as a venue for cultural and other events. There are concerts and theatre performances almost every day. *5 Edinburgh Place | 愛丁堡廣場 5 | tel. 29 21 28 40 | MTR Central*

CULTURAL CENTRE (文化中心)
(134 C6) (*E9*)
Hong Kong's most modern and important venue has a concert hall (with Asia's largest pipe organ), a theatre and a studio theatre. *10 Salisbury Rd. | 梳士巴利道 10 | tel. 27 34 20 09 and 27 34 28 49 | MTR Tsim Sha Tsui*

INSIDER TIP FRINGE CLUB (藝穗會)
(137 D3) (*C12*)
This active cultural organisation provides a forum for contemporary, experimental creativity with theatre, performances, music, exhibitions and much more. *2 Lower Albert Rd. | 下亞厘畢道 2 | tel. 25 21 72 51 | www.hkfringeclub.com | MTR Central*

TEMPLE STREET (廟街) ★ ●
(134 C3) (*E7*)
Every evening there is open-air musical fun around the edge of this bustling market. Amateur and semi-professional musicians give all they've got in scenes from Cantonese operas and other Chinese folk music on the south side of Tin Hau Temple – free of charge (donations welcome!) Next to them, there is a row of fortune tellers – mainly physiognomists and palmists. Some others work with trained birds. *Daily from around 7pm | Market St. | 街市街 | at the multi-storey car park | MTR Jordan*

LOW BUDGET

Take advantage of the happy hour! The days when most bars sold two drinks for the price of one are over but there is at least a discount. Many bars start their happy hour when they open their doors. This can last until 9pm..

Ladies' Night: most discos in Hong Kong offer "the fairer sex" free admission and free sparkling wine on one night in the week (often Wed).

WHERE TO STAY

Hong Kong's hotel industry has high standards. Even in simple guesthouses, air conditioning, a private bathroom, telephone and colour television are a matter of course, as well as a restaurant or coffeeshop serving international dishes from early in the morning until late at night.

Even middle-of-the-range hotels often have a business centre and 24-hour service. In exclusive hotels there are more than two employees per room. However, real luxury in Hong Kong is not as much a matter of service or decoration as one of the liberal use of the rarest and most expensive commodity here: space. Rooms in hotels that are not top category are correspondingly much less spacious. Sometimes it can even be a problem to find a space for a large suitcase in a room.

As a rule, the comfort offered corresponds with the size of the hotel. "Good things come in small packages" is almost unknown. Of course, rooms with a view of the harbour are particularly popular but they are mostly found in luxury hotels. The "Executive", "Club" or similarly named floors with extra service, such as breakfast in your room, free tea and coffee, and broadband internet access, are aimed more at business people.

Hong Kong hotels are expensive – just how expensive depends on the date. The top hotels in particular have room rates that sometimes change daily depending on demand; in middle-of-the-range hotels prices change with the season.

 Photo: Four Seasons

Pleasant dreams: from luxury suites to hostels in leafy surroundings – the spectrum is wide and the standard often exceptionally high

his guidebook classifies hotels based on he rates offered by internet booking serices (not including breakfast, which nevrtheless is part of the rate in some hoels) and includes the extra 10% "service harge" levied in Hong Kong. The actul prices can be much higher or lower, epending on the season. Inexpensive uesthouses on the other hand often ave no leeway for offering lower rates. ou can find out more about most hols under *www.discoverhongkong.com/ ng/trip-planner/accommodations.html*. All licensed hotel and guesthouse owners are listed under *www.hadla.gov.hk/ en/hotels*.

HOTELS: EXPENSIVE

Air conditioning, private bathrooms, telephone and broadband internet access in the rooms and suites; WiFi, several restaurants (usually with Chinese and international food), coffeeshop and bar, business centre, conference rooms, hotel doctor, laundry service, babysitters,

The Intercontinental spoils its guests with a view of the harbour and excellent food

hotel video programme and travel agency are all standard in hotels in this category. Most also have a hairdresser's and gym.

EXCELSIOR (怡東酒店)

(139 D3) *(G11)*

With 887 rooms, the sheer size of the building may be intimidating, but the location is fantastic: Causeway Bay, the liveliest of all Hong Kong districts, lies behind, while on the front side you have an unobstructed harbour view. *281 Gloucester Rd. | 告士打道 281 | tel. 28 94 88 88 | www.mandarinoriental.com/excelsior | MTR Causeway Bay*

FOUR SEASONS (四季酒店)

(137 D2) *(C11)*

Hong Kong's premiere luxury hotel with the atmosphere and facilities of a health resort: 22,000ft² spa oasis! The 399 rooms have plasma televisions and DVD players. Direct access to the airport train. *8 Finance St. | 金融街 8 | tel. 31 96 88 88 | www.fourseasons.com/hongkong | MTR Central, Hong Kong*

HYATT REGENCY (尖沙咀凱悅酒店)

(134–135 C–D5) *(E9)*

This hotel with 381 rooms occupies the 3rd to 24th floors of the "Masterpiece" skyscraper; beneath is a shopping centre with direct access to the underground. Business people value the INSIDER TIP Club Floors with a private lounge, additional working space and a better view. *18 Hanoi Rd. | 河内道 18 | tel. 23 11 12 34 | www.hyatt.com | MTR Tsim Sha Tsui*

INTERCONTINENTAL ★

(134–135 C–D6) *(E9)*

This hotel not only attracts guests due to its fantastic location on the southern tip of Kowloon – there is even view of the harbour from some bathrooms – but also thanks to its excellent gastronomy. The hotel has 50 rooms including 87 suites. *18 Salisbu*

Rd. | 梳士巴利道 18 | tel. 27211211 | www.intercontinental.com | MTR Tsim Sha Tsui

MANDARIN ORIENTAL (文華東方酒店)
(137 E3) (*🕮 C11*)
A luxury liner on dry land! The spa area combines Chinese medicine, Ayurveda and Kneipp treatments. 502 rooms and suites up to 3150 ft² in size. ● Drinking tea in the hall is a wonderful way to pass the time of day; Hong Kong ladies like to recover here after a day's shopping. *5 Connaught Rd. Central | 干諾道中 5 | tel. 25220111 | www.mandarinoriental.com/hongkong | MTR Central*

MARCO POLO HONG KONG HOTEL (馬哥孛羅香港酒店)
(134 C6) (*🕮 E9*)
This is a time-honoured hotel in a prime location at the tip of Kowloon next to the Star Ferry. Unobstructed view of the harbour from most of the 667 rooms. *3 Canton Rd. | 廣東道 3| tel. 21130088 | www.marcopolohotels.com*

THE PENINSULA (半島酒店) ★
(134 C6) (*🕮 E9*)
A Hong Kong hotel legend; absolute luxury – especially in the skyscraper wing. Hi-fi equipment in the rooms, bathrooms with television and panoramic views. The hotel's Rolls Royce fleet is almost legendary. 300 rooms including the most expensive suite in Hong Kong – HK$ 68,000 a night. *Salisbury Rd.| 梳士巴利道 | tel. 29202888 | www.peninsula.com | MTR Tsim Sha Tsui*

RITZ-CARLTON (麗思卡爾頓酒店)
(134 A4) (*🕮 C8*)
Located on the 102nd–118th floors of the International Commerce Center, this noble 312-roomed hotel is currently the tallest on earth. Of course, there is a wonderful view from all the windows – even when you go swimming on the 118th floor. *1 Austin Rd. West | 柯士甸道西 1 | tel. 22632263 | www.ritzcarlton.com | MTR Kowloon*

HOTELS: MODERATE

Standard facilities in this category include: air-conditioned rooms and suites with private bathrooms as well as direct-dial telephones, a restaurant and coffee-shop, bar, business centre, WiFi, laundry service and excursion booking desk.

CARITAS BIANCHI LODGE (明愛白英奇賓館) (134 C2–3) (*🕮 E7*)
Enjoy a heavenly night's sleep in one of the hotel's 90 rooms run by the Roman Catholic Church. Located in a quiet side street off Nathan, non-believers can also book a night here. *4 Cliff Rd. | 石壁道 4 | Tel. 23881111 | www.caritas-chs.org.hk | MTR Yau Ma Tei*

MARCO POLO HIGHLIGHTS

★ Intercontinental
Front row, panoramic view of the harbour – in South Kowloon → p. 82

★ The Peninsula
The legendary hotel chauffeurs its guests in a Rolls Royce → p. 83

★ Holiday Inn Golden Mile
Oasis at the heart of the shopping district → p. 84

★ The Salisbury YMCA of Hong Kong
Family hotel in a prime location with many leisure activities → p. 85

INSIDER TIP **CITADINES (馨樂庭亞士厘服務公寓)** (134 C5) (🕮 E9)
Apartment hotel for self caterers. The 36 studios (390–625ft²) are equipped with a kitchen. *18 Ashley Rd. | 亞士厘道 18 | reservation tel. 22 62 30 62 | www.citadines.com | MTR Tsim Sha Tsui*

THE CITYVIEW (城景國際)
(134 C2) (🕮 E6)
Nomen est omen: views of the jungle of skyscrapers can be had from the 422 rooms. The former YMCA has been refurbished to 4-star luxury standards and has a swimming pool, a large gym and even a prayer room. It has been awarded for its sustainable management. *23 Waterloo Rd. | 窩打老道 23 | tel. 27 83 38 88 | www.thecityview.com.hk | MTR Yau Ma Tei*

LOW BUDGET

Most important tip for anyone who plans to stay longer than two or three days: ask for a reduced weekly rate!

Yesinn **(138 C4) (🕮 G12)** *(2/F, Nan Yip Building | 472 Hennessy Rd./entrance Tang Lung St. | tel. 22 13 45 67 | www.yesinn.com):* colourful and modern hostel in the bustling Causeway Bay, sometimes loud but with rooftop garden. Dormitory bed from HK$ 160, double rooms from HK$ 400.

Mei Ho House **(132 A3) (🕮 D3)** *(Block 41, Shek Kip Mei Estate | tel. 37 28 35 00 | www.yha.org.hk | MTR Sham Shui Po):* The city's only youth hostel is a converted social housing block. 129 spacious rooms, some available for families. Dormitory bed HK$ 200.

GARDEN VIEW (園景軒) ★
(137 D4) (🕮 C12)
Guests have a view over the zoo to the skyscrapers in the Central District from many of the 141 rooms (including 25 family suites) in this modest-sized tower with a swimming pool, gym, business centre and restaurant. You can walk downhill through the zoo (there is direct access) and take a minibus back up. Price: at the lower end of this category. *1 Macdonnell Rd. | 麥當勞道 1 | tel. 28 77 37 37 | www.yhk.com.hk*

THE HARBOUR VIEW (灣景國際)
(138 A4) (🕮 E12)
Interesting location between the Arts Centre and Convention Centre. 144 of the 320 rooms have an **INSIDER TIP** inexpensive harbour view. At the top of the category and sometimes even a bit above but discounts are given for longer stays.. *4 Harbour Rd. | 港灣道 4 | tel. 28 02 01 11 | www.theharbourview.com.hk | MTR Wan Chai*

HOLIDAY INN EXPRESS (銅鑼灣智選假日酒店)
(136 C2) (🕮 B11)
Affordable accommodation in a central location on a quiet side street. The hotel is just ten minutes away from the pub district of SoHo. The 38-storey tower with 272 rooms has won several eco awards. *83 Jervois St. | 蘇杭街 83 | tel. 34 17 88 88 | www.ihg.com/holidayinnexpress | MTR Sheung Wan*

HOLIDAY INN GOLDEN MILE (金域假日酒店) ★ (134 C5) (🕮 E9)
Well-established hotel in the heart of Tsim Sha Tsui. The *Delicatessen Corner* in the basement serves German-Austrian food. *600 rooms | 50 Nathan Rd. | 彌敦道 50 | tel. 23 69 31 11 | www.ihg.com | MTR Tsim Sha Tsui*

Not a spectacular location but you know what to expect in the Holiday Inn Express

INSIDER TIP L'HOTEL (銅鑼灣海景酒店)
(139 E3) (*H11*)
275 modern rooms in a 40-storey tower near the underground and Victoria Park. The main attraction is the swimming pool on the roof – with a panoramic view of the harbour. *18–24 King's Rd. | 英皇道 18–24 | tel. 35 53 28 98 | www.lhotelcausewaybay-hv.com | MTR Tin Hau*

OVOLO ABERDEEN HARBOUR (奥華酒店一香港仔)
(140 A3) (*B17*)
Aberdeen is becoming in vogue. This small, modern hotel tower block offers splendid views over the harbour and its generously sized 85 rooms are cleverly designed to save space. Its happy hour from 5pm to 7pm is a real hit with guests when wine, beer and spirits are served on the house. *100 Shek Pai Wan Rd. | 石排灣道 100 | tel. 37 28 10 00 | www.ovolohotels.com | buses 7, 71, 91*

THE SALISBURY YMCA OF HONG KONG (基督教青年會) ★
(134 C6) (*E9*)
Intelligently planned, comfortable hotel. 365 rooms, kindergarten, swimming pool area, gym, comprehensive programme of games, sports and courses – and all in a luxurious location next to the Peninsula (many rooms with a harbour view). The perfect choice for families with children. Be sure to INSIDER TIP book early! *41 Salisbury Rd. | 梳士巴利道 41 | tel. 22 68 70 00 | www.ymcahk.org.hk | MTR Tshim Sha Tsui*

HOTELS: BUDGET

Standard facilities in this category include: air-conditioned rooms and suites with private bathroom and telephone, as well as a coffeeshop or simple restaurant, laundry service and usually an excursion booking desk.

HOTEL BENITO (華國酒店)
(134 C5) *(🕮 E9)*
New and modern hotel with 74 small rooms in a central location. Free internet (plug-in) but no restaurant. *7–7B Cameron Rd. | 金馬倫道 7–7B | tel. 36 53 03 88 | www.hotelbenito.com | MTR Tsim Sha Tsui*

BOOTH LODGE (卜維廉賓館)
(134 C2) *(🕮 E7)*
44 rooms in a cheerful little hotel run by the Salvation Army. Centrally located, but peaceful. *11 Wing Sing Lane | 永星里 11 | tel. 27 71 92 66 | www.salvationarmy.org.hk/en/services/booth | MTR Yau Ma Tei*

BUTTERFLY ON HOLLYWOOD (晉逸好萊塢酒店) (136 C2) *(🕮 B11)*
The walls of all 142 rooms in this savvy hotel are decorated with Hollywood legends and film stars. Located in an interesting corner of the city between Hollywood Park and antique shops. *263 Hollywood Rd. | 荷李活道 263 | tel. 28 50 88 99 | www.butterflyhk.com | MTR Sheung Wan*

IBIS NORTH POINT (宜必思世紀軒)
(139 F1) *(🕮 O)*
Skyscraper with ferry and tram access, 275 small but modern rooms, many with

MORE THAN A GOOD NIGHT'S SLEEP

Hospitality at its best
The *T Hotel (T酒店)* **(142–143 C–D4)** ***(🕮 O)*** is maybe not the most perfect of hotels but it is definitely the city's most hospitable. This training hotel is part of Hong Kong's Hotel and Tourism Institute and its highly motivated students deliver a unique brand of hospitality. It also offers a quiet location with sea views and an excellent value for money. The buses (many lines) which stop in front of the gate take 20 to 40 minutes to reach the centre. *30 rooms | Pokfulam Training Centre Complex | 職業訓練局 | 145 Pok Fu Lam Rd. | 薄扶林道 145 | tel. 37 17 73 88 | www.thotel.edu.hk* | Budget

Guarded treasure
A luxury hotel in green surroundings with no road access. To reach the *Tai O Heritage Hotel (大澳文物酒店)* **(142 A4)** ***(🕮 O)*** you can walk 1.3km/0.8mi on foot from the Tai O bus station (end of street) or take a ferry. Nestling in the far-west of Lantau, this tranquil hotel is a former police station, built in 1902 to combat pirates prevalent in neighbouring waters. It has been restored as a prestigious 13-room hostel serving the finest food. This hotel takes you back in time, far away from the hustle and bustle of Hong Kong. *Shek Tsai Po St. | Tai O | Lantau Island | 大嶼山大澳石仔埗街 | tel. 29 85 83 83 | www.taioheritagehotel.com* | Expensive

Appearances are deceptive
The building may appear nothing special but the *Wontonmeen Hostel* **(132 A5)** ***(🕮 D4)*** is home to Hong Kong's young creative scene where the city's artists live and work. Beds are available for HK$ 250 a night in the large dormitory or double room. If you like meeting new people, the hostel's common kitchen is the place to hang out. Book early! *135 Lai Chi Kok Rd. | 荔枝角道 135 | tel. 69 04 09 18 | www.wontonmeen.com | MTR Prince Edward* | Budget

an INSIDER TIP inexpensive harbour view. Another plus: non-touristy, authentic surroundings. *138 Java Rd. | 渣華道 138 | tel. 25 88 11 11 | www.accorhotels.com | MTR North Point*

LARGOS HOTEL (朗逸酒店)
(134 C3) *(E7)*
Cheerful hotel in a central, fairly quiet, location. Most of the 100 rooms are small but have internet. *30 Nanking St.| 南京街 30 | tel. 27 83 82 33 | www.largos.com.hk | MTR Jordan*

HOTEL SÁV (逸·酒店)
(135 F3) *(G7)*
Innovative, fresh and unbeatable value for money. Although the hotel is not located in one of the most popular areas (but close to an underground station), there are plus points. The rooms are designed by Hong Kong fashion designers (in the "floor of fashion") and have a free mini bar (to be emptied once per stay) and mobile phone for local calls. *388 rooms | 83 Wuhu St. | 蕪湖街 83 | tel. 22 75 88 88 | www.hotelsav.com | MTR Whampoa, Ho Man Tin*

SILKA SEAVIEW (香港海景絲麗酒店)
(134 C3) *(E7)*
Only a handful of the 268 rooms offer a distant view of the sea yet this comfortable accommodation is next to the Tin Hau Temple of Yau Ma Tei in a district full of local colour. *268 Shanghai St. | 上海街 268 | tel. 27 82 08 82 | www.silkahotels.com | MTR Yau Ma Tei*

STANFORD HILLVIEW HOTEL (仕德福山景酒店)
(135 D4) *(E8)*
177 rooms in a surprisingly quiet, green corner of the tourist district. Prices are at the upper end of the price bracket. *13–17 Observatory Road | 天文臺道 13–17 | tel. 27 22 78 22 | www.stanfordhillview.com | MTR Tsim Sha Tsu*

WHERE TO STAY OUTSIDE THE CITY CENTRE

INSIDER TIP **CONCERTO INN** (浪濤軒)
(U A6) *(0)*
Feel like a beach holiday? This well-kept guesthouse with 8 rooms with balconies on Lamma Island 1.5 km (1 mile) from the village of Yung Shue Wan (ferry stop) is right on the beach. Peaceful and inexpensive during the week; cannot be recommended on Sat. *28 Hung Shing Ye Beach | 洪聖爺灣 28 | tel. 29 82 16 68 | www.concertoinn.com.hk | Budget*

YOUTH HOSTELS
Apart from the inner city Mei Ho House, Hong Kong's youth hostels are all located in rural surroundings – most of them are intended for hikers. The lovely *Mount Davis hostel* (U A3) *(0) (123 Mount Davis Path | tel. 28 17 57 15 | www.yha.org.hk | www.hihostels.com)* is larger, closer to the city and has a shuttle bus 4 times a day. Overnight stay in a dorm HK$ 180, double from HK$ 480.

WARWICK HOTEL (華威酒店)
(142 C5) *(0)*
This comfortable hotel with a bar, restaurants and swimming pool is located right on the beach. The 66 rooms all have balconies. It is only a 10-min. walk to the harbour. Reduced rates during the week. *East Bay | Cheung Chau | 長洲東灣 | tel. 29 81 00 81 | www.warwickhotel.com.hk | Budget*

DISCOVERY TOURS

1 HONG KONG AT A GLANCE

START: ① **Victoria Park** **END:** ⑯ **Aqua Spirit**	**1 day** Walking time (without stops) 3 hours
Distance: **47 km/29 mi, 9 km/5.5 mi of which on foot**	

COSTS: 72 HK$ for public transport services
WHAT TO PACK: umbrella to shade against the sun and rain, rucksack for shopping

IMPORTANT TIPS: If possible take the tour on weekdays. The waiting times for the ⑩ **Peak Tram** at the weekend can spoil any well-made plans. An alternative is to take bus 15 (from Queensway) or a taxi.
⑮ **Kung Tak Lam:** Reserve a window seat!

→ p. 2/3

Vould you like to explore the places that are unique to this city? Then he Discovery Tours are just the thing for you – they include terrific tips or stops worth making, breathtaking places to visit, selected restau-ants and fun activities. It's even easier with the Touring App: download he tour with map and route to your smartphone using the QR Code on ages 2/3 or from the website address in the footer below – and you'll ever get lost again even when you're offline.

This one-day discovery tour shows you the many contrasting sides of Hong Kong. It takes you from the seafront beach to the Peak, from food markets to art dealers, from the traditional (tea house, early-morning gymnastics) to the ultra-modern (shopping temple IFC Mall) and ends with a panoramic view from the cocktail bar.

08:00am Hong Kong awakens to gymnastics in the morn-ng – a Chinese tradition that you can experience best in **1 Victoria Park** → p. 39 Then it's time for *yam cha* (a cup of tea): a Hong Kong breakfast with dim sums in the **2 Jade Garden** → p. 57, a few steps away. **Stroll along**

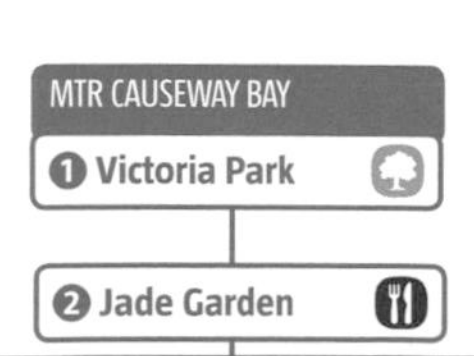

hoto: Statue Square

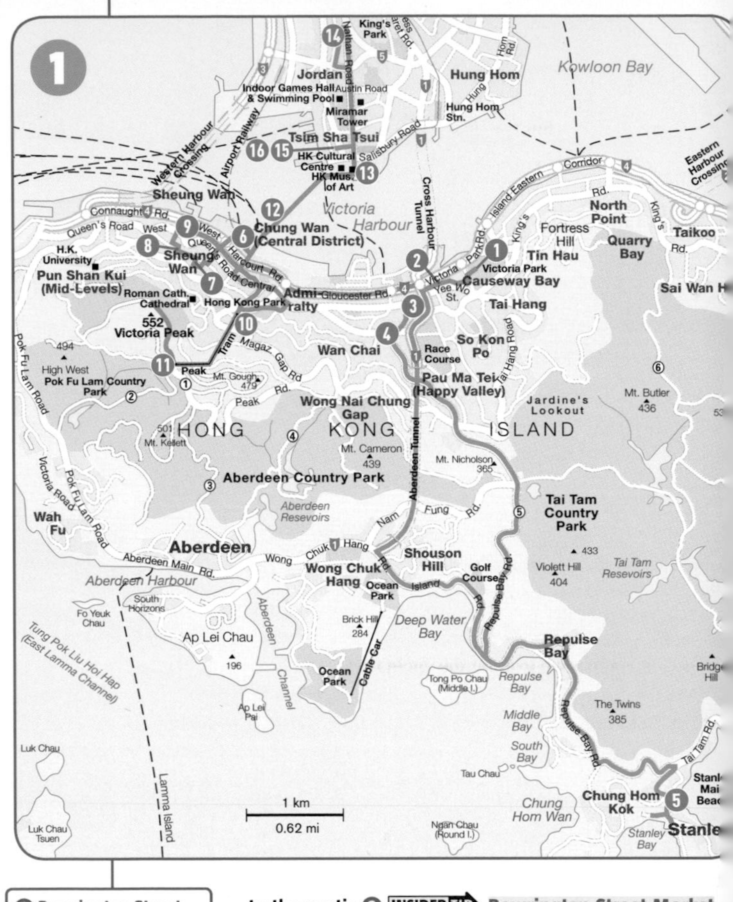

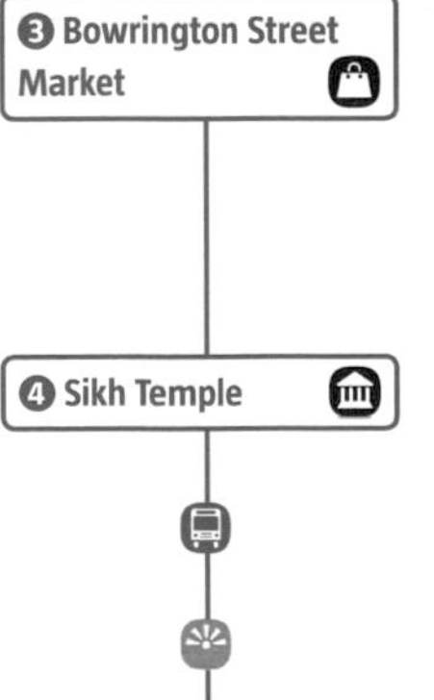

to the exotic 3 INSIDER TIP Bowrington Street Market, where you can explore the ingredients used in Hong Kong cuisine.

10:00am **Head west along Wan Chai Road, take a left into Tak Yan Street, along Oi Kwan Road and then up the steps to Queen's Road East.** You are now standing in front of the **4 Sikh Temple**, one of several non-Chinese religious centres in the district. **A little further on your right, take a line no. 6 bus.** If you sit at the top of the bus on the left, you will have great views from the bendy Stubbs Road onto Happy Valley → p. 37 with the horse racetrack below. On the other side of the pass, the view on the right stretches to the South China Sea and the green hills. Hong Kong's high society lives here. The bus takes you past the large beach for swimming at Repulse Bay → p. 48 and along many curves until you reach ⑤ **Stanley** → p. 48. **Get off when you reach the main bus terminal here.**

11:00am **towards the sea along the short Stanley New Street until you see the popular Stanley Market** → p. 71. Enjoy the view from the promenade and admire the old **Murray House** and the **Tin Hau Temple** on the large, modern Stanley Plaza. Choose a veranda from the many restaurants where you can enjoy a lunchtime snack. **Take the bus 260 back to the Central at around 12.45pm.** This bus line passes through the Aberdeen Tunnel and is a little faster than the 6; it doesn't matter really because both take you into the heart of the city.

01:30pm **at Statue Square → p. 28 and walk past Jardine House (with the portholes) to Exchange Square → p. 30 and along the footbridge above the road into the ⑥ IFC Mall → p. 30.** This exclusive, air-conditioned and expensive shopping centre is slightly sterile but the rooftop panorama is amazing (access on the side facing the sea through the Oval Atrium). **Head westwards on the footbridge and cross Connaught Road to enter the upper floor of the Central Market and continue until you reach the Central Escalator which gradually takes you up to Staunton Street.**

02:30pm **In SoHo (South of Hollywood Road) follow the row of stores along Staunton Street to the ⑦ PMQ** → p. 34. Half an hour is enough to have a quick browse around Hong Kong's design centre **before heading down to Hollywood Road → p. 70** where you can take a well-earned break for a coffee in ⑧ **Classified** *(No. 108)*. **Walk a few metres and go down the steps at the Man Mo Temple → p. 32. Turn left into Cat Street → p. 70, then right down to Morrison Street and straight on to the Western Market → p. 36.**

04:00pm **Catch one of the ⑨ trams** → p. 26 that turn around here and take a front seat at the top, heading east through the Central District **to Admiralty (eighth stop). Go into the Pacific Place Shopping Centre → p. 67 and straight up the escalator to Hong Kong Park → p. 30.** Now you should time everything exactly so that you catch the sunset. **Go straight to the lower terminal of the ⑩ Peak**

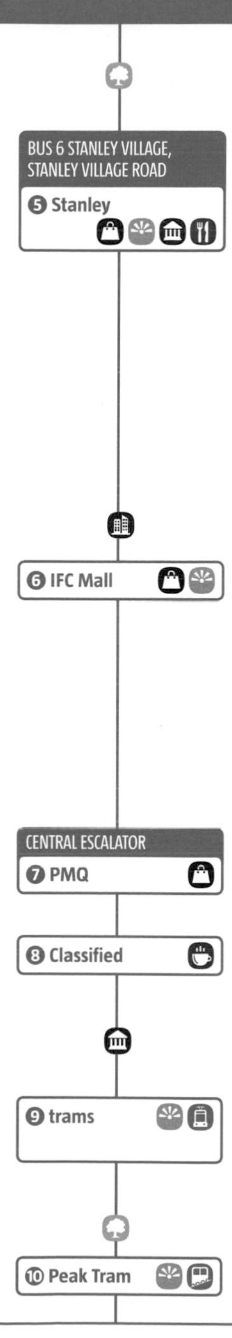

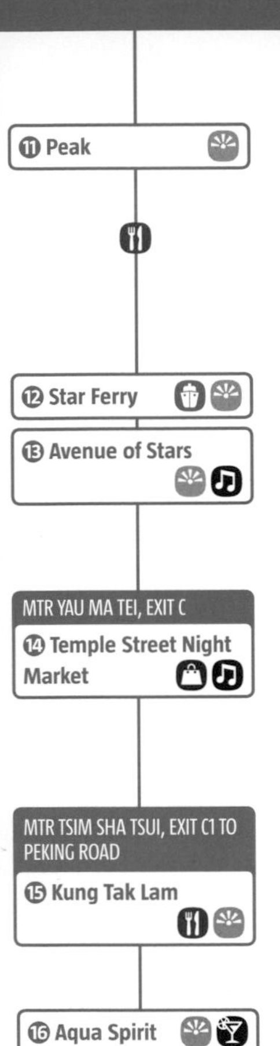

Tram → p. 33. You will probably have to wait here at least half an hour. **Then float upwards to the ⑪ Peak → p. 33** and to the highlight of any trip to Hong Kong: the panorama of the city in twilight. Split your dinner in two today: anybody who visits The Peak should not miss out on a drink at the **Peak Lookout → p. 62** (if sunset is late, stop off here first).

07:15pm After a starter and a glass of wine, **catch the Peak Tram again downhill, change onto the bus 15C to the ⑫ Star Ferry → p. 26 and cross over to the ⑬ Avenue of Stars → p. 40** on the other side of the water. The next highlight is the **Symphony of Lights → p. 75**. The panorama of the port is always great, though – even before or after the laser show.

08:30pm **From the MTR Tsim Sha Tsui train station, travel to ⑭ Temple Street Night Market→ p. 79** to see bargain hunters, amateur singers and even fortune tellers at work. The south end of the market is close to Jordan Road. **From here, take the MTR one station further southwards again.**

09:30pm Dinner, part 2: you can eat a light, healthy and not very expensive vegetarian Chinese meal in **⑮ Kung Tak Lam → p. 58**. Those who book ahead have the chance of getting a window table with a view of the harbour. You will for sure get the view from the top of the same building in **⑯ Aqua Spirit → p. 77**, the bar with a stunning panorama. Admittedly it's not cheap but you are not in Hong Kong every day. After that, everybody will be more than ready for bed.

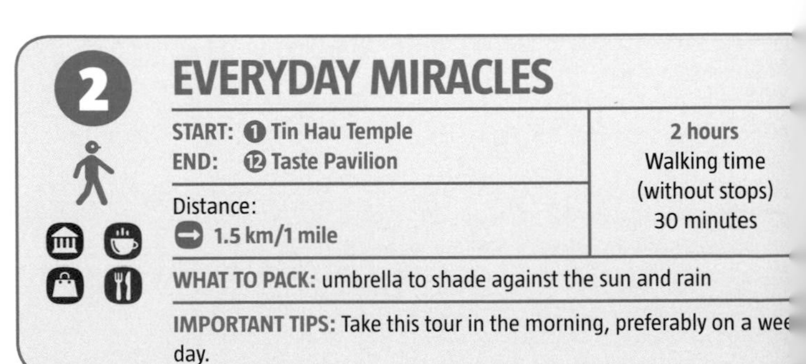

2 EVERYDAY MIRACLES

START: ① Tin Hau Temple
END: ⑫ Taste Pavilion

Distance: 1.5 km/1 mile

2 hours
Walking time (without stops) 30 minutes

WHAT TO PACK: umbrella to shade against the sun and rain

IMPORTANT TIPS: Take this tour in the morning, preferably on a weekday.

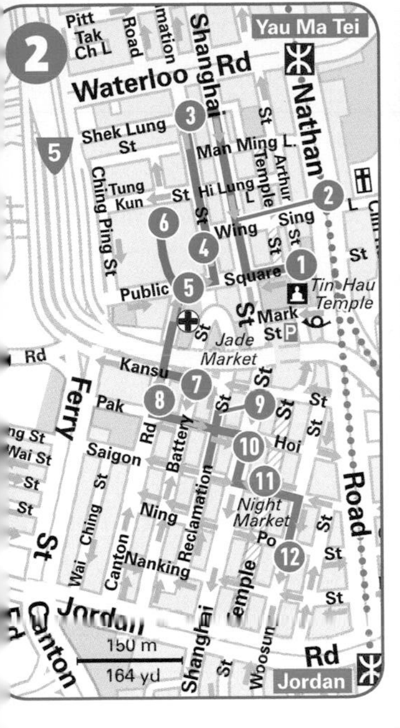

In the Tin Hau Temple of Yau Ma Tei: Guan Yin, the goddess of mercy

Explore Hong Kong's exotic sides far away from the air-conditioned consumer world. On this walking tour you'll spot house altars, chopping blocks, mah-jong salons, smell a fruit and vegetable market and marvel at the beauty of Chinese jade jewellery.

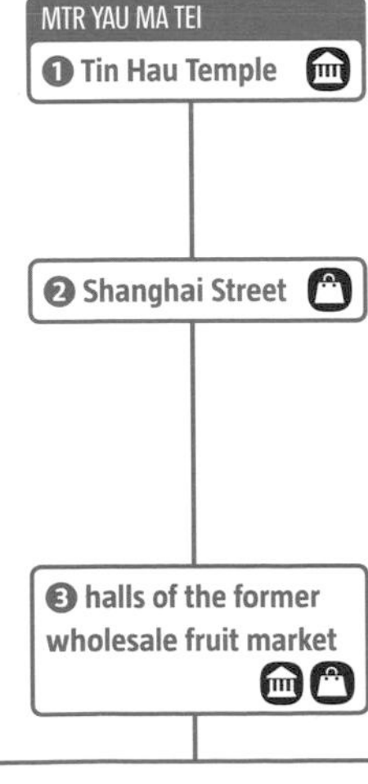

The walk starts at the popular ① **Tin Hau Temple → p. 44** in INSIDER TIP **Yau Ma Tei** with its shady forecourt. Shops selling devotional objects such as figures of saints and house altars – a unique mixture in combination with others carrying household goods and hardware – **line both sides of** ② **Shanghai Street that leads north.** You will see a bizarre collection of Chinese fondue sets, scissors, gas lanterns, scales, lazy Susan turntables, clay pots, chopping boards and wooden stools, money for offerings and geomantic compasses on the street that is only a little more than 200 m/650 ft long. Look on the back wall of many shops and you will see shrines dedicated to the patron saint Guan Yu, usually with an offering of a bowl of fruit in front of the figure.

Walk a block further west along Shanghai Street to the ③ **halls of the fromer wholesale fruit market**. The main

❹ Reclamation Street

❺ Yau Ma Tei Police Station

❻ Cafe Kubrick

❼ jade market

❽ Canton Road

❾ Reclamation Street Fruit and Vegetable Market

❿ Shanghai Street

⓫ Saigon Street

market has been relocated and the building now houses individual traders. The ancient buildings are to be maintained, some are overgrown with plants and a real tree can be seen growing out of one of the gables..

Now, continue south. There are more metalware shops with articles for household and professional kitchens – some of them produced on the spot – on **❹ Reclamation Street.** When you get to the shop at no. 181, you will ask yourself how they manage to get the gigantic steel coils in and out. There is a construction dating from 1923 **at the northern end of Canton Road:** the three-storey **❺ Yau Ma Tei Police Station** with arcades on the ground floor. ❻ INSIDER TIP **Cafe Kubrick** (next to the arthouse cinema) in the Prosperous Garden housing complex **opposite the police station** serves food and drinks for the "western" palate (many different types of tea!) and offers a pleasant setting for a break.

Our walk now takes us further southwards to the ❼ jade market → p. 73. **Go in through the second entrance (underneath the elevated highway)** and you will not find more typical Chinese jewellery on such a small space anywhere else. There is a row of shops selling minerals **to the south along ❽ Canton Road.** Here, you will be able to buy beautiful rock crystals, fossils and pearls. **The next stop (to the left along Pak Hoi Street) is the ❾ Reclamation Street Fruit and Vegetable Market** – a whole symphony of harmonious aromas with some fishy dissonances.

After you have looked around, return to Pak Hoi Street and go further as far as ❿ Shanghai Street. Have a look at house no. 189 with **jade and wooden carvings**, no. 185 where **incense** is sold and the **cookhouse** at no. 183 which serves a welcome snack of wonton dumpling soup for less than 4 pounds. There is a typical **pawnshop** in an ancient Hong Kong-style building (with an enormously high counter and barred windows) at no. 178 on the corner of Saigon Street.

Turn into ⓫ Saigon Street. Your eyes will be drawn to the two large tin kettles in the **herbal chemists** on the next corner with a photograph of the firm's owner hanging above them. Cups of medicinal tea will have been brewed just waiting to be tasted. Cross Temple Street → p. 72, 79 during the day and you will find it hard to believe that there is so much activity here at night. **Immediately on the corner to the right, Mahjong games** are played. A magnificent large mahjong salon – its façade covered in yellow marble – follows at nos. 70–72 **Woosung Street** with another one opposite it. **Follow the street until you reach Ningpo Street** and enjoy the authentic range of sweet and savoury Hong Kong snacks at the ⑫ **Taste Pavilion** on the corner. Or try their fruit desserts – tasting fresh, cool and delicious.

TRACES OF HISTORY

START: ① Statue Square END: ⑫ Lock Cha Tea House	1½ hours Walking time (without stops) 50 minutes
Distance: 2.7 km/1.5 miles	

WHAT TO PACK: umbrella to shade against the sun and rain

IMPORTANT TIPS: Take this walk around lunchtime, preferably on a week day.
At the end of the tour, walk through the Pacific Place shopping centre to the underground, tram and bus terminal.

The Hong Kong you see on old photos has now disappeared. But not completely: take this tour and trace Hong Kong's history to the sites of the early colonial period that have been preserved between the city's skyrises.

Start out in Hong Kong's "front room" ① **Statue Square** → p. 28 where you will see an ugly skyscraper opposite the elegant **Mandarin Oriental** → p. 83. It is the seat of the time-honoured **Hong Kong Club**, the former unofficial headquarters of the colony after the Jockey Club and before the city's Governor. **Now cross Chater Road.** Until well into the 1950s, it ran along the shore and was itself created around 1900 on reclaimed land. The old domed building is the **Old Supreme Court Building** → p. 33. Other Hong Kong financial institutes look down on you from above: on the right, the **Standard Chartered Bank**, in the centre the **HSBC Main Building** → p. 35 and on your left the **Bank of China Tower** → p. 35, soaring up like a gigantic geometrical sculpture behind the HSBC's old offices. If the cricket club hadn't kept its cricket pitch behind the Supreme Court until 1977, highrises would have been erected here a long time ago. Instead the – very, very expensive – ground was made into an inner-urban park: **Chater Garden**.

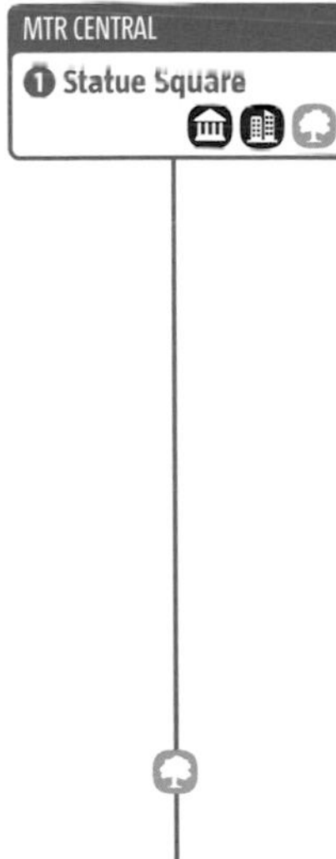

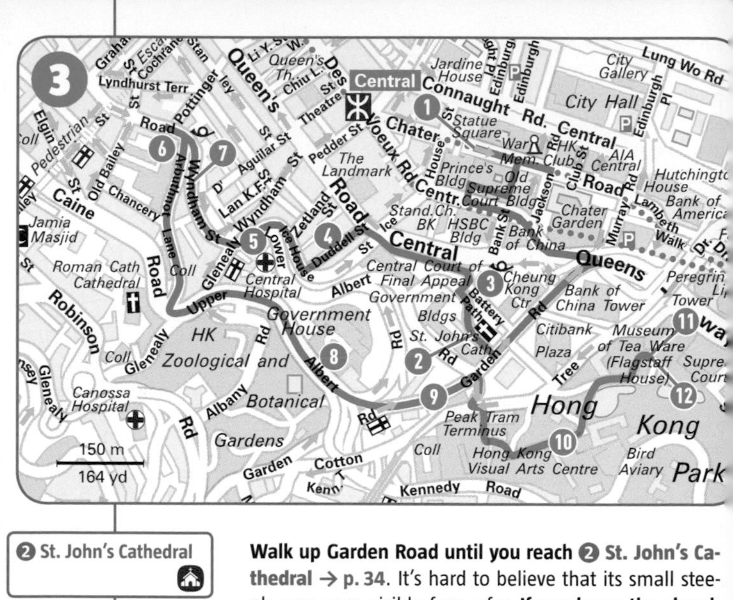

❷ St. John's Cathedral

Walk up Garden Road until you reach ❷ St. John's Cathedral → p. 34. It's hard to believe that its small steeple was once visible from afar. **If you leave the church through the main entrance,** you will catch sight of the stately, historic **❸ French Mission Building** to the right, once the seat of the French Foreign Mission and later of the Supreme Court.

❸ French Mission Building

❹ Duddell Street

Now follow Battery Path, shaded by old trees, down until you reach ❹ Duddell Street. The beautiful wide flight of steps at its southern end was laid out in 1880 and is decorated with four old gas lanterns. **The steps lead to Ice House Street** named after the ice from the USA that was stored here in summer and used by the dairy Lower Albert Road 2. Today, this is the location of the foreign correspondents' club. The neighbouring building (today, the home of the **❺ Fringe Culture Club → p. 79**) was built in the same style in 1913. If you are passing by at lunch time on a weekday, treat yourself to the INSIDER TIPP vegetarian lunch menu at **Colette's → p. 62**.

❺ Fringe Culture Club

The art and antique dealers' district starts **on the flat section of Wyndham Street.** Today this district houses the city's exclusive gastronomic scene, which becomes particularly crowded in the evening, but a few of the old galleries can still be found. Now you are not far away from

Hong Kong's largest complex of colonial buildings: the former ❻ **Central Police Station** → p. 30 on your left. Pottinger Street, coming up from the right, still has its old road surface.

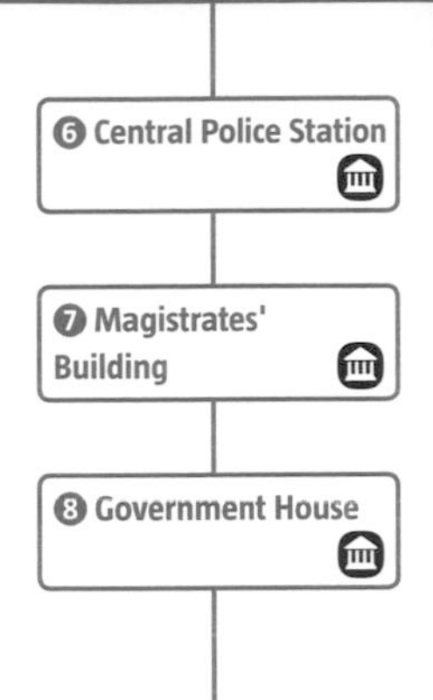

The impressive portal of the ❼ **Magistrates' Building** built in 1914, dominates **Arbuthnot Road.** The next destination is ❽ **Government House**: This former seat of the Governor dates back to 1855 but has been enlarged many times since. Hong Kong's chief administrator made a fuss about taking up his official residence here until 2006 although the last Governor, Chris Patten, had already vacated the premises on 30 June, 1997. To see over the high, barbed-wire fencing, **climb up a few of the stairs on the opposite side of the road.**

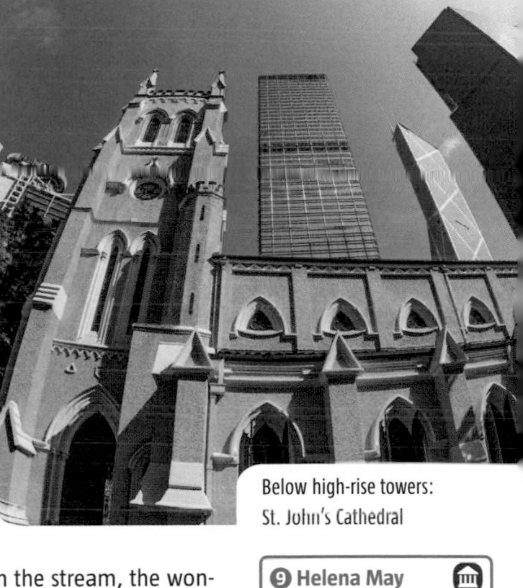

Below high-rise towers: St. John's Cathedral

Follow the route along the Upper Albert Road, down the stairs to return to the Garden Road where you will see a white building opposite: the ❾ **Helena May**, a club for women dating from 1916. Since 1888, the Peak Tram has departed from the lower floor of the next skyscraper down the hill. **Go under the elevated highway until you reach** ❿ **Hong Kong Park** → p. 30. Take a well-earned break by looking for an empty park bench and enjoying all the smells, sounds and sights around you: the trickle of water in the stream, the wonderful sights and smells of the blossoming flowers, high-rise buildings, the twittering of birds and often a wedding couple having their photos taken. The area is thankfully free from skyrise buildings because the British military held their garrison here. **Now follow the signs to** ⓫ **Flagstaff House** → p. 31, erected 1844–46 as the residence of the captain of the garrison. End your tour with a tea and delicious dim sum **next door in the** ⓬ **Lock Cha Tea House** → p. 73!

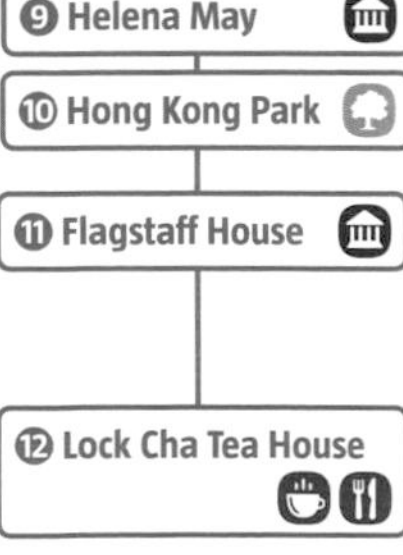

GINSENG, ART AND SWALLOWS' NESTS

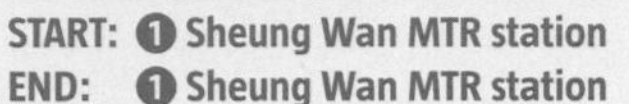

START: ❶ Sheung Wan MTR station END: ❶ Sheung Wan MTR station	2½ hours
Distance: 2.5 km/1.2 mile	Walking time (without stops) 40 minutes

WHAT TO PACK: umbrella for protection from the rain or sun

IMPORTANT TIPS: Do not take this tour early morning or in the evening or on a Sunday or bank holiday when the stores are closed.

The Sheung Wan district awaits you with enigmatic products and ancient art, amazing smells and fascinating sights – yet another exotic area of this diverse city.

After you leave exit A1 of the ❶ Sheung Wan MTR station turn right and right again onto ❷ Man Wa Lane where you will find a row of small stands run by people who carve seal stamps and print business cards. **Continue until you reach ❸ Bonham Strand, then turn right.** Just past the next crossing, you will see the first of many wholesalers selling dried mushrooms, ginseng and swallows' nests. The nests are packed in round transparent plastic containers. Dried abalones and shark fins can also be seen in tightly sealed jars. **Turn right towards the ❹ Western Market** → p. 36 from 1906. **Two streets further south,** there are two floors of groceries in the ❺ **Sheung Wan Market** and a cookhouse market above.

Up a few steps (Tung Street) and you have arrived at ❻ **Cat Street** → p. 70 where bric-a-brac items and fakes are sold alongside first-rate antiques. The street stands invite you to take a leisurely stroll around. The next highlight is the popular ❼ **Man Mo Temple** → p. 32. With its antique shops and large shop windows, ❽ **Hollywood Road** → p. 70 **towards the west** is a single, gigantic art gallery. **Then walk through Upper Station Street and take a left at the top to Tai Ping Shan Street no. 16** where ❾ INSIDER TIP **Hipster** will serve you a second breakfast or coffee and cake. **Then return to where you came from and follow the road straight on.** You pass by the ❿ **Kwun Yum**

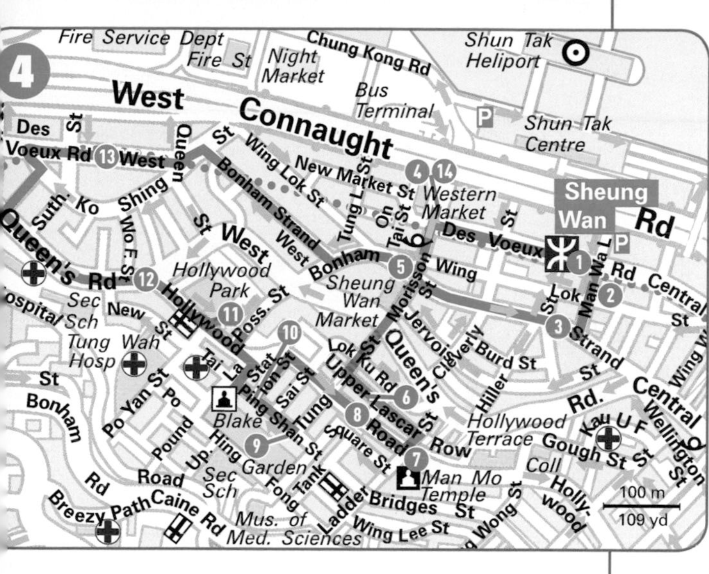

ong ("Guan Yin hall") temple with golden carvings hanging in front of the entrance. There is another Guan Yin hall **down the steps** on the right; this one has 60 gold-plated gods of the years on the left wall and a wheel of fortune. **Now go down on the right to the junction with Possession Street.** Its name reminds one that it was here that the British first raised the Union Jack on 26 January, 1841.

's time for a rest in ⑪ **Hollywood Park**. Opposite the entrance stand two shops selling enigmatic products: they are in fact Chinese wooden coffins. More shops selling dried food, herbs and ginseng are **on ⑫ Queen's Road West.** On the other side of the street, you can buy everything (from sports shoes to mobile phones) made of paper to offer as gifts to your ancestors. After you **reach house no. 181** (with amazing bracket fungus mushrooms in its side window), go down to **⑬ Des Voeux Road West, then turn right:** The next 100 metres are lined with dried fish wholesalers who attack all of your sensory organs with their codfish, shrimps, mussels, seahorses, fish lips, etc. **You can reach the underground through Bonham Strand West.** At the Western Market, treat yourself to a fruity refreshment at ⑭ **Honeymoon Dessert** → p. 57 – the best ones are with mango! The tour ends where it started, at the ① **Sheung Wan MTR-Station**.

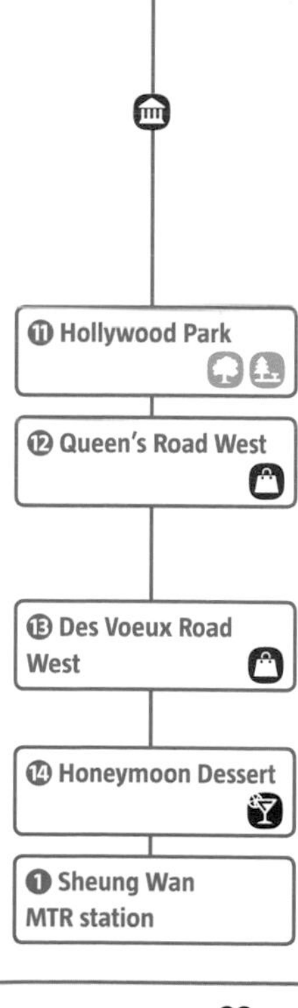

MACAU

> **CITY WHERE TO START?**
> **Largo do Senado (148 C4)** ***(c4)***: Before you get hooked on gambling, take a look at the historical centre – most attractions in the Old Town can easily be reached on foot from Senate Square. The buses on Largo do Senado can take you to more distant locations and the islands.

MAPS ON P. 148–151

From Hong Kong to Portugal in an hour? Hydrofoils really don't take longer than that to cover the 65 km/40 miles across the estuary of the Pearl River.

The former Portuguese overseas province was founded in 1557 as a trade an
mission station and is the oldest Europe
an settlement in East Asia. 650,000 pec
ple live here on one third of the area c
Hong Kong Island. During Hong Kong'
ascent, Macau existed in a kind of limbo
What visitors see today is a curious mi
ture of a medium-sized Chinese towr
a small Portuguese settlement and
bombastic Las Vegas although Maca
has now outstripped the original in th
USA in terms of turnover from gamblin
The city was returned officially to China
1999. Although Portuguese is still the c
ficial language along with Chinese, En
lish is much more important.
Those who prefer to hang on to the
money rather than support the ga

 Photo: Largo do Senado

Churches and casinos: Europe's oldest outpost in the Far East cultivates its very own traditions

bling industry will be more attracted by the highlights from the European colonial past. Almost all important historical buildings have been restored including some from a period long before Hong Kong even existed.

25 historical buildings have been declared ★ *Unesco World Heritage Sites (www.wh.mo)* as witnesses to the early interaction between the East and West. They include the São Paulo Ruins, Protestant Cemetery, Guia Fort, A Ma Temple (Ma Kok Miu), the buildings around Largo do Senado in the centre, the Mandarin's House, as well as several churches and temples. Detailed information (with an interactive layout plan) can be found under *www.culturalheritage.mo*.

SIGHTSEEING

It is best to explore the historical centre around Town Hall Square, *Largo do Senado*, as far as the Protestant Cemetery on foot. It is also worth walking around the southern tip (with the Museu Maritimo and A Ma Temple). The Guia Hill and Jardim de Lou Lim Ieoc are also within walking distance of each other. You can find well thought-out suggestions for INSIDER TIP strolls under *portal.gov.mo/web/guest/tourist* (menu: "Sightseeing") – complete with maps and descriptions in English.

"homecoming" *(www.macaupanda.org.mo)*. The tip of the island is dominated by a monumental statue of Tin Hau or A Ma, the patron saint of mariners, together with the obligatory opulently decorated temple.

The INSIDER TIP *village of Coloane* has kept its traditional appearance. It is only a few yards from the bus stop to the wa-

The venerable racing cars in the Grand Prix Museum will make motorsport fans' hearts beat faster

COLOANE (路環) ★ (150–151 B–E 4–6) *(🕮 b–e 10–12)*

The government decreed that this rural island should remain casino-free. It also has Macau's only bathing beaches. Idyllic *Cheoc Van Beach* in the south lies in a park and has a swimming pool and restaurant/bar. *Hac Sa Beach* in the east has dark sand and a swimming pool; it is located next to a golf course. The island's newest visitor attraction can be found in *Seac Pai Van Park* on the road from the north of the island to Coloane village: an enclosure for two giant pandas that the Chinese government presented to Macau to commemorate the first 10 years of its ter – on the way, you will pass *Lord Stow's bakery* that sells delicious cream cakes, *pasteis de natas*. Take the street on the left to *St Francisco Xavier Church*. The monument in front of the building commemorates the victory the villagers had over pirates who had abducted their children in 1910. *Café Nga Tim* on the corner near the church serves typical Macanese dishes. Follow the road along the coast until you reach *Tam Kung Temple* at the end. On the way back, take the small street that runs parallel to the shore from the church near Café Nga Tim where you will find some interesting shops. Then go back to the shore road which leads northwards to as series of shipyards where traditional wooden junks used to be made. Today, however, very few are built. *Buses 15, 21A, 25, 26A*

COTAI (路氹城) (150–151 B–D 2–4) (🕮 b–d 8–10)

The Las Vegas of the East is being developed on the newly reclaimed land between the islands of Coloane and Taipa. You will be astonished at the six giant complexes that already exist; others will fill the empty spaces in the coming years.The bombastic ★ ● *The Venetian (www.venetianmacao.com)* will immediately catch your eye. When it was opened in 2007, it dwarfed the rest of Macau – 2900 hotel suites, 350 shops, more than 25 acres for conferences and exhibitions, a theatre for shows, a 15,000 seat arena, the world's largest casino with 850 gambling tables and much more – not to forget, the Campanile, Rialto Bridge, Doge's Palace and the possibility to ride in a genuine gondola through an air-conditioned fake Venice! And, the neo-baroque kitsch in the interior is even more spectacular than the outside.

The entrance to the ● *City of Dreams* (148 C4) (🕮 *c4*) is opposite the Doge's Palace. In addition to the obligatory casino and shopping arcade, there are three hotels and a 2000-seat theatre with *The House of Dancing Water* show every evening (see p. 111). To the east (after the new elevated section of railway) is *Wynn Palace* where you can ride on the skycab, which lifts you into the sky and past enormous dragons. There are flowers everywhere in the hotel and casino complex – with amazing floral arrangements made from tens of thousands of naturally preserved flowers. The hotel even features a bouquet of enormous tulips sculpted by the pop artist Jeff Koons. And if you are still left wanting more, head to equally bombastic *The Parisian* complex to the south of the *Venetian*. The splendour of the hotel's reception is on a par with Versailles itself. Outside you can take a ride up the half-size replica of the Eiffel Tower. If you find yourself lost in this gigantic complex, you will be left wondering if the outside world still exists. Note: the minimum age for the casino is 21. *Free buses to the City of Dreams from Hotel Sintra (to the west of the Grand Lisboa Hotel) every 15–30 mins. from around 8.30am–10pm; or city buses 15, 21A, 25, 26A*

GRAND PRIX MUSEUM AND WINE MUSEUM (大賽車博AND物館) 葡萄酒博物館 (149 D4) (🕮 d4)

At the ● *Grand Prix Museum,* original racing cars, photos, videos and other documents tell the story of the car and motorbike races that have been held

MARCO POLO HIGHLIGHTS

★ **Unesco World Heritage Sites**
The historic face of the city
→ p. 101

★ **Coloane**
Rural island with Macau's only beaches for swimming → p. 102

★ **The Venetian**
The casino palace of superlatives
→ p. 103

★ **Macau Museum and Fortaleza do Monte**
The charming museum in a mighty fortress is the best introduction to old Macau → p. 106

★ **The House of Dancing Water**
The spectacular show in the City of Dreams → p. 111

since 1954. The highlight is a "ride" in the INSIDER TIP driving simulator. Next door at the *Wine Museum*, photos and equipment inform visitors of the Portuguese winegrowers' art. *Wed–Mon 10am–6pm | admission free, short wine tasting 15 Ptcs | Tourism Activities Centre | Rua de Luis Gonzaga Gomes 431 | 高美士街 431*

GUIA HILL (松山)
(149 D3–4) *(d3–4)*

In 1638, a fortress was built on the highest point in Macau. Since 1865, it has been towered over by a lighthouse, the *Farol da Guia*. There is a pretty little chapel next to it, on the rear side there's an air-raid shelter from 1931. *Daily 10am–5pm | cableway from Flora Garden (near Jardim de Lou Lim Ieoc), at the top, go to the right*

LOW BUDGET

Casinos: Entrance is free and visitors can see what is going on and breathe in the atmosphere. The most interesting and busy are the large, new, bombastic buildings. Don't forget to take your passport with you!

Accommodation: If you book in advance through the travel agencies in the *Shun Tak Centre* **(136–137 C–D1)** *(**B10**)* in Hong Kong, you will receive considerable reductions in the better hotels during the week.

San Va Hospedaria **(148 B4)** *(**b4**) (Rua da Felicidade 67 | tel. 28 57 37 01 | www.sanvahotel.com):* Stay in a romantic old building on Rua de Felicidade! Most of the 33 rooms are tiny (many without bathrooms) and the walls are made of cardboard but you only have to pay from HK$ 220 per night.

HISTORICAL BUILDINGS IN THE CITY CENTRE
(148 B–C4) *(b–c4)*

The centre of Macau is the pedestrian precinct *Largo de Senado*, Senate Square. With its uniform, perfectly restored buildings, it exudes a feeling of dignity even though a well-known American hamburger chain and similar shops have moved in and replaced local colour with standard international fare – as everywhere else. The most distinctive building on the south side is the *Leal Senado (daily 9am–7pm)*, the "loyal senate": the former town hall. You will not see this written on the building but instead "Institute for Civil and Urban Affairs" which has given rise to its new name of IACM Building. It was built at the end of the 18th century. Have a look at the distinguished panelled rooms on the upper floor: the Senate Library, which is open to the public, and the Council Hall. Painted tiles in the courtyards show historical views of the town. The rooms on the ground floor are used for temporary exhibitions.

If you take the small street on the right past the Leal Senado and walk uphill you will come to an ensemble of beautifully restored old buildings around the *Santo Agostinho Church*. Opposite this lies the classicistic *Teatro Dom Pedro* from 1860; it is the oldest western-style theatre in the Far East.

When you return to Largo do Senado, you will see *São Domingos*, Macau's most beautiful Baroque church, at the northern end. It was built by the Dominicans in the 17th century and magnificently restored in 1996/97. The highlight is the main altar. The picture of the Fátima in the left side chapel is taken out of the church on a procession held on 13 May every year. The church museum is located in the bell tower *(daily 10am–6pm)*.

JARDIM DE LOU LIM IEOC (盧廉若公園) ● (149 D3) (*🗺 d3*)

The most attractive park in Macau was established in the 19th century as the private garden of a Chinese merchant. He combined classic Chinese garden artistry with Macanese colonial architecture to create something very special. Visitors stroll through a miniature landscape of artificial mountains, bamboo groves and a goldfish pond with lotus flowers. Amateur musicians often perform in the pavilions. Sit under the porch roof of the garden villa for a relaxing break. A museum on tea culture has been set up in a lovingly restored building on the edge of the garden. *Garden daily 6am–9pm, museum Tue–Sun 9am–7pm| Estrada de Adolfo Loureiro | 羅利老馬路*

KUN IAM TONG (觀音堂) (149 D2–3) (*🗺 d2–3*)

Guan Yin Hall, Macau's most important Buddhist temple, has its origins in the 17th century. The first American-Chinese treaty was signed here in 1844. The goddess of compassion stands in the last hall of the central wing of the large complex whose individual small buildings are topped with colourfully decorated roofs in the typical Cantonese style. Offerings are made to the recently deceased in two side halls. A passage on the eastern edge of the complex first leads out and then back to the rear temple garden. That is where the famous "Lover's Tree" has been re-cultivated. The original of this strange tree with several trunks died in 1994. *Avenida do Coronel Mesquita | 美副將大馬路*

Jardim do Lou Lim Ieoc – miniature landscape and Macau's most beautiful park

LARGO DO LILAU AND THE MANDARIN'S HOUSE (阿婆井前地 AND 鄭家大屋)

(148 B5) (*b5*)

Atmospheric Lilau Square is bordered by an ensemble of restored houses. The small street going down the hill leads to the entrance of the *Mandarin's House,* the impressive property once in the possession of a learned and wealthy Chinese family. Its most famous member was Zheng Guanying (1842–1921), an industrialist, writer and reformer. The once dilapidated buildings have been painstakingly renovated and visitors can now see some script tablets, furniture and fine carvings. *Thu–Tue 10am–6pm | admission free | Travessa de Antonio da Silva | 龍頭左巷 10 | www.wh.mo/mandarinhouse*

LAS VEGAS HOTELS IN THE CENTRE

(148–149 C–D 4–5) (*c–d 4–5*)

You can see it from far away: *Gran Lisboa's* crazy 258 m/847 ft tower. This eyecatcher reminds some people of a Brazilian dancing girl with a feather boa and others of a lotus blossom. Moving pictures run across the surface of the balloon-like base at night.

The next station is the *Wynn*. Every 15 minutes, colourful fountains of water start to play in front of its entrance. Once an hour, the golden "Tree of Prosperity" grows up out of the floor in a round hall in the shopping centre while a chandelier with 21,000 crystals, illuminated by LEDs, descends from the ceiling. Half an hour later, the "lucky dragon" floats up out of the mist.

The neighbouring *MGM Grand* thought up something completely different: an atrium with the façades of magnificent Lisbon houses. In all three cases – if you don't like kitsch, steer clear!

MACAU MUSEUM AND FORTALEZA DO MONTE (澳門博物館 AND大炮台)

★ (148 C3–4) (*c3–4*)

Escalators whisk visitors up from the ruins of São Paulo to the City Museum that has found its home in the Mountain Fortress *Fortaleza do Monte (platform daily 7am–sunset)* – the largest in Macau. It was built by the Jesuits between 1617 and 1626 and provides a lovely panoramic view. In 1622, a siege by the Dutch was warded off from here. A good collection of well-presented originals and models, together with audiovisual media and dioramas of the highest standard, breathes new life into old Macau at the ● *Macau Museum (Tue–Sun 10am–6pm, last admission 5.30pm | admission 15 Ptcs | www.macaumuseum.gov.mo)*: – with façades of houses, shops and even the calls of street traders.

MACAU TOWER (澳門旅遊塔)

(148 B6) (*b6*)

This 338 m/1008 ft-high tower was erected on reclaimed land and, with its congress centre and new parliament building, makes a – not very convincing – contrast to the old city. But, the view form the top is magnificent. The adventurous climb outside to the Skywalk in the open air – or make the deepest bungee jump on earth: 233 m/765 ft. *Daily 10am–9pm, revolving restaurant until 10pm | observation platform 135 Ptcs | www.macautower.com.mo*

MA KOK MIU (A MA TEMPLE) (媽閣廟)

(148 B5) (*b5*)

The oldest temple in the city. The name Macau can be traced back to the patron saint of seafarers who is worshipped here (*A Ma Gao*: A Ma Bay). The irregular, shady complex is made up of several small buildings on a steep slope above the sea. The main temple is at the bottom and there is a Guan Yin Temple higher up. *Largo do Pagode da Barra | 媽閣廟前地*

MUSEU DE ARTE AND HANDOVER GIFTS MUSEUM (藝術博物館 AND 澳門回歸賀禮陳列館) (149 E5) (*🕮 e5*)

The MAM – the abbreviation used for Macao's art museum *Museu de Arte (www.mam.gov.mo)* – is part of a culture centre and has a not very large permanent collection of Macanese paintings as well as space for temporary exhibitions. The *Handover Gifts Museum (handovermuseum.iacm.gov.mo)* adjoins it to the north. It stores the presents Macau received from all the other Chinese provinces when it "returned" in 1999 – a show of Chinese splendour that is astonishing and frightening at the same time. *Tue–Sun 10am–7pm, entry until 6.30pm | admission MAM 5 Ptcs, Handover Museum free | Avenida Xian Xing Hai | 冼星海大馬路*

MUSEU MARÍTIMO (海事博物館) (148 A–B5) (*🕮 a–b5*)

The splendid Maritime and Seafaring Museum is located opposite A Ma Temple (Ma Kok Miu). There are four sections: fishing in the South China Sea, sea travel and discoveries, marine biology, and harbour technology and hydrography. The exhibits – models, dioramas, aquariums, maritime maps, tools – have explanations in three languages. *Wed–Mon 10am–6pm, entry until 5.30pm | admission 10 Ptcs, Sun 5 Ptcs | Largo do Pagode da Barra | 媽閣廟前地 | www.museumaritimo.gov.mo*

Not a stroll for the faint-hearted: the skywalk on the Macau Tower

PAWN HOUSE MUSEUM (典當業展示館) (148 B–C4) (*🕮 b–c4*)

The fortress-like warehouse of pawned articles is impressive and it is interesting to see how the boss kept his eye on the people working there. The house is part of the Culture Club with an excellent souvenir shop and tearoom. *Daily except 1st Mon in the month 10.30am–7pm | admission free | Avenida Almeida Ribero 396| 新馬路 396*

PORTAS DO CERCO (關閘) (149 D1) (🗺 d1)

This border gate to China was built in 1870 but today it is merely a monument in front of the gigantic checkpoint build-

Do not miss the ruins of São Paulo, a landmark in Macau

ings. The dates from "August 1849" on the front commemorate the murder of a governor of the city by rebellious Chinese and the subsequent retaliation campaign by the Portuguese. The inscription "Honour your fatherland because it is watching you" warns those passing through the gate to remain faithful to Portugal. *At the northern edge*

PROTESTANT CEMETERY AND JARDIM LUIS DE CAMÕES (基督教墳場 AND 白鴿巢公園) (148 C3) (🗺 c3)

The shady *Jardim Luis de Camões* park recalls the great poet who lived in Macau for several years from 1558 and sang the praises of Portuguese conquests in his "Os Lusiadas". The humble *Protestant cemetery* to the north-east of the park entrance is a history book in stone: plagues and pirates cut short the lives of merchants and sailors living here. *Praça Luís de Camões | 白鴿巢前地*

SÃO PAULO (大三巴牌坊) (148 C3–4) (🗺 c3–4)

The impressive façade of the cathedral that was destroyed by fire in 1835 is Macau's symbol and a cultural-historical monument of the first order. Japanese and Cantonese Christians erected it in the years 1620–27 to plans drawn up by an Italian Jesuit. This is a mission to Christianise the heathens in stone: the dove, as the symbol of the Holy Ghost, hovers at the top below the Cross; Jesus stands beneath it with Mary lower down who can be seen conquering a dragon further to the right; to the right of this, there is a *memento mori* in Chinese: "If you think of death, you will not sin". This is a counterpart to the inscription "The devil leads man to sin" on the left next to the merchant ship. A subterranean *museum (daily 9am–6pm)* at the end of the long vanished nave has exhibits of Christian art as well as the bones of Japanese and Vietnamese martyrs from the 17th century.

TAIPA (氹仔)
(150–151 A–D 1–2) (*a–d 7–8*)

The racetrack, university, airport and a satellite town are all located on the island that can be reached by crossing over a series of three bridges. A stroll through *Taipa Village* in the south is very pleasant. The traffic-free lanes are lined with two-storey houses, the main street Rua du Cunha – no cars here either – is well-known for its *pastelerias* (cake shops), cafés and restaurants. At the end, turn left and then right and go up the steps to reach the Carmelite Church built in the Classicist style in 1885. You now walk through a well cared-for park down to a body of water that was once part of the ocean from where you can see the hotel and casino palaces in Cotai. A row of five superbly restored villas on the shore, shaded by ancient trees, forms the *Taipa House Museum*. This is where you will be able to see how the "better people" lived around 1900. You can walk from here to *The Venetian* on a moving walkway. *Buses 11, 15, 28A, 33*

FOOD & DRINK

Once you get away from the large hotels, the restaurants in Macau are much more easy-going and European than their bombastic competitors in Hong Kong – and cheaper too, especially when it comes to wine. The Macanese dishes are really unique – they are a combination of Portuguese and Cantonese cuisine with African chicken, Macau sole, codfish, shrimps and pigeon among the specialities.

ANTÓNIO (安東尼奧餐廳)
(150 B2) (*b8*)

António Coelho cooks at a level to satisfy gourmets in his simple 7-table restaurant in Taipa Village. The chef himself prepares many dishes in front of the guests at their table. *Rua dos Clérigos 7 | 氹仔木鐸街 7 | tel. 28 88 86 68 | www.antoniomacau.com* | Expensive

INSIDER TIP CAFÉ OU MUN
(澳門咖啡) (148 C4) (*c4*)

Typical café-restaurant in a side street off Largo do Senado. Inexpensive set meals, Portuguese baked items and a wide range of sandwiches. *Travessa de São Domingos 12 | 板樟堂巷 12 | tel. 28 37 22 07* | Budget

CLUBE MILITAR (澳門陸軍俱樂部)
(148 C4) (*c4*)

There is no need to be afraid: the only things shooting around in this lovely old building are champagne corks. You will be served Portuguese cuisine in artistic surroundings. *Avenida da Praia Grande 975 | 南灣大馬路 975 | near Hotel Lisboa | tel. 28 71 40 10* | Moderate

FERNANDO (法蘭度餐廳)
(151 D5) (*d11*)

This fashionable restaurant lies hidden behind a bower of bougainvilleas at Hac Sa Beach. This is the place to enjoy spectacular seafood dishes. Terrace bar – no reservations! *Coloane | 路環黑沙海灘* | Budget

LITORAL (海灣餐廳)
(148 B5) (*b5*)

A top address for Macanese cuisine and one of the best places to try African Chicken. *Rua do Almirante Sergio 261a 河邊新街 261a | near the Museu Marít[illegible]mo | tel. 28 96 78 78* | Moderate

INSIDER TIP **NOODLE AND CONGEE CORNER** (粥麵莊)
(148 C4–5) *(📖 c4–5)*
In the casino – and still good and inexpensive? Hard to believe, but it's true. And there is more than just noodles and rice soup as the name seems to suggest. The open kitchen let's you see how soup is prepared with a single 10-foot-long noodle. *1st floor, Grand Lisboa | 新葡京酒店 | tel. 88 03 77 55 | Budget*

SHOPPING

The shopping arcades in the large hotels are full of international luxury articles. The *Rua de Nossa Senhora de Amparo* **(148 C4)** *(📖 c4)* and the adjacent streets is a good place for antiques and there is also a small flea market. *Artesanatos Fai Long (Rua São Paulo 33B)* sells first-rate painted porcelain figures made in the Shiwan ceramic centre.

ENTERTAINMENT

CENTRO CULTURAL (文化中心)
(149 E5) *(📖 e5)*
It is impossible not to notice Macau's Cultural Centre with the floating roof of the theatre and concert building curving upwards. Artists from China and around the world make guest appearances here. *Avenida Xian Xing Hai | 冼星海大馬路 | tel. 28 55 55 55 | credit-card ticket sales tel. 28 40 05 55 | www.ccm.gov.mo*

INSIDER TIP **COTAI AT NIGHT**
(150–151 C–D 2–3) *(📖 b–d 8–10)*
Experience Asia's equivalent to Las Vegas. The bright lights of the *Cotai Strip* in Macau are most dazzling at night. The most spectacular sights lie in close vicinity: *The Venetian* (gondola ride), *The Parisian* (up the Eiffel Tower), *City of Dreams* (Vquarium – for free admission to the mermaid show) and *Wynn*

Optical illusions in Macau: more Venetian than Venice

Palace (skycab dragon ride). There are simply too many breath-taking sights to list them all here. If the signature attraction *The House of Dancing Water* is already sold out, there are many other shows to take your pick from. Simply inquire at the tourist information as soon as you arrive in Hong Kong for a program of events.

THE HOUSE OF DANCING WATER
(水舞間) ★ (150 C2) (*c8*)
The most spectacular show in the eastern hemisphere. In an instant, the ring in the 2000-seat theatre changes into a pool of water out of which ships emerge and into which people disappear. The motorbike stunts in particular are really breathtaking. *City of Dreams | Cotai | Thu–Sun 5pm und 8pm, Mon 8pm (changes possible) | tickets from HK$ 580 | ticket tel. 88 68 67 67 | www.thehouseofdancingwater.com*

WHERE TO STAY

Prices are always higher at weekends than on workdays. Hotels in Macau: *www.macautourism.gov.mo/en/info/accommodation.php.*

EAST ASIA (東亞酒店)
(148 B4) (*b4*)
Hotel with 98 rooms in the Old Town. The location is ideal for going on strolls to explore old Macau. *Rua da Madeira 1 | 新埗頭街 1 | tel. 28 92 24 33 | eastasiahotelmacau.com* | Budget

GRAND COLOANE BEACH RESORT
(豪華家庭度假酒店)
(151 D5) (*d11*)
Awarded as a "green hotel" by Macau's environmental agency, the resort offers 208 rooms all with sea and beach views and veranda set in subtropical gardens. *Coloane | Estrada de Hac Sa 1918 | 黑沙马路 1918 | tel. 28 87 11 11 | www.grandcoloane.com* | Moderate

MANDARIN ORIENTAL
(文華東方酒店) (149 D5) (*d5*)
This hotel consciously resists trying to out-do the Las Vegas hotels and appearing just that little bit more bombastic. Instead, the Mandarin Oriental stresses refined elegance. There are wonderful views over the water from all 213 bedrooms – and some bathrooms! *Avenida Dr Sun Yat Sen | 孫逸仙達馬路 | tel. 88 05 88 88 | www.mandarinoriental.com* | Expensive

INSIDER TIP POUSADA DE MONG-HÁ
(望厦宾馆) (149 D2) (*d2*))
The romantic hotel run by the tourism college is the most highly-praised in the city: it has been lovingly decorated in Macanese style and the service and gastronomy is of the same excellent standard. The peaceful location on a green hill makes up for the less-than-ideal location. *Colina de Mong Há | 望厦山 | tel. 28 51 52 22 | www.ift.edu.mo/pousada* | Budget

RIVIERA HOTEL (濠濠酒店)
(148 B5) (*b5*)
Tranquil, sea views, inexpensive and only a short walk from the Old Town – these are the advantages of this 160-room hotel. *Rua Comendador Kou Ho Neng 7–13 | 高可寧紳士街 7–13 | tel. 28 33 99 55 | www.macauctshotel.com* | Moderate

WYNN (永利澳门酒店)
(149 C–D5) (*c–d5*)
Centrally located Las Vegas hotel with 1009 rooms. The suites in particular revel in luxury. Large casino, spacious spa area and really excellent dim sums in the INSIDER TIP Chinese Restaurant. *Rua Cidade de Sintra | 仙德麗街 | tel. 28 88 99 66 | www.wynnmacau.com* | Expensive

TRAVEL WITH KIDS

Hong Kong is probably not really one of the first destinations tourists think of visiting with children – but voilà: it is more interesting for the young ones than you may expect! It starts with the parks: the Avarium in Hong Kong Park, the bird pond in Kowloon Park and the zoo are all pleasant places to visit, and educational too, and no admission is charged to any of them. There is also a large open-air swimming pool at the northern end of Kowloon Park.

The Science Museum is also a good choice – especially if the weather is bad, as the many young visitors go to prove. The sophisticated presentation technology in the Museum of History makes it especially interesting for school children *(admission for pupils and students: Science Museum and Museum of History free | identification required)*.

Ocean Park: although the area after the entrance is no longer officially called *Kid's World*, the most important activities for children can still be found there – and provide a great variety of entertainment and education *(admission for children from 3–11, HK$ 193)*.

APE COLONY AT THE SHEK LEI PUI RESERVOIR (石梨貝水庫)
(143 D3) *(🕮 O)*

Rhesus monkeys which now live on the northern edge of Kowloon used to be common in Hong Kong – but most of them had been wiped out by the middle of the 20th century. It is possible that all the monkeys frolicking around between the bus stop and reservoir are descendants of some who managed to escape their fate. This funny gang has made their own swimming baths directly behind the "no swimming" sign. Take the ban on feeding them seriously: the animals can become aggressive. This little excursion – a bus trip and short walk – takes about 2 hours. *Bus 81 from MTR Yau Ma Tei/exit A1 to Shek Lei Pui Reservoir*

CITY PLAZA ICE PALACE (太古城中心冰上皇宮) (U D3) *(🕮 O)*

No, it's is not a joke! Hong Kong's largest shopping centre, City Plaza, even has an ice-skating rink. You can rent skates there. *Tue, Wed, Fri 9.30am–10pm, Mon, Thu 9.30am–9.30pm, Sat 12.30–10pm, Sun 12.30–5pm (changing exceptions) | admission from HK$ 55 | www.icepalace.com.hk | MTR Tai Koo, exit E1*

The jungle of skyscrapers offers more for children than you possibly thought – and some attractions are even free

DISNEYLAND (迪士尼樂園)

(142 C4) (*🕮 0*)

The first Asian Disneyland outside Japan is divided into four sections: *Main Street USA* takes visitors back to around 1900 with a street theatre and a lot of music; in *Adventureland* visitors take a ride on a raft through the jungle to Tarzan's tree house and take part in the Lion King's Festival; Mickey Mouse is the guide through a fairy tale world of roundabouts and Sleeping Beauty's Castle in *Fantasyland*, while children and adults will marvel at the peaceful and exciting future in *Tomorrowland*. Add to that the mysterious *Mystik Point* and the exciting *Grizzly Gulch* with a rollercoaster that runs partly underground. *Daily 10.30am–8.30pm, during the summer holidays 10am–8.30pm | admission HK$ 539, children (3–11) HK$ 385, senior citizens (over 65) HK$ 100 | limited number of tickets, advance bookings: tel. 183 08 30 or www.hongkongdisneyland.com | MTR Disneyland Resort*

SNOOPY'S WORLD (史諾比開心世界)

(143 D3) (*🕮 0*)

Charlie Brown is here and so are Schroeder, Linus, Lucy, Woodstock, and of course Charlie's philosophical beagle, as well as all the other figures from the comic series – more than 60 in all, two and three-dimensional and up close. *Daily 10am–8pm | admission free | Sha Tin New Town Plaza | 新城市廣場 | Phase One, Level 3 | Sha Tin station, exit A*

WITH CHILDREN IN MACAU

While the little ones try out the hands-on displays at the *Science Center* (149 E5) (*🕮 e5*) (*Fri–Wed 10am–6pm, last entrance 5.30pm | admission 25 Ptcs, 2–11 years 15 Ptcs | opposite the Culture Centre*), the adults take a break at the café with sea views. Several casinos in Cotai offer creches for a small fee, e.g. *Kid's Club* at the *Galaxy Macau* (150 C2) (*🕮 b8*) or *Qube Kingdom* at *The Parisian* (150 D3) (*🕮 c9*).

FESTIVALS & EVENTS

CHINESE FESTIVALS

Roman numerals = lunar months.

1. I. CHINESE NEW YEAR

This festival is just as important for Chinese families as Christmas is for us. Most shops close for 2 days or longer. The decorations in banks and department stores are really spectacular and there is a magnificent flower market in Victoria Park before the festival. There is a New Year's Parade on the 2nd day and fireworks over the harbour in the evening. It is forbidden to use fireworks yourself. The festival season ends on the 15th day with the lantern festival to celebrate the first full moon.

CHING MING FESTIVAL

Festival to commemorate the dead: families sweep the graves of their ancestors and bring offerings of food and drink.

23 III BIRTHDAY OF TIN HAU

(8 May 2018, 27 April 2019) Decorated ships go to Tin Hau Temple on the southern end of the Clear Water Bay peninsula on the INSIDER TIP goddess' birthday. There, the seafarers make sacrifices to their patron saint, enjoy themselves with lion dances and have their boats' shrines blessed for the coming year (143 E4) (*🗺 O*). *Special ferries from North Point* (139 F1) (*🗺 O*).

8 IV BIRTHDAY OF TAM KUNG AND BUDDHA

(22 May 2018, 12 May 2019) Celebrations for Tam Kung, the Ruler of the Weather, in his main temple in Shau Kei Wan *(MTR Shau Kei Wan, north end of Main St.)* (U E3) (*🗺 O*). This is also the day when Buddha's birthday is celebrated in Buddhist temples by washing the statues.

IV MONTH: BUN FESTIVAL IN CHEUNG CHAU

The INSIDER TIP Bun Festival in honour of the God of the North (the main god of the island) lasts 3 days. The exact date is determined by an oracle. There is a lot of "gods' entertainment" going on in front of the temple; the procession is spectacular; colourfully costumed children, supported by hidden frames, seem to float on the hands of other children. Pink buns which bring good luck are hung from three 20 m/66 ft-high towers and distributed by the priests on the last evening. (142 B–C5) (*🗺 O*)

5 V DRAGON BOAT FESTIVAL (TUEN NG FESTIVAL)

People eat sticky rice wrapped in leaves and organise spectacular dragon boat races. The international races in Sha Tin are held one or two weeks later.

15 VIII MID-AUTUMN FESTIVAL (MOON FESTIVAL)

(24 Sept 2018, 13 Sept 2019) Coloured lanterns glow, people look at the moon and eat rich moon cakes. The dances by the INSIDER TIP fire dragons made of glowing incense sticks that wind their way through the lanes near Wun Sha Street on three evenings are an unforgettable sight. *(139 E4) (H12)*

9 IX DOUBLE NINTH (CHUNG YEUNG FESTIVAL)

Hong Kongers make offerings at the graves and excursions into the surrounding hills.

FESTIVALS & SPORTS

FEBRUARY/MARCH

Arts Festival *(www.hk.artsfestival.org:* varied programme with performances by top artists from around the world. Music, ballet and theatre

NOVEMBER

Macau Grand Prix: Classic car race *(www.macau.grandprix.gov.mo)*

NATIONAL HOLIDAYS

1 Jan	New Year's Day
16 Feb 2018, 5 Feb 2019	Chinese New Year (three days)
4 or 5 April	Ching Ming Festival
30 March–2 April 2018, 19–22 April 2019	Good Friday to Easter Monday
18 June 2018, 7 June 2019	Dragon Boat Festival
1 July	Foundation of SAR Hong Kong
3rd Mon in August	Liberation Day
25 Sept 2018, 14 Sept 2019	Day after Mid-Autumn Festival
17 Oct 2018, 7 Oct 2019	Double Ninth
25/26 Dec	Christmas

If a holiday falls on a Sunday, the following Monday is a day off.

LINKS, BLOGS, APPS & MORE

LINKS & BLOGS

m.discoverhongkong.com Free access to the tourism sites of the Hong Kong Tourism Board at the 7000 hotspots of the provider PCCW

www.hongkongextras.com A non-commercial English guide with a mass of detailed information on construction projects, changes to public transport connections, ferry fares, etc.

gohongkong.about.com Another independent English travel guide; less detailed but more focused on recommendations and – a big plus – Macau is also included

www.openrice.com/english Hong Kong's most comprehensive online gourmet guide with guest reviews, photos, recipes and search function

www.hongkonghustle.com Art, parties, fashion, music; in short, this is where you can find out about the lifestyle of the metropolis

www.travelblog.org/Asia/Macau Overview of current Macau blogs

community.justlanded.com/en/Hong-Kong A comprehensive forum aimed at people who intend to stay in Hong Kong for a lengthy period

www.hkdigit.net Photo-blog in English, a variety of subjects seen from the Hong Kong perspective

therealnewshk.wordpress.com A blog on politics which was set up with the goal of filtering the Chinese language newspapers to find out what the majority of Hongkongers are reading and what is really going on in Hong Kong

hong-kong-blogs-review.com Overview of Hong Kong blogs, especially by expatriates living there

Regardless of whether you are still preparing your trip or already in Hong Kong: these addresses will provide you with more information, videos and networks to make your holiday even more enjoyable

www.flickr.com/groups/hongkong Hong Kong forum for hobby photographers – useful tips and wonderful pictures

foodcraverhk.tumblr.com The sub-heading "A blog on Hong Kong delicacies" reveals what the site is about. Its author Nini takes her readers on a tour of Hong Kong's new culinary experiences. Extremely informative site with appealing photos and Chinese letters

VIDEOS & MUSIC

www.youtube.com/user/HongKong Reality channel of the Hong Kong Tourism Board with dozens of well-made short films

www.tripfilms.com/Tourism-l62489-Hong_Kong-Travel_Videos.html Mainly amateur videos; special sections are devoted to hotels and restaurants

www.tripfilms.com/search.sdo?keywords=Macau&x=0&y=0 A small selection of videos on Macau – including a gondola ride in *The Venetian* casino palace

www.goandroam.com/webcams/china/hk Collection of Hong Kong webcams with photos changing every 15 minutes; with a Macau link

APPS

Discover Hong Kong mobile app series An entire collection of Hong Kong apps commissioned by the Hong Kong Tourism Board

KMB Bilingual app from Kowloon Motor Bus for iPhone and Android

MTR Mobile This app (iOS and Android) provides you with plans of the underground and tram networks, information on the right exits to take and timetables to help plan your journey

Hong Kong eTransport provides a one-stop service of point to point public transport route enquiry for the MTR, bus, tram and ferry. Available for iOS and Android

Learn Cantonese A teach yourself program for basic Cantonese conversation, useful for anyone who wants to exchange a few simple words with the taxi driver or fruit and vegetable stall owner. Available for Windows phone

TRAVEL TIPS

ARRIVAL (HONG KONG)

There are a great number of flights to Hong Kong; either direct from London or with stopovers. Compare the price of flights offered by major airlines on the Internet. As a rule, a nonstop flight from Europe takes around 12 hours. All planes land at *Chek Lap Kok Airport.* If you do not have a pressing engagement, you should take one of the INSIDER TIP airport buses to the inner city (instead of the Airport Express) as they travel over three elevated bridges with spectacular views. In addition, it is possible to reach many destinations without having to change.

Airport Express train: The trip to the terminus in Central (137 E2) (*C11*) costs HK$ 100, to the Kowloon stop HK$ 90 (travel time 23 and 19 minutes respectively). Onward travel by underground (change at Tsing Yi and Hong Kong stops) and special shuttle buses that travel on several routes to around 50 hotels from the Kowloon and Hong Kong stations is free of charge.

Buses: Air-conditioned buses travel on over two dozen lines directly to all districts and many hotels. Line 11A makes the journey via Causeway Bay to North Point in 70 minutes (HK$ 40), line A21 to Hung Hom station (HK$ 33, 65 minutes). The exact fare has to be inserted when you get on. In addition, comfortable hotel buses connect the airport with several major hotels; tickets are available at the counter C15 in Terminal 2.

Taxis: Green cabs only drive to the New Territories; blue ones on Lantau. Count on paying HK$ 350 to reach Central and Causeway Bay and HK$ 280 for Tsim Sha Tsui (incl. bridge and tunnel fees).

Trains arriving directly from China end at the Kowloon/Hung Hom station (135 E4) (*F–G8*), where passport and customs control takes place. From there, it is only a 5-minute taxi ride to the Kowloon hotels and 5–15 minutes to the island. The tunnel buses that stop at the railway station are a much cheaper way of reaching the island but they are often overcrowded and hardly practical if you have much luggage with you.

Cruise liners dock at Ocean terminal (134 B6) (*D9*) or the new Kai Tak terminal; ferries from China at the China Ferry Terminal (134 B5) (*D8–9*). Taxis and buses leave from the lower floor.

RESPONSIBLE TRAVEL

It doesn't take a lot to be environmentally friendly whilst travelling. Don't just think about your carbon footprint whilst flying to and from your holiday destination but also about how you can protect nature and culture abroad. As a tourist it is especially important to respect nature, look out for local products, cycle instead of driving, save water and much more. If you would like to find out more about eco-tourism please visit: *www.ecotourism.org*

ARRIVAL (MACAU)

Jet-propelled catamarans and hovercraft operated by the *Turbo*

From arrival to weather

Holiday from start to finish: the most important addresses and information for your Hong Kong and Macau trip

jet Shipping Company *(7am–midnight, every 15 mins. | travel time 60 mins. | HK$ 165 from Hong Kong, 135 Ptcs/ HK$ from Macau (one way economy fare, incl. exit fee | information: Hong Kong tel. 28 59 33 33 | Macau tel. 28 55 50 25 | www.turbojet.com.hk)* depart round the clock from Macau Ferry Terminal (136–137 C–D1) *(🕮 B10)* to Macau's main ferry port, the Macau Maritime Ferry Terminal. There are higher fares at weekends and at night and an extra charge for large pieces of luggage (more than 10 kg).

From 7am–10.30pm, Turbojet runs from China Ferry Terminal (134 B5) *(🕮 D8–9)* every half hour, fares are similar.

A third alternative is *Cotai Water Jet (www.cotaiwaterjet.com)* to Taipa Ferry Terminal; from there, it is not very far to the Las Vegas casinos in Cotai. Departures from the Macau Ferry Terminal every 30 mins. between 7am and 11.30pm; return journeys also at midnight and 1am. The prices are the same as with Turbojet. Bookings for the ferries can be made at the docks, in travel agencies and some underground stations, as well as on the Internet. During the week, there are usually spaces free but a reservation is advisable at the weekend. It is not worth paying the additional money for a first-class ticket.

In Macau, buses 3, 3A and 10A depart from the ferry terminal (149 E3–4) *(🕮 e3–4)* for the centre and pass several hotels on the way. The larger hotels and casino hotel complexes on Cotai provide free shuttle buses. There are similar connections to the airport. Taxis from the ferry landing to the centre cost around 25 Ptcs.

CURRENCY CONVERTER

£	HKD	HKD	£
1	12.5	10	0.80
3	23	30	2.4
5	63	50	4
13	163	130	10.4
40	500	400	32
75	940	750	60
120	1500	1200	96
250	3140	2500	200
500	6280	5000	400

$	HKD	HKD	$
1	8	10	1.25
3	23.5	30	2.50
5	39	50	6.3
13	102	130	16.3
40	315	400	50
75	590	750	94
120	940	1200	150
250	1965	2500	313
500	3930	5000	625

For current exchange rates see www.xe.com

There are no direct flights to Macau from Europe. You can reach Macau from the airport in Hong Kong without actually entering the SAR by using the *Turbojet* and *Cotai Water Jet* services. Those in a real hurry can take a *helicopter (20 flights daily, between the two main terminals only, 10am–11pm | flying time 15 mins. | HK$ 4300 one way | Hong Kong tel. 20 18 98 98, Macau tel. 28 72 72 88 | www.skyshuttlehk.com)*.

BANKS & CURRENCY EXCHANGE

Several exchange offices on arrival level 5 at the airport | daily 7am–10.30pm. The most convenient way to get cash is from an ATM. Charges vary depending on your bank or credit card. If you change money or cash travellers' cheques elsewhere, the fees can be higher than the difference in the exchange rate. You can pay with your credit card in all hotels and most restaurants.

BEACHES

42 beaches are looked after and patrolled by the city. During the official bathing season (April–Oct), they provide showers, changing rooms, toilets, pontoons and other conveniences that can be used free of charge. The beaches are accessible throughout the year. As there are no strong currents and little surf, children can also swim safely.

CLIMATE, WHEN TO GO

The ideal period is between the middle of Oct and the end of Dec when it is almost always warm and dry. The weather can be damp and chilly in Feb and March. Summers are muggy and hot, a strain on circulation. The typhoon season is July–Oct; when signal level 8 is sounded, schools, offices and shops close, ferries and planes stop running, followed a little later by bus and rail transport.

COMPLAINTS

The Consumer Council can help if you feel that you have been cheated shopping: *tel. 29 29 22 22 | www.consumer.org.hk*

CUSTOMS

1 litre of spirits (30+% alcohol content) and 19 cigarettes can be imported duty free into Hong Kong. In Macau, this is 1 litre of wine or spirits (30% alcohol content), 1 litre of spirits with a higher alcoholic content and 200 cigarettes. When you return to the EU, the same tax-exemption limit for cigarettes applies as it does in Macau and, in addition, 1 litre of sprits above 22% or 2 litres with less alcohol. Passengers are also allowed to carry purchases worth up to £ 390. For allowances, *see: www.gov.uk/duty-free-goods/arrivals-from-outside-the-eu*

ELECTRICITY

The power supply in Hong Kong and Macau is the same as in Europe: 220V. Hong Kong uses the British three-pin rectangular blade plug although there are other plug variations too. If your hotel does not have multiple wall sockets, they will usually provide adapters (also available cheaply from electrical shops).

EMBASSIES & CONSULATES

BRITISH CONSULATE-GENERAL

1 Supreme Court Rd. | Hong Kong | tel. +8 52 29 0130 00 | ukinhongkong.fco.gov.uk/en/

CONSULATE GENERAL OF THE UNITED STATES OF AMERICA

26 Garden Rd. | Hong Kong | tel: +852 25 23 90 11 | hongkong.usconsulate.gov/contact.html

CONSULATE GENERAL OF CANADA

12th–14th Floor | One Exchange Square | Hong Kong | tel. +852 37 19 47 00 | www.canadainternational.gc.ca/hong_kong

EMERGENCY SERVICES

Fire Brigade, Ambulance, Assault: tel. 999 (without coins)
Police (for tourists; also for taxi complaints): tel. 23 27 71 77

EVENT INFORMATION

www.discoverhongkong.com ("Events & Festivals"). Information for partygoers and pub crawlers is provided by *www.bcmagazine.net* and *www.hkclubbing.com.* Printed information is supplied by the daily newspaper *South China Morning Post.* Flyers on cultural events are available at the Cultural Centre and in City Hall.

HEALTH

No vaccinations are prescribed for Hong Kong. You should not drink large quantities of tap water that has not been boiled. The following hospitals have 24-hour emergency services: *Queen Mary Hospital* (U A4) (*🗺 O*) (*102 Pokfulam Rd. | Hong Kong Island | tel. 28 55 38 38*) and *Queen Elizabeth Hospital* (135 D3) (*🗺 E–F7*) (*30 Gascoigne Rd. | Kowloon | tel. 29 58 88 88*). *St John Ambulance (tel. 1 87 80 00)* is a free ambulance service. The consulate can provide information on English-speaking doctors. Medication is provided directly by doctors and hospitals. Medicine can also be purchased at some *Watson's* branches, e.g. *Melbourne Plaza | 33 Queen's Rd. Central* (137 D3) (*🗺 C11*), *11 Cameron Rd.* (134 C5) (*🗺 E9*).

IMMIGRATION

Full British citizens with a valid passport can stay for up to 180 days visa-free as visitors; citizens from British Overseas Territories, the USA and Canada for up to 90 days. You will also need your passport if you intend to travel between Hong Kong and Macau. Normally, formalities are handled quickly but you will have to fill out a small form. You should be at the departure counter 15 minutes before your ferry (or helicopter) leaves. A visa is still required to enter mainland China from Hong Kong.

BUDGETING

Beer, wine	£5.50/$7 *for a draught beer or glass of wine*
Lunch	£4.10/$5.30 *for a Chinese noodle soup*
Dinner	£18–26/$24–33 *in an average standard Chinese restaurant*
Peak Tram	£4.10/$5.30 *for a return trip to The Peak*
Bus fare	32p/¢42 *In the city in Macau*
Ferry	£32/$41.50 *to Macau and back during daytime*

INFORMATION BEFORE THE TRIP

HONG KONG TOURISM BOARD (HKTB)
www.discoverhongkong.com/eng/index.html

MACAU GOVERNMENT TOURIST OFFICE
www.macautourism.gov.mo

INFORMATION IN HONG KONG

HONG KONG TOURISM BOARD (HKTB)

– *Visitor tel. 25 08 12 34 | daily 9am–6pm*
Visitor Information:
– *at the airport (only for arriving passengers) | daily 8am–9pm*
– *at the Star Ferry Dock | Kowloon | daily 8am–8pm* (134 C6) (*B E9*)
– *at the Peak Piazza (between the Peak Tower and Peak Galleria) | daily 11am–8pm* (136 C5) (*B B13*)

– *Lo Wu | 2/F, Arrival Hall (only for passengers arriving from Shenzhen)*

MACAU TOURIST INFORMATION BUREAU

– *Shop 336–337, Shun Tak Centre | 200 Connaught Rd. | daily 9am–10pm | tel. 28 57 22 87 | MTR Sheung Wan* (136–137 C–D 1–2) (*B B10*)
– *Hong Kong International Airport | counter A06, arrival level 5, terminal 1* (0) (*B 0*)

ACCOMMODATION SERVICE

At the airport (only for arriving passengers)

INFORMATION IN MACAU

MACAU GOVERNMENT TOURIST OFFICE

– *Visitor tel. 28 33 30 00*
– *Largo do Senado 9 | daily 9am–6pm | tel. 83 97 11 20* (148 C4) (*B c4*)
– *additional counters (some with accommodation service) in the Macau Ferry*

WEATHER IN HONG KONG

	Jan	Feb	March	April	May	June	July	Aug	Sept	Oct	Nov	Dec
Daytime temperatures in °C/ °F	18/64	18/64	20/68	24/75	28/82	30/86	31/88	31/88	30/86	27/81	24/75	20/68
Nighttime temperatures in °C/ °C	13/55	13/55	16/61	19/66	23/73	26/79	26/79	26/79	25/77	23/73	19/66	15/59
Sunshine hours/day	5	4	3	4	5	5	7	6	7	7	6	6
Precipitation days/month	4	5	7	8	13	18	17	15	12	6	2	3
Water temperatures in °C/ °F	18/64	18/64	21/70	24/75	25/77	27/81	28/82	28/82	27/81	26/79	24/75	21/70

 Sunshine hours/day Precipitation days/month Water temperatures in °C/ °F

Terminal (149 E3–4) *(🗺 e3–4), Taipa Ferry Terminal* (151 D1) *(🗺 d7) and at the airport* (151 D1–2) *(🗺 d7–8)*

INTERNET & WIFI

All better hotels and shopping centres provide wireless internet access (WiFi); however, you will sometimes have to pay extra for this service. Internet terminals that can be used free of charge can be found on the second floor of the *China Hong Kong City (China Ferry Terminal)* (134 B5) *(🗺 D–E8)*. Internet access is free in most government buildings including the foyer of *City Hall* (137 E3) *(🗺 D11)*.

In these public WiFi networks, access is time-limited and some addresses could be blocked. All government hotspots are listed under *www.gov.hk/en/theme/wifi/location/index.htm*, others at *www.ofta.gov.hk/en/consumer_interest/main.html*.

You will be able to surf the net while drinking coffee in the branches of *Pacific Coffee, e.g. Shop 4, The Center | 99 Queen's Rd. Central* (137 D2) *(🗺 C11) and 1/F Silvercord Shopping Arcade | 30 Canton Rd.* (134 C5) *(🗺 E9)*.

OPENING HOURS

The shops in Tsim Sha Tsui and Causeway Bay are usually open from 11am–9pm, some until 10pm, also at weekends; in Central only until around 7.30pm. Many specialist shops remain closed on Sunday. The opening hours in Macau are similar. The shops in the arcades in the casino palaces all close before 11pm.

PHONE & MOBILE PHONE

Your mobile phone will connect automatically to a Hong Kong network. The best option is to buy a *Tourist SIM Card (HE$ 88 for 5 days, HK$ 118 for 8 days incl. Macau | available in 7-Eleven and Circle K stores)* which offers internet connection and diverse discounts on excursions and sightseeing tours. More information can be found at *www.discoverhongkong.com*, by clicking "Plan your trip – Traveller information – Communications". Calls within Hong Kong's fixed-line network are free but cost HK$ 1 from a payphone. The international dialing code to the UK is *0044*, US/Canada *001*. The code for Hong Kong is *008520*, for Macau *008530*.

POST

The *General post office* (137 E2) *(🗺 C11) (Mon–Sat 8am–6pm, Sun 9am–5pm | MTR Central)* is located near the Star Ferry.

PRICES & CURRENCY

The Hong Kong dollar, abbreviated here as HK$, is pegged to the US dollar with a range of 7.75 to 7.85 (US$ 1 = HK$ 7.75–7.85) and the exchange rate to other currencies fluctuates accordingly. The bank notes are issued by three different banks, have the same size but different designs. Prices in Macau (calculated in Patacas – Ptcs) are comparable to those in Hong Kong. You can pay with Hong Kong currency in Macau (the rate is almost 1:1) but make sure you get your change in Hong Kong dollars.

PUBLIC TRANSPORT

IN HONG KONG

The magic word for comfortable travel in Hong Kong is the INSIDER TIP *Octopus Card*. It costs HK$ 100 – that is the stored credit – plus HK$ 50 deposit, is valid in most means of public transport and can be used as soon as you leave the airport. You can return it at the airport (or in underground stations) and any credit remaining plus the deposit will be refunded in cash (minus a small service charge). When you go through a barrier (e.g. in an MTR station) or get on a bus, you put the card on a sensor and a beep lets you know that the fare has been deducted. You can increase the credit by HK$ 50 or HK$ 100 at machines in underground stations or in *7-Eleven* shops.

The *Octopus* bonus: you don't have to have loose change with you when you take a bus and can go through the gates at the train stations without buying a ticket. In addition, the MTR grants a reduction. The senior citizen *Octopus* card is a bargain for anyone over 65 years old. A journey costs just HK$ 2 (40 percent discount when travelling with the airport express). The expensive Airport Express Travel Pass is not really recommendable; it is only valid on the MTR, not on buses.

Mass Transit Railway: MTR for short, is the name of Hong Kong's underground and suburban railway company. If an MTR station is near an address, it is named in this guide. A single ticket from a machine costs from HK$ 4.50. It is only permitted to go to the two border stations Lo Wu and Lok Ma Chau with travel documents. *www.mtr.com.hk*

Buses: There are several companies. The lines through the harbour tunnels are noted with red, three-digit numbers. You have to insert the exact fare (usually HK$ 4–10) when you get on a bus. A display shows the name of the next stop in most buses.

Services stop at around midnight but some buses run throughout the night. Minibuses with green stripes (maxi cabs) operate like the big buses but those with red stripes stop wherever needed, like a taxi – but without any knowledge of Cantonese and the route, you will never end up where you want to go.

Trams: Very inexpensive. You pay when you get off (HK$ 2.30, no change). Stations are not called out.

Light Rail Transit: A modern tram in the west of the New Territories.

Peak Tram: Buy a return ticket when you get on if you don't plan to walk down the hill (single fare HK$ 32, return HK$ 45). You will have a better view if you sit on the right. There is no need to buy the expensive *Peak Tram Sky Pass* including the fee for the observation terrace that, in no way, offers the best panoramic view.

Ferries: The last Star Ferry sails at 11.30pm. Most ferries to the islands depart from the piers in Central (137 D–E 1–2) (*C10–11*). The tariffs are higher at the weekend. The expensive express ferries to Cheung Chau and Lantau are not especially attractive for tourists. *Information: Ferries to Lantau (Mui Wo) and Cheung Chau tel. 21318181, Lamma Island tel. 28156063, Tolo Harbour tel. 22722022*

IN MACAU

More than 50 bus lines guarantee good connections. Several buses to the islands stop at the Hotel Lisboa (148 C5) (*c5*); almost all of those to "Barra" (near the Museu Marítimo) (148 B5) (*b5*) come close to the city centre. *City tour 3.20 Ptcs, to Taipa 4.20 Ptcs, to Coloane Village 5 Ptcs, to Hac Sa Beach 6.40 Ptcs*

TOURS

The tours of the harbour organised by *Star Ferry (offices at the piers (Tsim Sha Tsui, Central, Wan Chai) | duration 1 hour, departures from Tsim Sha tsui hourly 11.55am–8.55pm, counters close 10 minutes before departure | tel. 61 18 62 01 | www.starferry.com.hk/tour)* cost from HK$ 100. *Watertours* (134 C5) (*E8*) *(6/F Carnarvon Plaza | 20 Carnarvon Rd. | tel. 29 26 38 68 | www.watertours.com.hk)* offers longer tours from 1 ½ hours.

The motorised junk ● *Aqua Luna (from Tsim Sha Tsui Pier 2 Mon–Fri hourly noon–4pm, HK$ 130, 5.30pm–10.30pm HK$ 195 including a drink, Sat and Sun tour to Stanley HK$ 280 | tel. 21 16 88 21 | www.aqualuna.com.hk)* (built in 2006) glides nostalgically through the water – with its sails als mere decoration. There is no better way to enjoy the city than relaxing on the divans on the upper deck. tours of the harbour also from Central, Wan Chai, Hung Hom.

Big Bus (ticket offices on the upper floor of the Star Ferry piers | tel. 21 67 89 95 | bigbustours.com) offers three hop-on-hop-off routes (north part of the island, Kowloon and Aberdeen/Stanley); every half hour with several stops *(HK$ 450 for a 24 hour ticket)*. Similar: *Rickshaw Bus (tel. 2136 88 88 | www.rickshawbus.com)* from Central Pier 6 with an island-Kowloon round trip *(day ticket HK$ 200, section HK$ 33)*. *Gray Line Tours (tel. 23 68 71 11 | www.grayline.com.hk)* organises tours of the New Territories.

TAXIS

All taxis are registered and use a taximeter minimum tariff in the inner city HK$ 22). Trips through tunnels cost twice the toll fee because the driver has to drive back. The green taxis in the New Territories do not drive into the city. A double yellow line on the curb shows that no stopping is allowed – this applies to taxis too. A single yellow line indicates that stopping is not permitted during peak hours. Very few taxi drivers understand English. Write the address of your destination in Chinese, if it is not included in this guide, and always have the Chinese name of your hotel with you. The same is true of Macau.

THEATRE & CONCERT TICKETS

Tickets for almost all performances can be ordered from *Cityline (tel. 21 11 53 33 | www.cityline.com | daily 10am–8pm)*. Tickets for events in the Cultural Centre and City Hall can be purchased from their box offices in advance or before performance. *Urbtix (booking tel. 21 11 59 99 | www.urbtix..com.hk)* provides information on events in city theatres and halls. Tickets for events in Macau are available under *www.macauticket.com | tel. in Macau 28 55 55 55 | tel. in Hong Kong 23 80 50 83*.

TIME

Hong Kong Time (HKT) is 8 hours ahead of GMT, during European summer plus 7 hours, 14 hours behind US Eastern Time (EST) and 3 hours behind Australian Eastern Time (AEST), one hour less during summers daylight saving time.

TIPPING

Most restaurants and bars charge 10% service charge. If that isn't the case or you want to honour good service with an extra tip, return part of your change on the small tray. Most people round up the taxi fare.

USEFUL PHRASES CANTONESE

IN BRIEF

Yes, correct/	係 [hai]/
Yes, okay	好 [hoe]
No, wrong/	唔係 [m hai/
No, not okay	唔好 [m hoe]
Maybe	可能 [haw nang]
Thank you/	多謝 [daw jeh]/
Nichts zu danken!	唔駛唔該 [m sai m goi]
Excuse me, please	對唔住! [doi m ju]
May I ...?	可唔可以 ...? [haw m haw-yee]
Pardon	你講乜嘢話? [nay gong mat yeh wa]
I would like to .../	我想要 ... [naw sung yiu]/
have you got ...?	有冇 ... [yao moe]
Where is ...?	... 係邊度? [hai bindoe]
How much is ...?	幾多錢? [gay daw tsin]
I like this/	唔錯呀 [m tsaw ah]/
I don't like this	唔係幾好 [m hai gay hoe]
good/bad	好/唔好 [hoe/m hoe]
broken/	壞咗 [wai joe]/
doesn't work	冇反應 [moe fanying]
too much/	多得滯 [dawdak jai]/
much/	好多 [hoe daw]/
little	少少 [syiu-syiu]
all/nothing	全部/全部唔要 [tsinbao/tsinbao m yiu]
Help!/Attention!/	救命!/睇住! [gaomeng/taiju]/
Caution!	小心! [syiu sam]
ambulance	白車 [bak cheh]
police/	差人 [tsai yan]/
fire brigade	消防員 [syiufonyeun]
prohibition/forbidden	唔俾 [m bay]
danger/dangerous	危險 [ai heem]

GREETINGS, FAREWELL

Good morning!/	早晨! [joe san]/
afternoon!	你好! [nay hoe]
Good evening!/night!	早抖! [joe tao]
Hello! (on the phone)	喂! [wai]
My name is ...	我叫 ... [naw gyiu]
What's your name?	你貴姓? [nay gwai sing]
I am ... [American/English]	我係 ... [naw hai]

Do you speak Cantonese?

This guide will help you to say the basic words and phrases in Cantonese

DATE & TIME

Monday/Tuesday	星期一/星期二 [singkay yat/singkay yee]
Wednesday/Thursday	星期三/星期四 [singkay sam/singkay say]
Friday/Saturday	星期五/星期六 [singkay m/singkay lok]
Sunday/ holiday	星期天 [singkay teen]/ 工作日 [goong jok teen]
today/tomorrow/ yesterday	今日/聽日[gammyat/tingyat]/ 噚日 [tsamyat]
hour/minute	鐘頭/分鐘 [joongtao/fenn joong]
day/night/ week	日抖/夜晚 [yat tao/ye man]/ 星期 [singkay]
month/year/ Holiday	月/年 [yiu/neen]/ 假期 [gah kay]
What time is it?	幾多點? [gay daw deem]
It's three o'clock	三點 [sam deem]
It's half past three	三點半 [sam deem boon]

TRAVEL

open/ closed	開門 [hoy moon]/ 唔開門 [m hoy moon]
entrance	入口 [yap hao]
exit	出口 [tsoot hao]
departure/ departure (flight)/ arrival	開車 [hoy cheh]/ 起飛 [hay fay]/ 到達 [daw daat]
toilets/restrooms/ ladies/gentlemen	洗手間 [sai sho gan]/ 女/男 [noy/nam]
(no) drinking water	(非)飲用水 [(fay) yam yoong soy]
left/right	左邊/右邊 [tsaw been/yao been]
straight ahead/back	直行/回去 [jik hang/wooey hoy]
close/far	遠/近 [yuen/gan]
bus/bus stop	巴士/巴士站 [ba see/ba see jam]
MTR/tram	地鐵/電車 [day tit/deen cheh]
taxi/cab	的士 [dek see]
street map/map	地圖 [day toe]
train station/ pier	火車站 [faw cheh jam]/ 碼頭 [ma tao]
airport	機場 [gay chang]
timetable/ticket	時刻表/車飛 [see hak beeou/cheh fay]
single/return	單程/來回 [dan tseng/loy wooey]

FOOD & DRINK

The menu, please	餐牌唔該 [tsanpai m goi]
Could I please have ...?	... 唔該 [m goi]
bottle/can/glass	樽/罐/杯 [joon/goon/booey]
knife/fork/spoon/chopstick	刀/叉/匙羹/筷子 [doe/tsah/tsee gang/faidsee]
salt/pepper/sugar/vinegar	鹽/胡椒粉/糖/醋 [yeem/hoo yieu fan/ton/tsoe]
soy sauce/milk/lemon	豉油/牛奶/檸檬 [see yao/ao nai/ning meung]
vegetarian/allergy	素食/敏感 [soe sek/man gam]
May I have the bill, please?	唔該你埋單 [m goi nay mai dan]
bill/receipt/tip	帳單/收條/貼士 [jeung dan/sao tieu/tip see]

SHOPPING

pharmacy/chemist	藥房 [ye fong]/Watson's
baker/market	麵包鋪/街市 [min bao paw/gai see]
shopping centre/department store/supermarket	購物中心/百貨公司/超級市場 [cao mat joong sam/bak foe goong see/tsiu kap see tsun]
camera shop/newsagent	影視鋪/報攤 [ying see paw/boe taan]
100 grammes/1 kilo	一百克/一公斤 [yat bak hak/yat goonggan]
expensive/cheap/price	貴得滯/平/價錢 [gwai/peng/gatseen]
more/less	多/少 [doe/syiu]

BANKS, MONEY & CREDIT CARDS

bank/ATM	銀行/柜員機 [nan hong/gwai yeung gay]
pin code	密碼 [mat ma], PIN

NUMBERS

0	零 [ling]	15	十五 [sap m]
1	一 [yat]	16	十六 [sap lok]
2	二 [yee]	17	十七 [sap tsat]
Two of those	兩個 [leunggoe]	18	十八 [sap bat]
3	三 [sam]	19	十九 [sap gao]
4	四 [say]	20	二十 [yee sap]
5	五 [m]	70	七十 [chat sap]
6	六 [look]	80	八十 [baat-ssap]
7	七 [tsat]	90	九十 [gao sap]
8	八 [bat]	100	一百 [yat bak]
9	九 [gao]	200	二百 [yee bak]
10	十 [sap]	1000	一千 [yat chin]
11	十一 [sap yat]	2000	兩千 [leung tseen]
12	十二 [sap yee]	10 000	一萬 [yat man]
13	十三 [sap sam]	½	一半 [yat boon]
14	十四 [sap say]	¼	四分一 [say fan yat]

STREET ATLAS

The green line indicates the Discovery Tour "Hong Kong at a glance"
The blue line indicates the other Discovery Tours

All tours are also marked on the pull-out map

 Photo: The shore promenade in Kowloon with a view of Hong Kong Island

Exploring Hong Kong

The map on the back cover shows how the area has been sub-divided

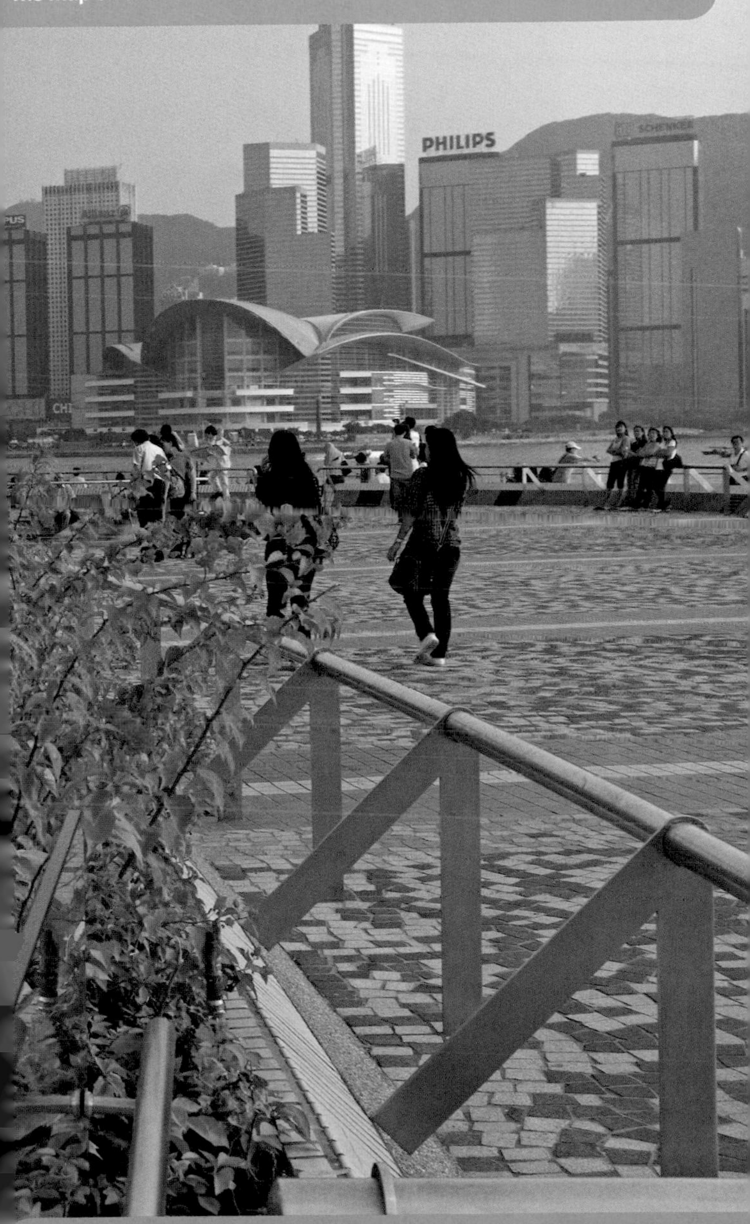

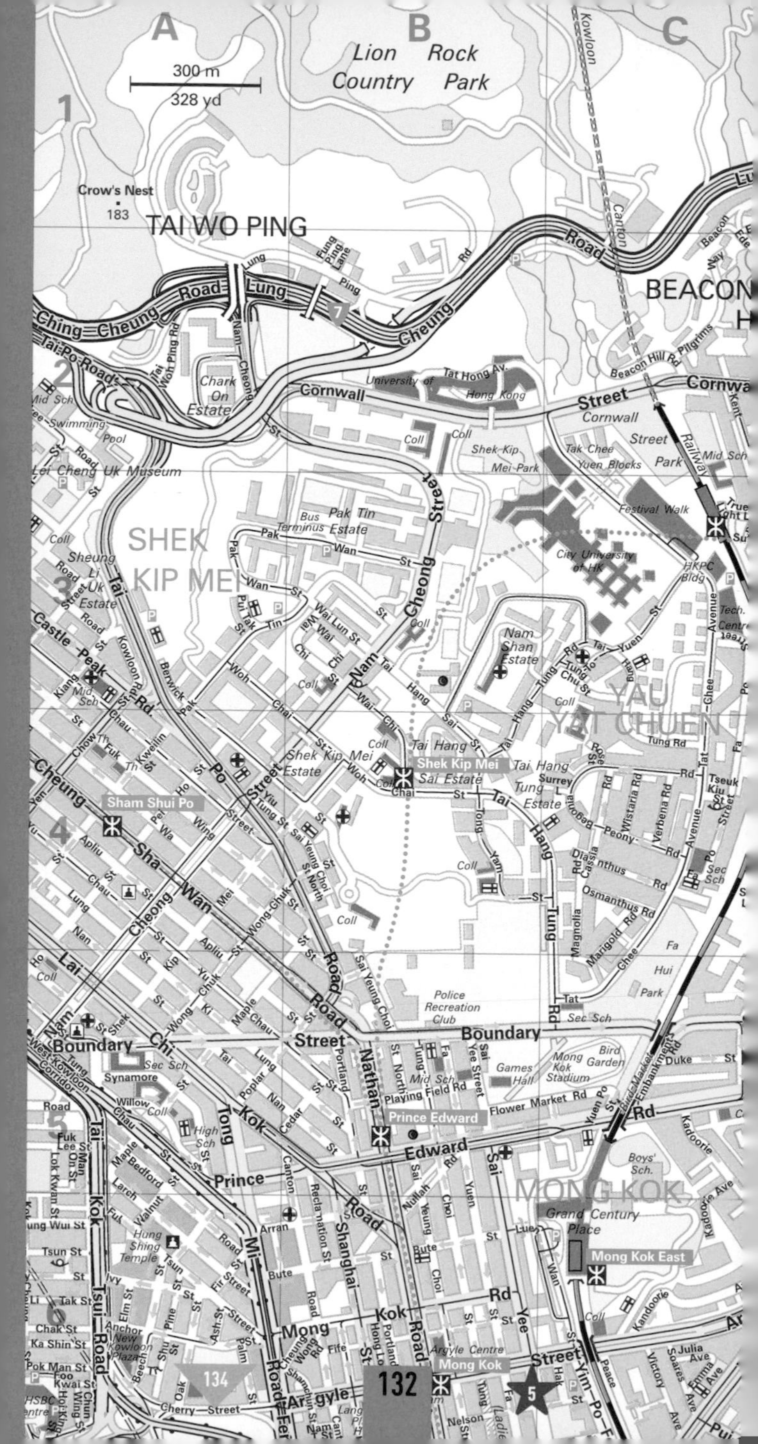

A
B
C
1
2
3
4
5
6
300 m
328 yd
Lion Rock Country Park
Crow's Nest
183
TAI WO PING
BEACON HILL
SHEK KIP MEI
YAU YAT CHUEN
MONG KOK
Ching Cheung Road
Lung Cheung Road
Tai Po Road
Cornwall Street
University of Hong Kong
Tat Hong Av.
Chark On Estate
Lei Cheng Uk Museum
Shek Kip Mei Park
Tak Chee Yuen Blocks
Cornwall Street Park
Festival Walk
City University of HK
HKPC Bldg
Pak Tin Estate
Bus Terminus
Nam Cheong Street
Nam Shan Estate
Shek Kip Mei Estate
Tai Hang Sai Estate
Tai Hang Tung Estate
Shek Kip Mei
Sham Shui Po
Castle Peak Rd.
Cheung Sha Wan Rd
Boundary Street
Police Recreation Club
Mong Kok Stadium
Bird Garden
Games Hall
Flower Market Rd
Prince Edward
Prince Edward Road
Nathan Road
Grand Century Place
Mong Kok East
Mong Kok
Argyle Street
Argyle Centre
Anchor New Kowloon Plaza
Hung Shing Temple
Tai Kok Tsui Road
West Kowloon Corridor
Kowloon Canton Railway
Fa Hui Park
Boys' Sch.
Kadoorie Ave
Waterloo Rd

134

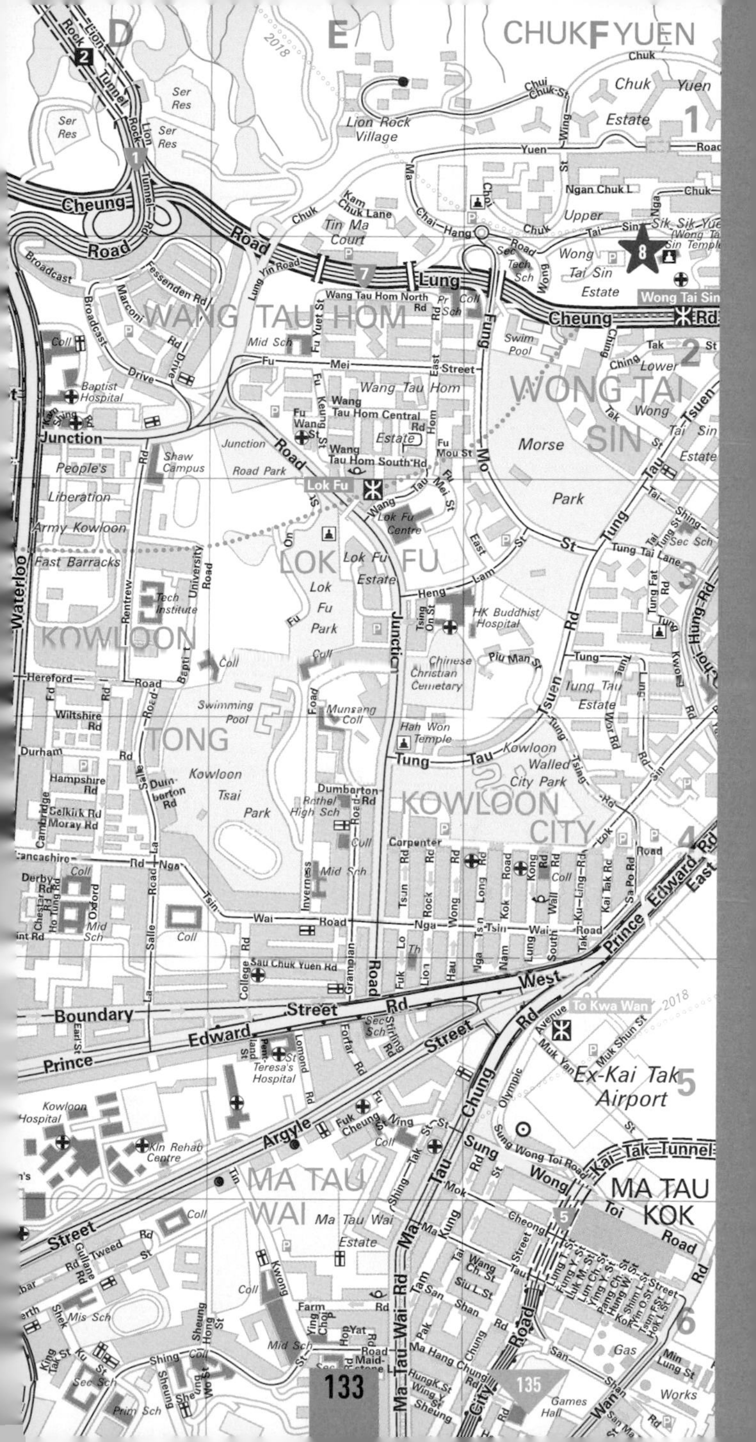
D
E
F
CHUK YUEN
1
2
3
4
5
6
Lion Rock Tunnel
Ser Res
Lion Rock Village
Chuk Yuen Estate
Ngan Chuk L
Upper Wong Tai Sin Estate
Sik Sik Yuen (Wong Tai Sin Temple)
Wong Tai Sin
Kam Chuk Lane
Tin Ma Court
Cheung Road
Lung Cheung Rd
Lung Yin Road
Broadcast Drive
Fessenden Rd
Marconi Rd
WANG TAU HOM
Wang Tau Hom North Rd
Fu Mei Street
Wang Tau Hom Estate
Wang Tau Hom Central Rd
Wang Tau Hom South Rd
Fung Mo St
Swim Pool
WONG TAI SIN
Lower Wong Tai Sin Estate
Morse Park
Baptist Hospital
Junction Road
Junction Road Park
Shaw Campus
People's Liberation Army Kowloon East Barracks
Lok Fu
Lok Fu Centre
LOK FU
Lok Fu Estate
Lok Fu Park
Tung Tau Tsuen Rd
Tung Tai Lane
Heng Lam St
HK Buddhist Hospital
Tech Institute
University Road
Renfrew Rd
Waterloo Rd
KOWLOON
Hereford Road
Chinese Christian Cemetery
Piu Man St
Tung Tau Estate
Swimming Pool
Munsang Coll
Hah Won Temple
Kowloon Walled City Park
TONG
Kowloon Tsai Park
Dumbarton Rd
Bethel High Sch
KOWLOON CITY
Carpenter Road
Prince Edward Rd East
Prince Edward Rd West
Boundary Street
Wiltshire Rd
Durham Rd
Hampshire Rd
Selkirk Rd
Moray Rd
Cambridge Rd
Derby Rd
Oxford Rd
Nga Tsin Wai Road
La Salle Road
Sau Chuk Yuen Rd
Grampian Road
St Teresa's Hospital
Kowloon Hospital
Kln Rehab Centre
Argyle Street
To Kwa Wan
Muk Yan St
Muk Shun St
Ex-Kai Tak Airport
Olympic Avenue
Chung Road
Sung Wong Toi Road
Kai Tak Tunnel
MA TAU WAI
Ma Tau Wai Estate
Ma Tau Wai Rd
MA TAU KOK
Ma Tau Kok Road
Mok Cheong St
Ma Hang Chung Rd
Gas Works
Games Hall
135

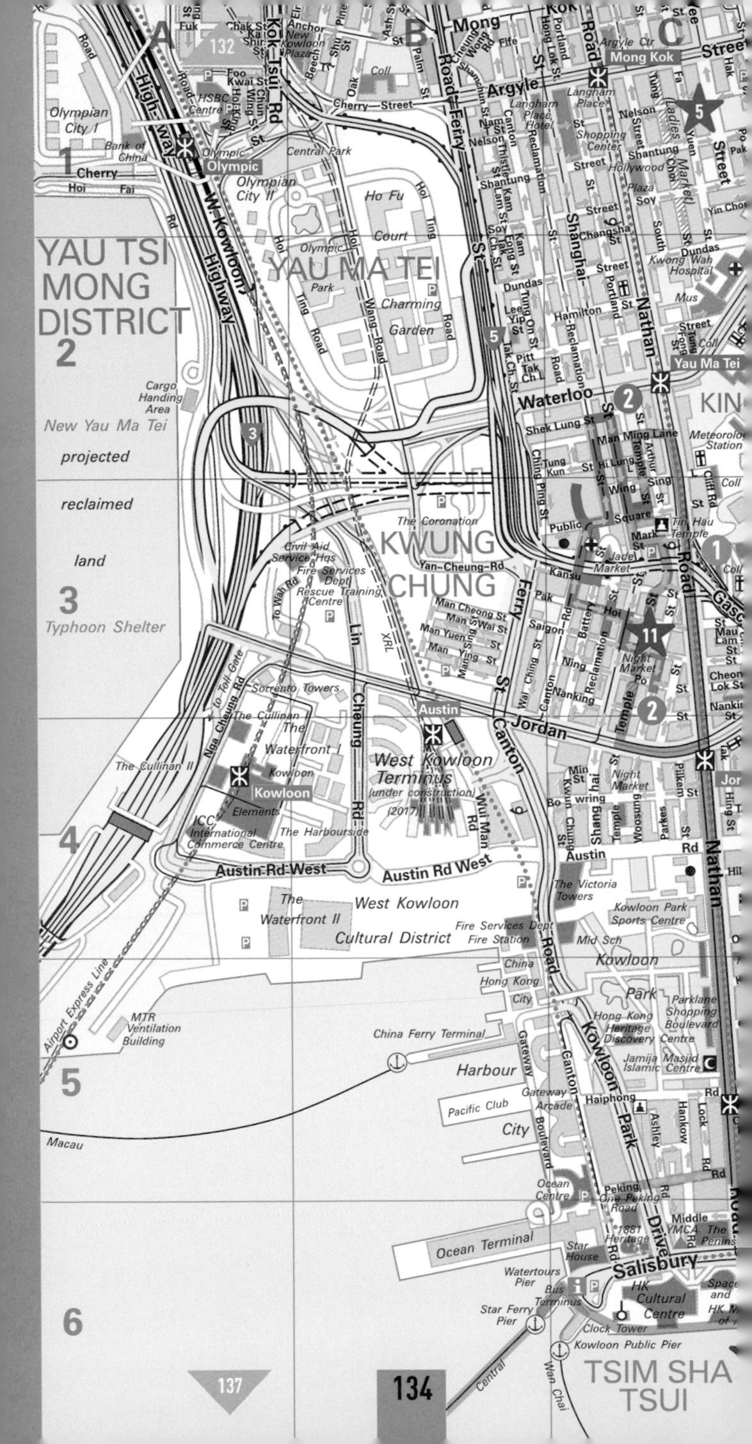

A
B
C
132
1
2
3
4
5
6
Mong Kok
Olympic
Olympian City I
Olympian City II
Bank of China
HSBC Centre
Cherry Street
Argyle Street
Central Park
Ho Fu Court
YAU MA TEI
Charming Garden
YAU TSIM MONG DISTRICT
W. Kowloon Highway
Cargo Handing Area
New Yau Ma Tei projected reclaimed land
Typhoon Shelter
Langham Place
Langham Place Hotel
Shopping Center
Hollywood Plaza
Ladies Market
Kwong Wah Hospital
Yau Ma Tei
Waterloo
Shanghai
Reclamation
Nathan
Portland
Kok Tsui Rd
Ferry
Dundas
Shantung
Nelson
Man Ming Lane
Meteorological Station
Tin Hau Temple
Jade Market
Public Square
Civil Aid Service Hqs
Fire Services Dept
Rescue Training Centre
KWUNG CHUNG
The Coronation
Yan Cheung Rd
Night Market
Temple
Jordan
Austin
Canton
XRL
Lin Cheung Rd
Sorrento Towers
The Cullinan
The Cullinan II
The Waterfront I
Kowloon
Elements
ICC International Commerce Centre
The Harbourside
West Kowloon Terminus (under construction) (2017)
Wui Man Rd
Austin Rd West
The Waterfront II
West Kowloon Cultural District
Fire Services Dept Fire Station
The Victoria Towers
Kowloon Park Sports Centre
Kowloon Park
China Hong Kong City
China Ferry Terminal
Harbour City
Hong Kong Heritage Discovery Centre
Parklane Shopping Boulevard
Jamija Masjid Islamic Centre
MTR Ventilation Building
Airport Express Line
Macau
Pacific Club
Gateway Arcade
Gateway Boulevard
Haiphong Rd
Kowloon Park Drive
Ashley
Hankow
Lock Rd
Ocean Centre
Ocean Terminal
Peking Rd
One Peking Road
1881 Heritage
Middle Rd
YMCA
The Peninsula
Salisbury Rd
Star House
Watertours Pier
Bus Terminus
Star Ferry Pier
HK Cultural Centre
Clock Tower
Kowloon Public Pier
TSIM SHA TSUI
137

D
E
F
133
1
2
3
4
5
6
HO MAN TIN
TO KWA WAN
HUNG HOM
JORDAN
T-S-T EAST
Ma Tau Wai
Ho Man Tin
Hung Hom
Whampoa
East Tsim Sha Tsui
Waterloo Rd
Pui Ching Road
Princess Margaret Rd
Argyle
Julia Ave
Emma Ave
Man Wan Rd
YWCA
Mid Sch
Sec Sch
Prim Sch
Mis Sch
Mid Sch
Kwong
Good Shepherd St
Carmel Village St
Chun Man Court
Oi Man Estate
Leisure Centre
Chung Yee St
HK Housing Authority Exhibition Centre
Ho Man Tin Estate
Sheung Lok St
Lok Man Sun Chuen
Maidstone Rd
Ko Shan Rd
Ko Shan Theatre
Park
Ma Tau Wai Rd
Chi Kiang St
Ma Tau Corridor
Kowloon City Road
To Kwan Wan Rd
Games Hall
Ngan Hon St
Hung Fook St
Kai Ming St
Wing Kwong St
Bailey St
Hok Yuen St
Man Yue St
Sung On Road
Block 1
Valley Road Estate
Hung Hom Estate
Kun Yam Lane
Pr. Sch
Hutchinson Park
Dock St
Tak Man St
Whampoa Garden
Gillies Ave
Wuhu St
Bulkeley St
Station Lane
East Rd
Cheong Wan Rd
Funeral Parlour
Royal Peninsula
Hung Hom South Rd
Harbourview Horizon
Harbour Place
Hung Luen Rd
Bus Terminal
Hung Hom Ferry Pier
Kowloon City
North Point
Hung Hom Bypass
Harbourfront Horizon
Metropolis Tower
Bus Term.
Hung Hom Station
Harbour Plaza Metropolis
Hong Kong Coliseum
Int. Mail Centre
Hung Hom Rd
Chong Rd
Hong Kong Polytechnic University
Gun Club Hill Barracks
King's Park Sports Ground
Brit Mil Hospital
Elizabeth Hospital
Wylie Road
Rise Park
HK Mus. of History
HK Science Museum
Science Museum Rd
Tourist Bus Term
New Mandarin Plaza
Granville Rd
Energy Plaza
Granville Square
Peninsula Center
Auto Plaza
Mody Square
Empire Centre
Mody Lane
Houston Center
TST Centre
Wing On Plaza
Mody Rd
Salisbury Rd
Chatham Rd
Tsim Sha Tsui East Promenade
Cross Harbour Tunnel
300 m
328 yd
135
138

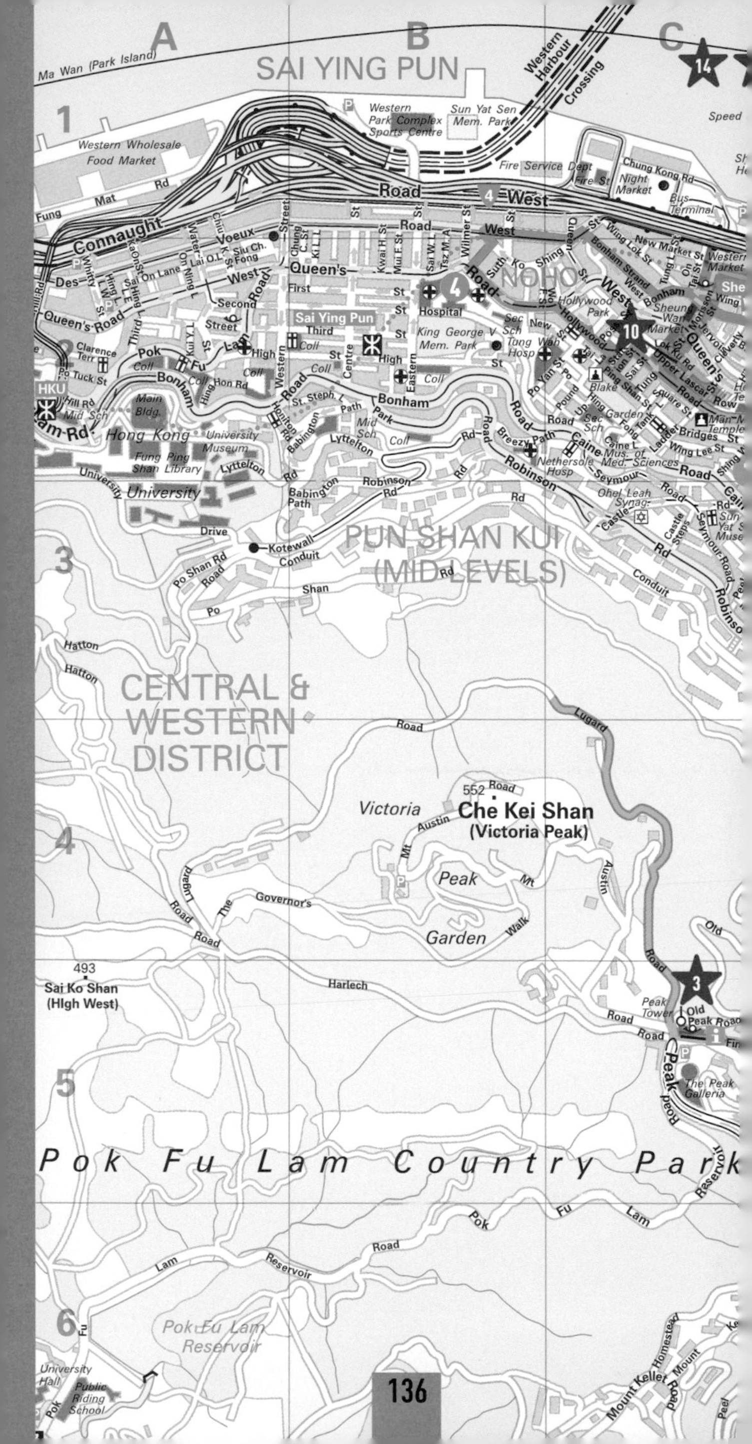

SAI YING PUN
Western Wholesale Food Market
Western Park Complex Sports Centre
Sun Yat Sen Mem. Park
Western Harbour Crossing
Connaught Road West
Des Voeux Road West
Queen's Road West
Sai Ying Pun
Bonham Road
Pok Fu Lam Road
Hospital
King George V Mem. Park
Tung Wah Hosp
NOHO
Hollywood Park
Sheung Wan Market
HKU
Main Bldg.
University Museum
Fung Ping Shan Library
Hong Kong University
Robinson Road
Caine Road
Mus. of Med. Sciences
Nethersole Hosp
Ohel Leah Synag.
Sun Yat Sen Muse
Man Mo Temple
PUN SHAN KUI (MID LEVELS)
Conduit Road
Po Shan Road
CENTRAL & WESTERN DISTRICT
Lugard Road
Victoria
Che Kei Shan (Victoria Peak)
552
Mt Austin Road
Victoria Peak Garden
Governor's Walk
493
Sai Ko Shan (High West)
Harlech Road
Peak Tower
Old Peak Road
The Peak Galleria
Peak Road
Pok Fu Lam Country Park
Pok Fu Lam Reservoir Road
Pok Fu Lam Reservoir
University Hall
Public Riding School
Mount Kellet Road

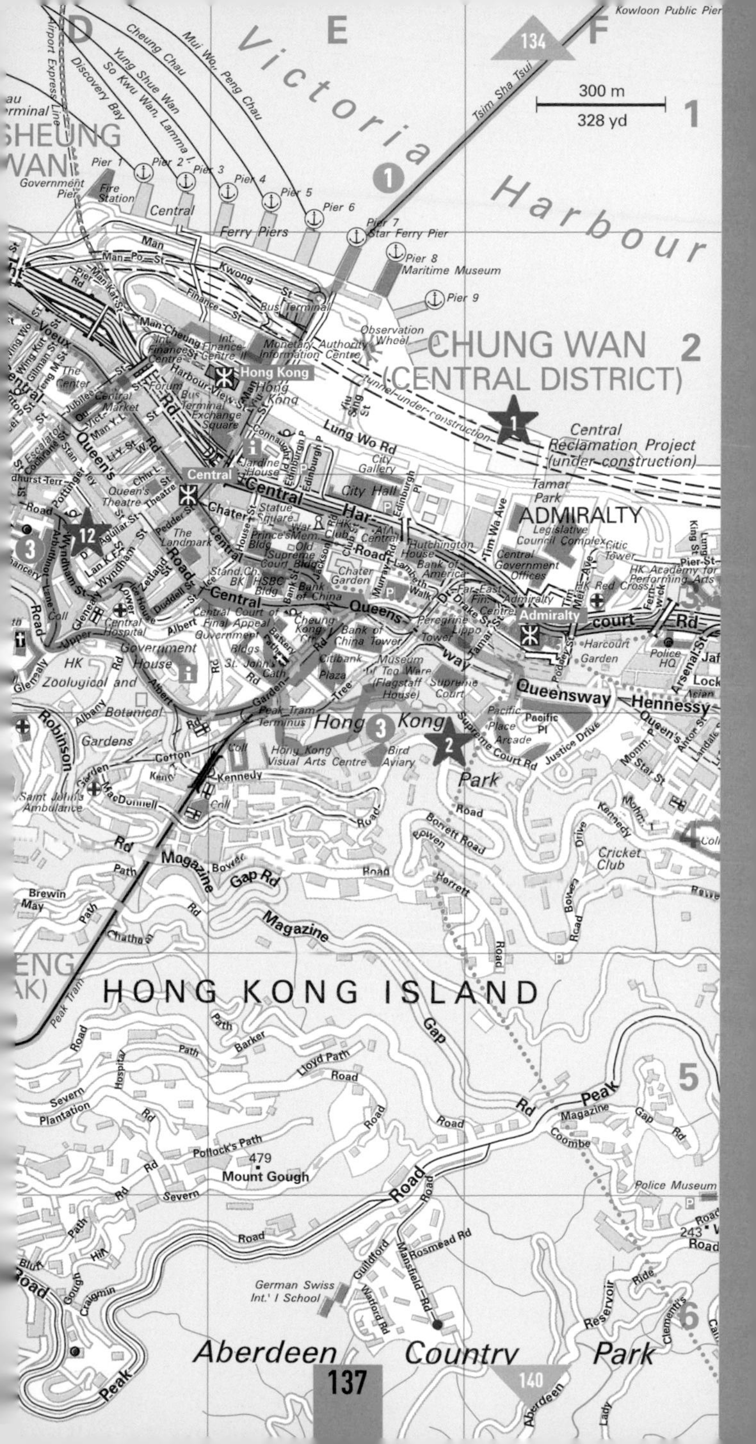
Kowloon Public Pier
D
E
F
134
Victoria Harbour
300 m
328 yd
1
2
3
4
5
6
Airport Express Line
Cheung Chau
Mui Wo, Peng Chau
Yung Shue Wan
So Kwu Wan, Lamma I.
Discovery Bay
Tsim Sha Tsui
SHEUNG WAN
Government Pier
Fire Station
Pier 1
Pier 2
Pier 3
Pier 4
Pier 5
Pier 6
Pier 7
Star Ferry Pier
Pier 8
Maritime Museum
Pier 9
Central Ferry Piers
Man Kwong St
Man Po St
Finance St
Bus Terminal
Observation Wheel
Monetary Authority Information Centre
Int. Finance Centre II
Int. Finance Centre
Hong Kong
CHUNG WAN
(CENTRAL DISTRICT)
Tunnel under construction
Central Reclamation Project (under construction)
Lung Wo Rd
City Gallery
Connaught Rd
Harbour View St
Exchange Square
The Forum
Central Market
Jubilee St
Queen's Rd
Escalator
Jardine House
Central
City Hall
Tamar Park
ADMIRALTY
Legislative Council Complex
Citic Tower
Central Government Offices
HK Academy for Performing Arts
HK Red Cross
Tim Wa Ave
Tim Mei Ave
Chater Rd
Statue Square
Prince's Bldg
Old Supreme Court Bldg
HK Club
AIA Central
Hutchington House
Bank of America
Chater Garden
Murray Rd
Lambeth Walk
Far East Fin. Centre
Admiralty
Admiralty
Lippo
Peregrine Tower
Drake St
Tamar St
Harcourt Rd
Harcourt Garden
Police HQ
Arsenal St
Queensway
Hennessy
Queen's Rd East
Pacific Place Arcade
Pacific Pl
Justice Drive
Supreme Court Rd
Supreme Court
Museum of Tea Ware (Flagstaff House)
Cheung Kong Ctr
Bank of China Tower
Citibank Plaza
HSBC Bldg
Bank of China
Stand.Ch. BK
The Landmark
Pedder St
Queen's Theatre
Theatre Lane
D'Aguilar St
Wyndham St
Lan K.F.
Zetland St
Duddell St
Ice House St
Central Court of Final Appeal
Government Bldgs
St. John's Cath
Battery Path
Garden Rd
Peak Tram Terminus
Hong Kong Park
Hong Kong Visual Arts Centre
Bird Aviary
Cotton Tree Dr
Kennedy Rd
Central Hospital
Government House
HK Zoological and Botanical Gardens
Albany
Upper Albert Rd
Robinson Road
Glenealy
Arbuthnot
Lower Albert Rd
Glenealy
Saint John's Ambulance
MacDonnell Rd
Magazine Gap Rd
Bowen Road
Borrett Road
Kennedy Rd
Cricket Club
Monmouth
Star St
Bowen Road
Brewin Path
May Rd
Peak Tram
HONG KONG ISLAND
Barker Path
Lloyd Path
Hospital Rd
Severn Plantation
Pollock's Path
479
Mount Gough
Peak Road
Magazine Gap Rd
Coombe Road
Police Museum
243
Severn Road
Guildford Rd
Mansfield Rd
Rosmead Rd
Watford Rd
German Swiss Int.' l School
Bluff Path
Gough Hill Path
Craigmin
Peak Road
Reservoir Ride
Clementi's
Aberdeen Country Park
140
137

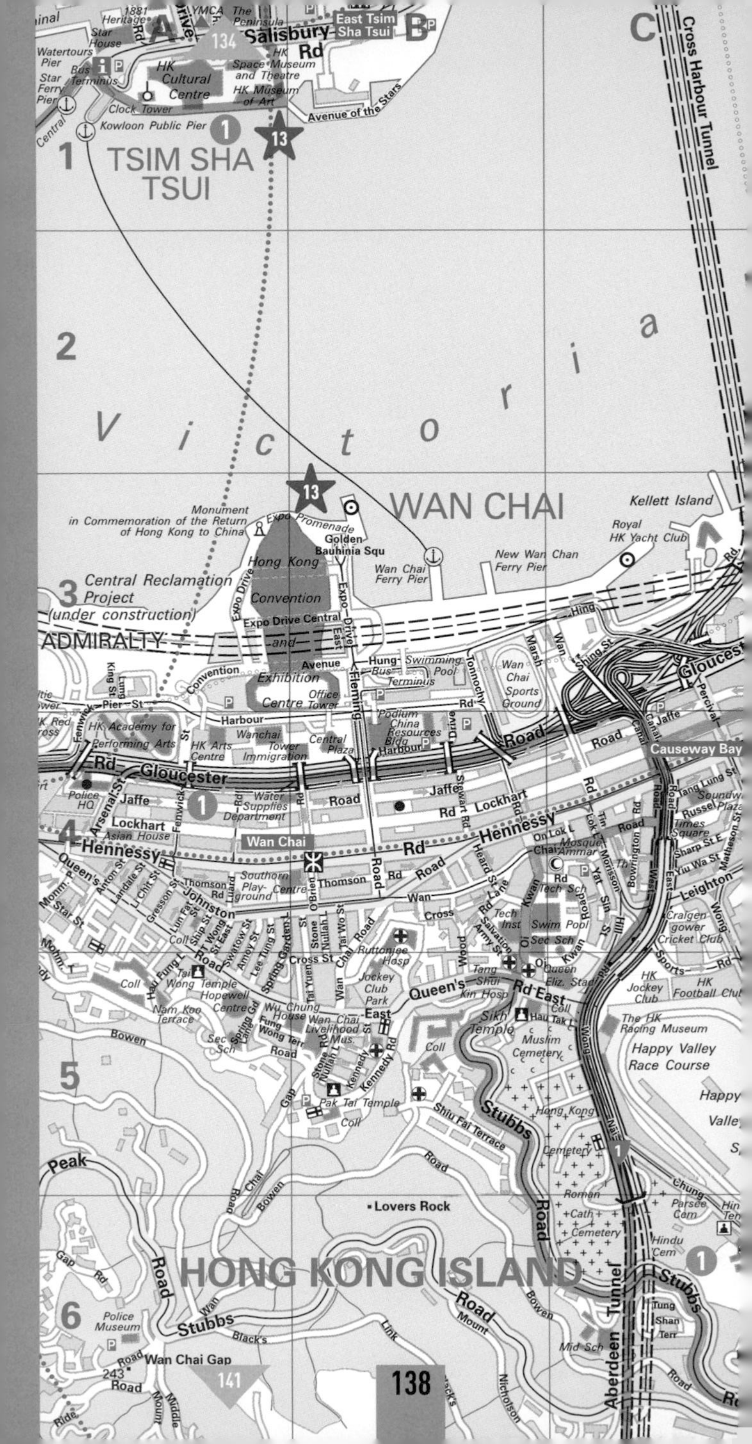
TSIM SHA TSUI
Victoria
WAN CHAI
ADMIRALTY
HONG KONG ISLAND
Salisbury Rd
East Tsim Sha Tsui
HK Cultural Centre
HK Space Museum and Theatre
HK Museum of Art
Clock Tower
Kowloon Public Pier
Avenue of the Stars
Star Ferry Pier
Cross Harbour Tunnel
Monument in Commemoration of the Return of Hong Kong to China
Expo Promenade
Golden Bauhinia Squ
Hong Kong Convention and Exhibition Centre
Wan Chai Ferry Pier
New Wan Chan Ferry Pier
Kellett Island
Royal HK Yacht Club
Central Reclamation Project (under construction)
Wan Chai Sports Ground
Causeway Bay
HK Academy for Performing Arts
HK Arts Centre
Police HQ
Gloucester Rd
Harbour Rd
Jaffe Road
Lockhart Rd
Hennessy Rd
Wan Chai
Queen's Rd East
Happy Valley Race Course
The HK Racing Museum
HK Jockey Club
HK Football Club
Craigengower Cricket Club
Pak Tai Temple
Sikh Temple
Muslim Cemetery
Hong Kong Cemetery
Roman Cath Cemetery
Parsee Cem
Hindu Cem
Aberdeen Tunnel
Stubbs Road
Peak Road
Lovers Rock
Police Museum
Wan Chai Gap
Bowen Road
Kennedy Rd
Tung Shan Terr
134
141

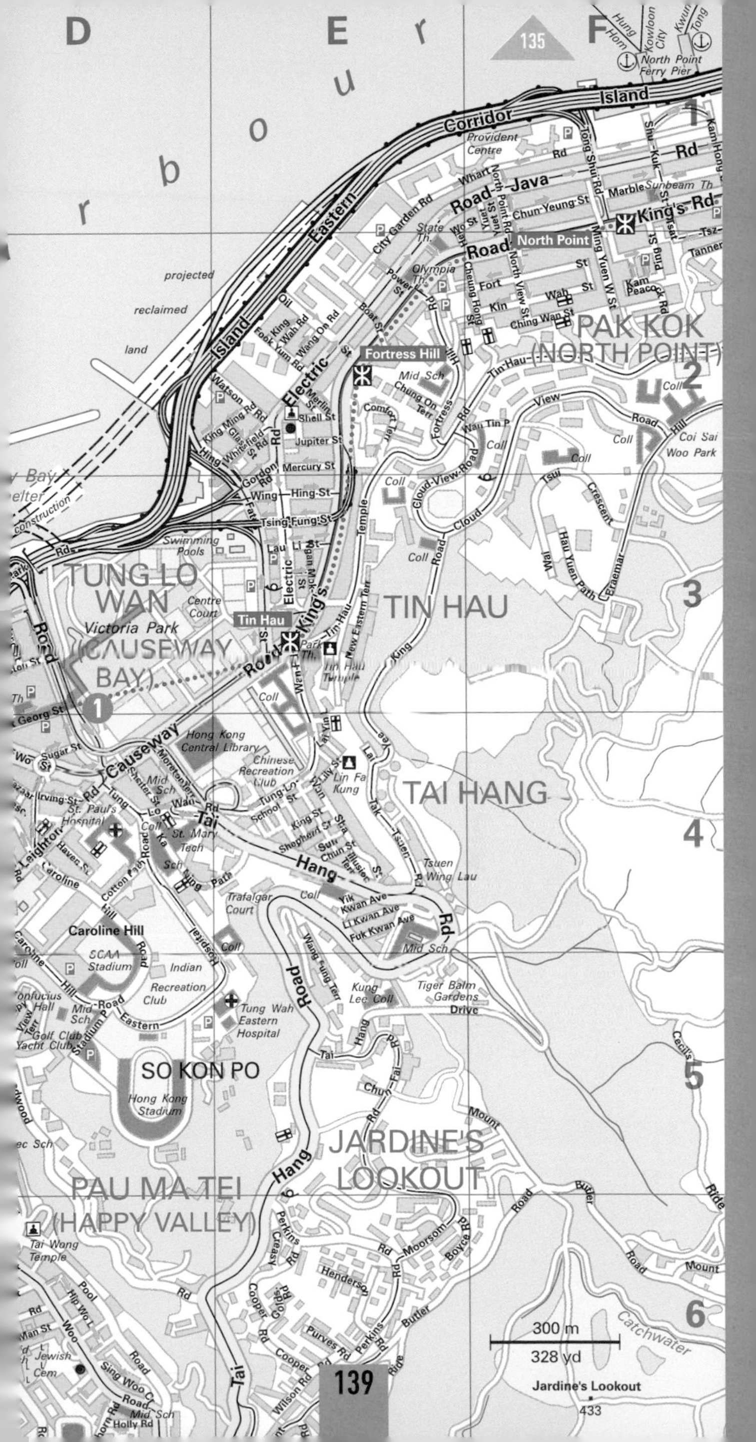
D
E
F
135
North Point Ferry Pier
Island Eastern Corridor
Provident Centre
Java Road
King's Rd
North Point
Fortress Hill
PAK KOK (NORTH POINT)
TIN HAU
Tin Hau
TUNG LO WAN
Victoria Park
(CAUSEWAY BAY)
Centre Court
Hong Kong Central Library
Chinese Recreation Club
TAI HANG
Lin Fa Kung
Tsuen Wing Lau
Caroline Hill
SCAA Stadium
Indian Recreation Club
Tung Wah Eastern Hospital
SO KON PO
Hong Kong Stadium
Tiger Balm Gardens
Coi Sai Woo Park
JARDINE'S LOOKOUT
PAU MA TEI (HAPPY VALLEY)
Tai Wong Temple
Jewish Cem
projected reclaimed land
300 m
328 yd
Jardine's Lookout
433
1
2
3
4
5
6

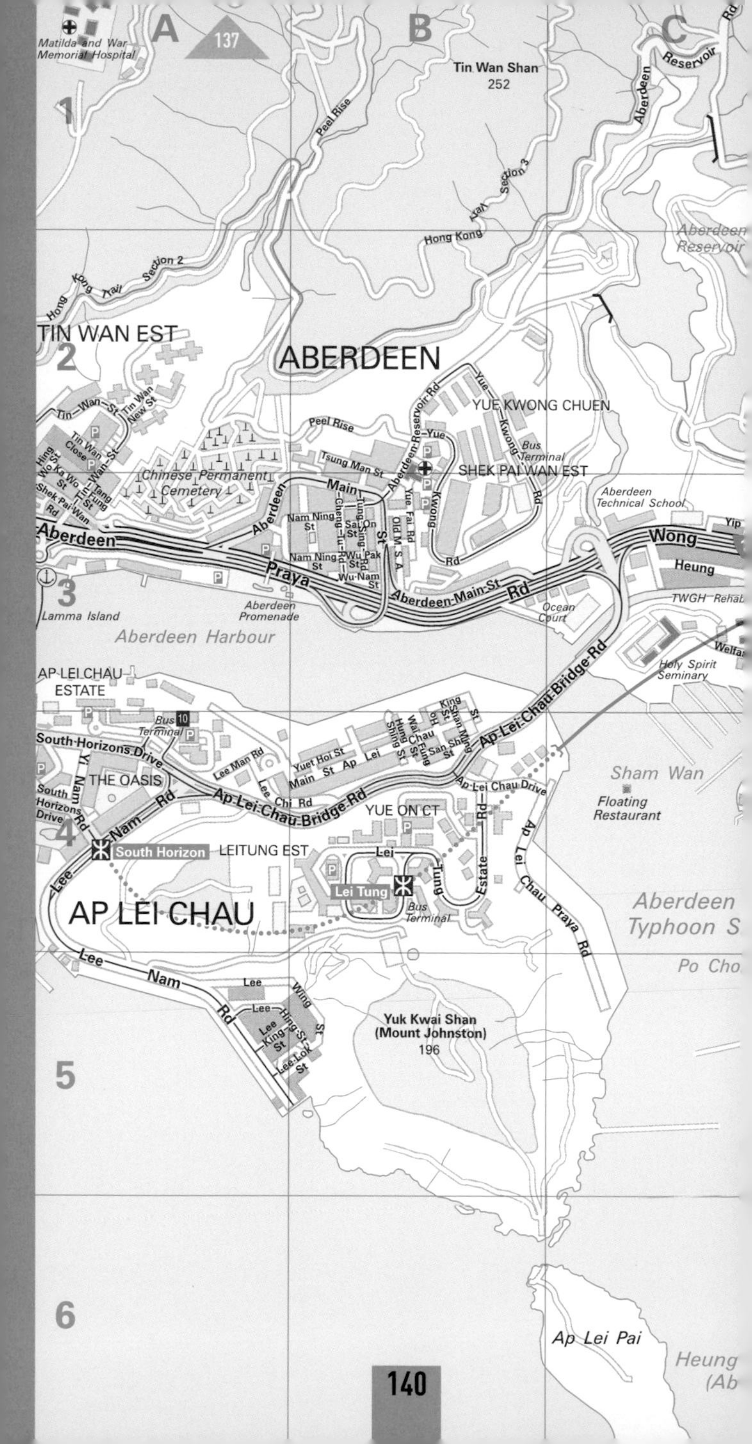
A
B
C
137
1
2
3
4
5
6
Matilda and War Memorial Hospital
Tin Wan Shan
252
Reservoir Rd
Aberdeen
Peel Rise
Hong Kong Trail Section 3
Hong Kong Trail Section 2
Aberdeen Reservoir
TIN WAN EST
ABERDEEN
Tin Wan St
Tin Wan New St
Tin Wan Close
Hing Wo St
Ka Wo St
Tin Wan St
Tang Fung St
Shek Pai Wan Rd
Chinese Permanent Cemetery
Peel Rise
Aberdeen Reservoir Rd
Yue Kwong Rd
YUE KWONG CHUEN
Bus Terminal
SHEK PAI WAN EST
Tsung Man St
Aberdeen Main St
Cheng Tu Rd
Tung Sing Rd
Nam Ning St
Sai On St
Wu Pak St
Wu Nam St
Yue Fai Rd
Old M. S. A.
Aberdeen Technical School
Yip
Wong Chuk Hang Rd
Heung
TWGH Rehab
Aberdeen Praya Rd
Aberdeen Promenade
Ocean Court
Lamma Island
Aberdeen Harbour
Welfare
Holy Spirit Seminary
AP LEI CHAU ESTATE
Bus Terminal
10
South Horizons Drive
Lee Man Rd
Yuet Hoi St
Main St Ap Lei Chau
Hung Shing St
Wai Fung St
Ping Lan St
San Shi St
King St
Shan Ming St
Ap Lei Chau Bridge Rd
Sham Wan
Floating Restaurant
Yi Nam Rd
THE OASIS
South Horizons Drive
Lee Chi Rd
Ap Lei Chau Drive
YUE ON CT
Estate Rd
Ap Lei Chau Praya Rd
Lee Nam Rd
South Horizon
LEITUNG EST
Lei Tung
Bus Terminal
AP LEI CHAU
Aberdeen Typhoon S
Po Cho
Lee Wing St
Lee Hing St
Lee King St
Lee Lok St
Yuk Kwai Shan (Mount Johnston)
196
Ap Lei Pai
Heung
(Ab

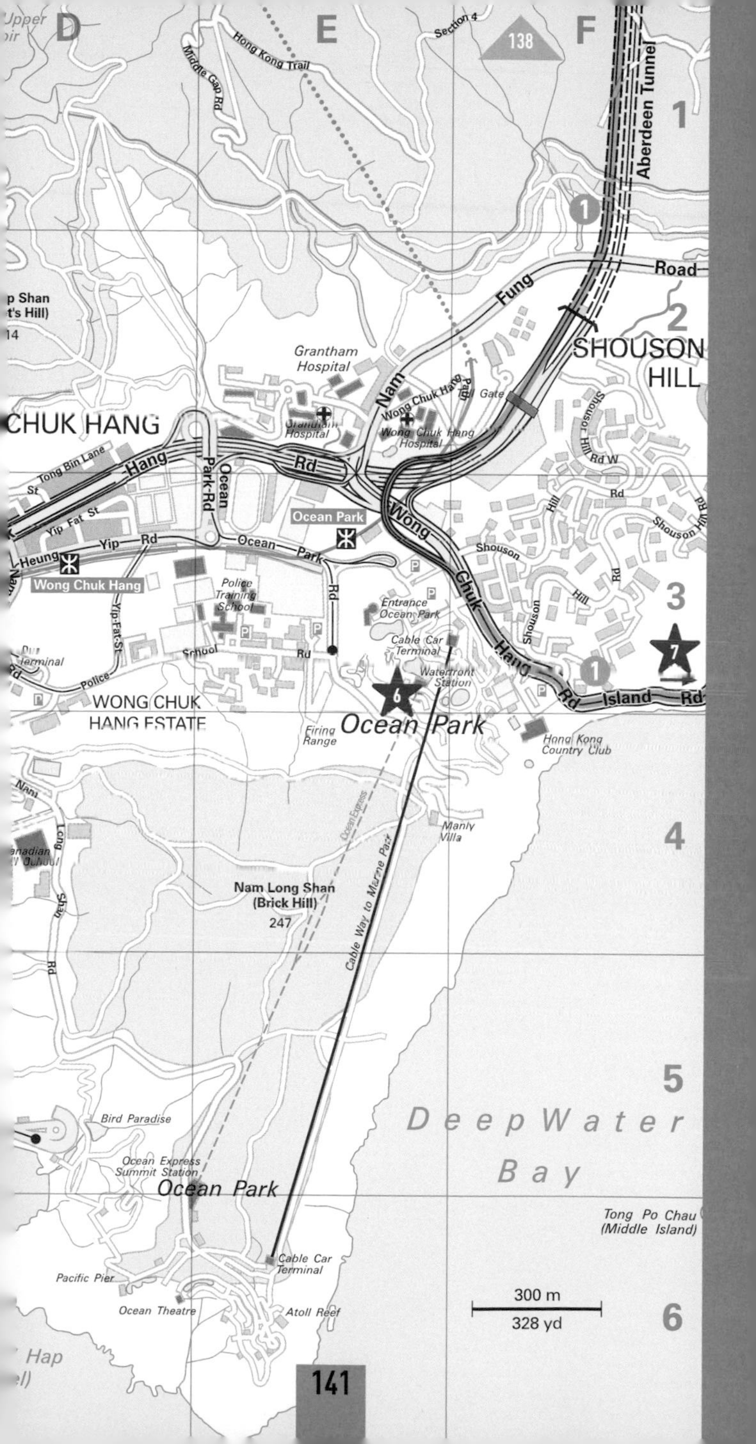
D
E
F
138
1
2
3
4
5
6
Hong Kong Trail
Section 4
Middle Gap Rd
Aberdeen Tunnel
Road
Fung
Nam
SHOUSON
HILL
CHUK HANG
Grantham
Hospital
Wong Chuk Hang
Hospital
Wong Chuk Hang Path
Toll Gate
Tong Bin Lane
Hang
Rd
Ocean
Park-Rd
Ocean Park
Wong
Chuk
Hang
Rd
Island
Rd
Shouson Hill Rd W
Shouson Hill Rd
Shouson
Hill
Yip Fat St
Yip
Rd
Ocean
Park
Heung
Wong Chuk Hang
Police
Training
School
Yip-Fat-St
School
Rd
Police
Entrance
Ocean Park
Cable Car
Terminal
Waterfront
Station
WONG CHUK
HANG ESTATE
Firing
Range
Ocean Park
Hong Kong
Country Club
Manly
Villa
Ocean Express
Cable Way to Marine Park
Nam Long Shan
(Brick Hill)
247
Long
Shan
Rd
Deep Water
Bay
Bird Paradise
Ocean Express
Summit Station
Ocean Park
Tong Po Chau
(Middle Island)
Cable Car
Terminal
Pacific Pier
Ocean Theatre
Atoll Reef
300 m
328 yd

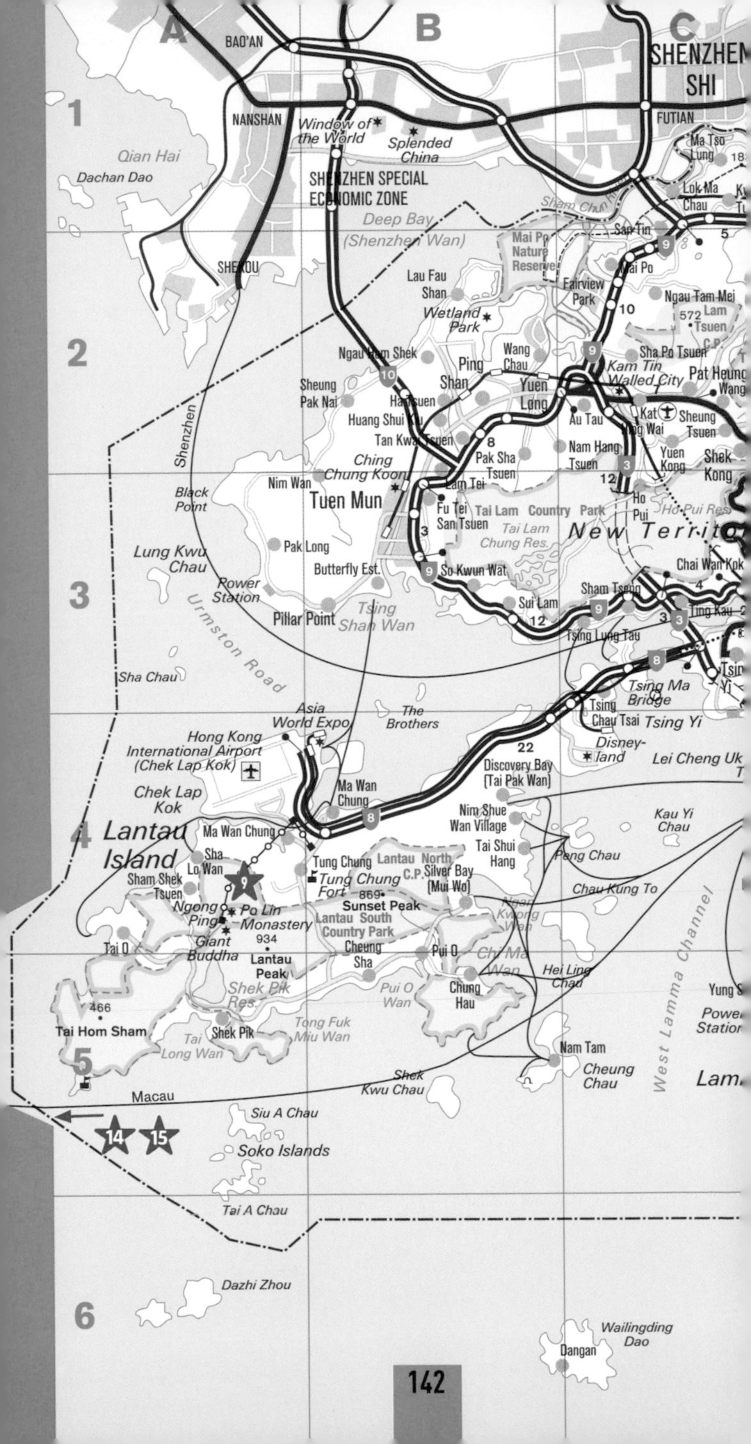

A
B
C
1
2
3
4
5
6
BAO'AN
SHENZHEN SHI
NANSHAN
Window of the World
Splended China
FUTIAN
Ma Tso Lung
Qian Hai
Dachan Dao
SHENZHEN SPECIAL ECONOMIC ZONE
Lok Ma Chau
Deep Bay (Shenzhen Wan)
San Tin
Mai Po Nature Reserve
Mai Po
SHEKOU
Lau Fau Shan
Fairview Park
Ngau Tam Mei
Wetland Park
572
Lam Tsuen C.P.
Ngau Tam Shek
Ping Shan
Wang Chau
Sha Po Tsuen
Kam Tin Walled City
Pat Heung
Sheung Pak Nai
Yuen Long
Hang Tsuen
Huang Shui Kiu
Au Tau
Kat Hing Wai
Sheung Tsuen
Tan Kwai Tsuen
Pak Sha Tsuen
Nam Hang Tsuen
Yuen Kong
Shek Kong
Shenzhen
Ching Chung Koon
Lam Tei
Nim Wan
Black Point
Tuen Mun
Fu Tei San Tsuen
Tai Lam Country Park
Ho Pui
Ho Pui Res.
Tai Lam Chung Res.
New Territo
Lung Kwu Chau
Pak Long
Butterfly Est.
So Kwun Wat
Chai Wan Kok
Power Station
Sham Tseng
Pillar Point
Tsing Shan Wan
Sui Lam
Ting Kau
Urmston Road
Tsing Lung Tau
Sha Chau
Tsing Ma Bridge
Tsing Yi
Asia World Expo
The Brothers
Tsing Chau Tsai
Hong Kong International Airport (Chek Lap Kok)
22
Disney-land
Lei Cheng Uk
Discovery Bay (Tai Pak Wan)
Chek Lap Kok
Ma Wan Chung
Nim Shue Wan Village
Kau Yi Chau
Lantau Island
Ma Wan Chung
Tai Shui Hang
Peng Chau
Sha Lo Wan
Tung Chung
Lantau North C.P.
Silver Bay (Mui Wo)
Tung Chung Fort
Sham Shek Tsuen
869
Chau Kung To
Sunset Peak
Ngong Ping
Po Lin Monastery
Lantau South Country Park
Ngan Kwong Wan
West Lamma Channel
Giant Buddha
Tai O
934
Cheung Sha
Pui O
Chi Ma Wan
Hei Ling Chau
Lantau Peak
Shek Pik Res.
Pui O Wan
Chung Hau
Yung S
Power Station
466
Tai Hom Sham
Tong Fuk Miu Wan
Tai Long Wan
Shek Pik
Nam Tam
Cheung Chau
Shek Kwu Chau
Lam
Macau
14
15
Siu A Chau
Soko Islands
Tai A Chau
Dazhi Zhou
Wailingding Dao
Dangan

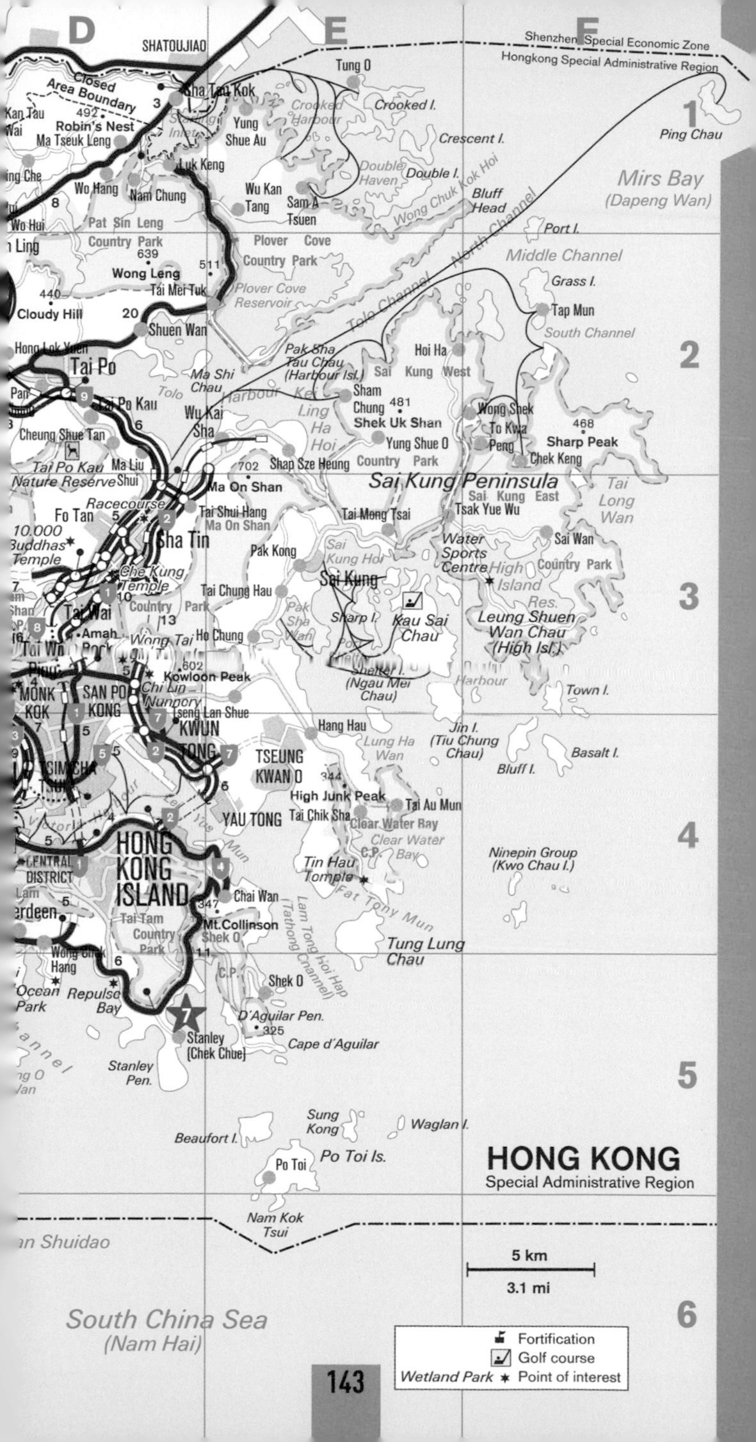

D
E
F
1
2
3
4
5
6
Shenzhen Special Economic Zone
Hongkong Special Administrative Region
SHATOUJIAO
Sha Tau Kok
Closed Area Boundary
Robin's Nest
Ma Tseuk Leng
Tung O
Crooked Harbour
Crooked I.
Yung Shue Au
Crescent I.
Ping Chau
Luk Keng
Wo Hang
Nam Chung
Wu Kan Tang
Sam A Tsuen
Double Haven
Double I.
Wong Chuk Kok Hoi
Bluff Head
Mirs Bay
(Dapeng Wan)
Pat Sin Leng
Country Park
Plover Cove
Country Park
Port I.
Middle Channel
North Channel
Wong Leng
Tai Mei Tuk
Plover Cove Reservoir
Grass I.
Tap Mun
Cloudy Hill
Shuen Wan
Tolo Channel
South Channel
Hong Lok Yuen
Tai Po
Ma Shi Chau
Tolo Harbour
Pak Sha Tau Chau
(Harbour Isl.)
Sai Kung West
Hoi Ha
Tai Po Kau
Wu Kai Sha
Kei Ling Ha Hoi
Sham Chung
Shek Uk Shan
Wong Shek
To Kwa Peng
Sharp Peak
Cheung Shue Tan
Yung Shue O
Chek Keng
Tai Po Kau Nature Reserve
Ma Liu Shui
Shap Sze Heung
Country Park
Ma On Shan
Sai Kung Peninsula
Tai Long Wan
Racecourse
Fo Tan
Tai Shui Hang
Ma On Shan
Sai Kung East
Tsak Yue Wu
Tai Mong Tsai
10.000 Buddhas Temple
Sha Tin
Pak Kong
Sai Kung Hoi
Water Sports Centre
Sai Wan
Country Park
High Island Res.
Che Kung Temple
Sai Kung
Tai Chung Hau
Country Park
Tai Wai
Pak Sha Wan
Sharp I.
Kau Sai Chau
Leung Shuen Wan Chau
(High Isl.)
Amah Rock
Wong Tai
Ho Chung
Kowloon Peak
Chi Lin Nunnery
Shelter I.
(Ngau Mei Chau)
Harbour
Town I.
MONK KOK
SAN PO KONG
Tseng Lan Shue
KWUN TONG
TSEUNG KWAN O
Hang Hau
Lung Ha Wan
Jin I.
(Tiu Chung Chau)
Basalt I.
Bluff I.
High Junk Peak
Tai Chik Sha
Tai Au Mun
YAU TONG
Clear Water Bay
Clear Water Bay
C.P.
HONG KONG ISLAND
CENTRAL DISTRICT
Lei Yue Mun
Ninepin Group
(Kwo Chau I.)
Tin Hau Temple
Fat Tong Mun
Chai Wan
Mt.Collinson
Tai Tam Country Park
Shek O
Lam Tong Hoi Hap
(Tathong Channel)
Tung Lung Chau
Hang
Ocean Park
Repulse Bay
C.P.
Shek O
D'Aguilar Pen.
Stanley
(Chek Chue)
Cape d'Aguilar
Stanley Pen.
Sung Kong
Waglan I.
Beaufort I.
Po Toi
Po Toi Is.
HONG KONG
Special Administrative Region
Nam Kok Tsui
5 km
3.1 mi
South China Sea
(Nam Hai)
Fortification
Golf course
Wetland Park
Point of interest

This index lists a selection of the streets and squares shown in the street atlas

A
B
C
1
2
3
4
5
6
Dong-
qiaocun
ZHUHAI
Chang-
shengwei
Estrada Marginal
Av. do Parque Industrial
Ilha Verde
Av. da Ilha Verde
Av. do Comendador
Av. do Cons
Rua Norte do Patane
Av. da Con-
Rua Cons. Borja
João Bele
Ivens F
Rua do Comandante
R. do Gen.
R. da Bacia
Praça das Orquídeas
Rua Sul do Patane
Nan-
shan
Avenida Marginal do Lam Mau
Avenida do
Santo
R. da Alegria
R. da Lin Kai
Estr.
Barca
Rua de Ribeira do Patane
R. da Palmeira
Luís de Camões Garden and Grotto
R. de Entre-Campos
Casa Garden
St. Anthony
R. de Coelho do Amaral
Repouso
R. do Tarrafeiro
Museum of Sacred Art
R. de T. Vieira
R. de Dom Belchior Carneiro
Na Tcha
R. da Ruins of St. Paul's
Hong Kung
Fortaleza do Monte
Calc. do Monte
St. Laz
Shijiaoju
Inner Harbour
R. do Visconde Paço de Arcos
R. das Lorchas
Av. de Almeida Ribeiro
Tercena
Sam Kai Vui Kun
St. Dominic
Na Cha
R. de Pedro Nolasco da Silva
Lou Kau Mansion
R. dos Mercadores
Senado Squ.
Holy House of Mercy
14
Cathedral
Rua do Campo
Huadi
Dom Pedro V Theatre
St. Augustine
St. Augustine's Squ.
Av. da Praia Grande
Central
Av. Infante D. Henrique
Casino Grand Lisboa
Rua do Almirante Sérgio
St. Joseph's Seminary
São Lourenço
St. Lazaro
Government Headquarters
Av. Dr. Mário Soares
Av. do
Av. Comercial de Macau
R. do Padre António
Mandarin's House
Lilau Squ.
R. da Penha
Travessa do Colégio
Rua da Barra
Ho
Stanley
Praça de F do Am
Cybernetic Fountain
Moorish Barracks
Calc. da Penha
Penha Hill
A-Ma
R. Comend. Kou Ho Neng
República
Nam Van Lake Nautical Centre
Av. Panorâmica do Lago
Maritime Museum
Nam Van Lake
Ponte Gov.
Santa Sancha
R. do Lago
Dr.
Av. Panorâmica do Lago Nam Van
Legislative Assembly Bldg.
Barra Hill
Estrada da Penha
Sai Van
The Court Bldg.
Avenida da
Sai Van Lake
Avenida
Sul de
R. Entre Lagos
Avenida Dr.
Ponte de Sai Van
Macau Tower
Convention and Entertainment Centre
Gate of Understanding

D
E
F
1
2
3
4
5
6
Border Checkpoint
Barrier Gate
Portas do Cerco
Avenida Norte do Hipódromo
Avenida da
Rua Central da Areia Preta
Nossa Senhora Fatima
St Joseph The Worker
Estr. Marginal do Hipódromo
Av. Leste do Hipódromo
R. Direita do Hipódromo
R. do Mercado
Rua de Iao Hon
Avenida da Longevidade
R. Oito do Bairro Iao Hon
R. dos Hortelãos
R. da Tranquilidade
Avenida 1. de Maio
Rua Nova do Canal Novo
Avenida do Nordeste
R. de Ma Kau Seak
da Areia Preta
1. de Maio
Ponte da Amizade
Pearl
Lin Zexu Mem. Mus.
Mong Ha Park
Mong-Ha Fort
Estr. Areia Preta
Av. de Venceslau Morais
Av. do M. Correia
Av. do Francisco Vieira Machado
Estr. Marginal da Areia Preta
Rampa dos Cavaleiros
Our Lady of Piety Cemetery
Montanha Russa Garden
Rua dos Pescadores
Kun Iam
Estrada de Dom Maria II
Museum of Communication
Estr. de Ferreira do Amaral
Ramal dos Mouros
Avenida da Amizade
Costa Cabral
Arriaga
Almeida
Mesquita
Silva Mendes
Sidónio Pais
Costa
Estr. do Reservatório
Reservoir
Cable Car
Flora Garden
Dr. Sun Yat Sen
Guia Tunnel
Municipal Park
Cacilhas
Rodrigues
Amizade
Grand Prix Stand
Estr. do Eng. Trigo
Guia Fort and Lighthouse
Rodrigo
Rua de Malaca
Avenida
Macau Ferry Terminal
Heliport
Estrada
Grand Prix Museum
Macau Forum
Golden Lotus Flower
Macau Palace Casino
Orient Arch
Dr.
Luís Gonzaga Gomes
Amizade
Av. Dr. Sun Yat Sen
Fisherman's Wharf
Outer Harbour
Alameda Dr. Carlos d'Assumpcao
R. de Xangai
Rua de Berlim
Av. do Governador Jaime Silvério Marques
Handover Gifts Museum
Av. Xian Xing Hai
Art Museum
Macau Cultural Centre
Av. Sir Anders Ljungstedt
24 de Junho
Sen
Yat
Grand
Kun Iam Statue
Macau Science Centre
Hong Kong
Macau
500 m
545 yd

A
B
C
1
2
3
4
5
6
Estrada Nordeste
University of Macau
R. de Choi Long
R. de Taipa
Tomas Pereira
Kun Iam Rock
Av. Padre
Estr. Alm. Marqu. Esparteiro
Av. do Oceano
Jardins do Oceano
Estr. de Sete Tanques
Av. dos Jogos
Estr. Sete Tanques
Taipa Pequena
Pou Tai Un Monastery
Rua dos Hortelãos
Av. Dr. Sun Yat Sen
Estr. Alm. Magalhaes Correia
Estr. da Ponta da Cabrita
Estrada
Taipa
Taipa Grand
R. do Minho
Av. de Kwong Tung
R. de Coimbra
R. de Seng Tu
Av. de Guimaraes
R. de Braganca
R. de Nam Keng
Four Faced Buddha
Cidade das Flores Garden
Estrada Governador Albano de Oliveira
Av. Olympica
Sam Po
Estr. Governador Nobre de Carvalho
Macau Jockey Club
Macau Olympic Complex
Macau Stadium
Ka Sin Tong
Carmo Square
Taipa Houses Museum
Our Lady of Carmel
Olympic Aquatic Centre
Pak Tai
Tin Hau
Museum of Taipa and Coloane History
Av. da Asia Oriental
Av. do Estadio
Avenida
Estr. da Baia de Nossa Senhora da Esperanca
Istmo
City of Dreams
Galaxy
The Venetian
15
Cotai
Sands Cotai
Avenida Marginal Flor de Lotus
Av. Cidade Nova
The Parisian
Avenida de Cotai
Studio City
Cotai Frontier Post
Ponte Flor-de-Lotus
Estr. Flor de Lotus
Estr. do Dique Oeste
ZHUHAI
Orient Golf Macau Club
Karting Track
Estrada
Reservoir
Estr. de Seac Pai Van
R. das arvores do Pagode
R. das Canforeiras
R. das Acacias Rubras
R. dos Zimbros
R. dos Bombaxes
Rua Marginal da Concordia
Seac Pai Van Park
Museum of Nature and Agriculture
Lai Chi Vun
Cushahuan
A-Má Go Statue
Macau Tin Hau
Estr. do Alto de Coloane
Estr. de Lai Chi Vun
R. de São Francisco Xavier
R. Entre Campos
Coloane Hill
Hengqinzhen
St. Francis Xavier
Coloane
Av. da República
R. do Estaleiro
Tam Kung
Tin Hau
Estrada de Cheoc Van
Nautical Club
Cheoc Van Swimming Pool
Cheoc Van Beach
R. Dois dos de Cheoc
Estrada da Aldeia

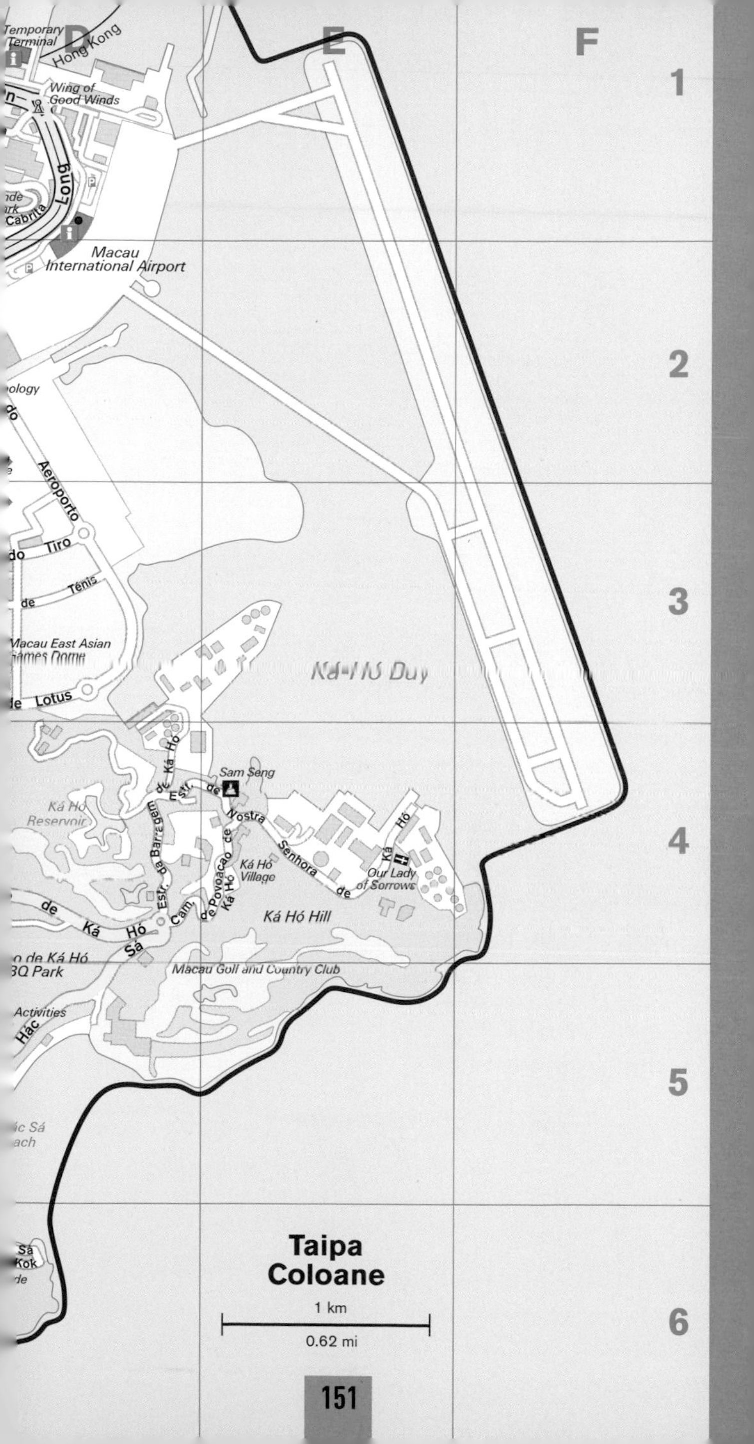
D
E
F
1
2
3
4
5
6
Temporary Terminal
Hong Kong
Wing of Good Winds
Long
Cabrita
Macau International Airport
Aeroporto
Tiro
Ténis
Macau East Asian
Lotus
Ká Hó
Sam Seng
Nostra
Senhora
Ká Hó Reservoir
Ká Hó Village
Our Lady of Sorrows
Ká Hó Hill
Estr. da Barragem de Ká Hó
Cam. de Povoação de Ká Hó
Macau Golf and Country Club
Activities
Taipa Coloane
1 km
0.62 mi

KEY TO STREET ATLAS

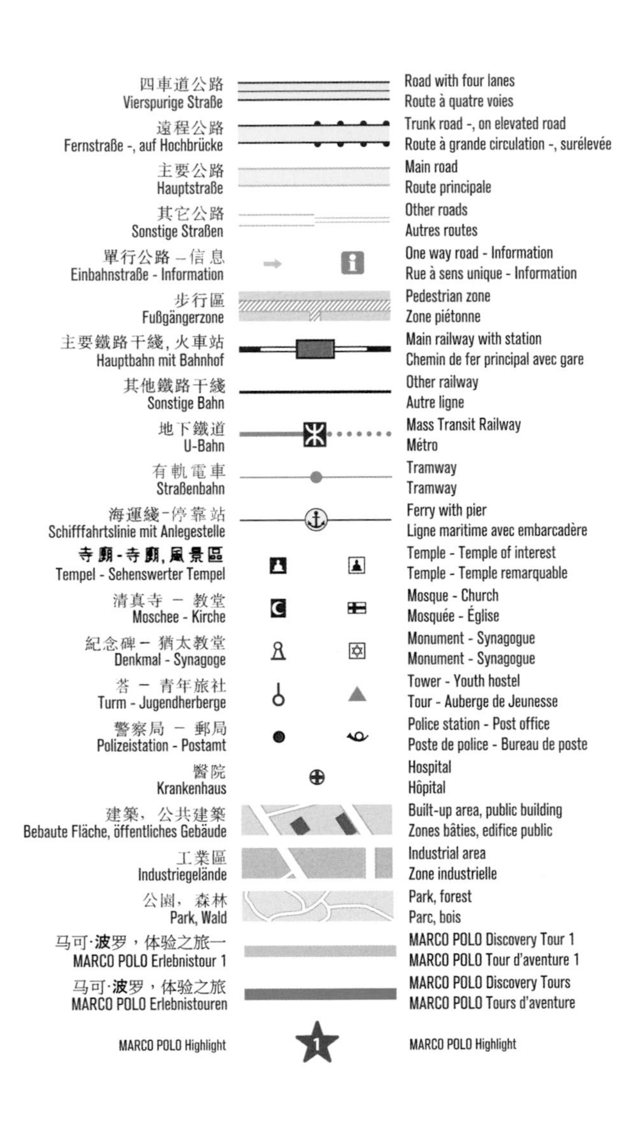
四車道公路
Vierspurige Straße
Road with four lanes
Route à quatre voies
遠程公路
Fernstraße -, auf Hochbrücke
Trunk road -, on elevated road
Route à grande circulation -, surélevée
主要公路
Hauptstraße
Main road
Route principale
其它公路
Sonstige Straßen
Other roads
Autres routes
單行公路 – 信息
Einbahnstraße - Information
One way road - Information
Rue à sens unique - Information
步行區
Fußgängerzone
Pedestrian zone
Zone piétonne
主要鐵路干綫, 火車站
Hauptbahn mit Bahnhof
Main railway with station
Chemin de fer principal avec gare
其他鐵路干綫
Sonstige Bahn
Other railway
Autre ligne
地下鐵道
U-Bahn
Mass Transit Railway
Métro
有軌電車
Straßenbahn
Tramway
Tramway
海運綫-停靠站
Schifffahrtslinie mit Anlegestelle
Ferry with pier
Ligne maritime avec embarcadère
寺廟-寺廟, 風景區
Tempel - Sehenswerter Tempel
Temple - Temple of interest
Temple - Temple remarquable
清真寺 – 教堂
Moschee - Kirche
Mosque - Church
Mosquée - Église
紀念碑 – 猶太教堂
Denkmal - Synagoge
Monument - Synagogue
Monument - Synagogue
荅 – 青年旅社
Turm - Jugendherberge
Tower - Youth hostel
Tour - Auberge de Jeunesse
警察局 – 郵局
Polizeistation - Postamt
Police station - Post office
Poste de police - Bureau de poste
醫院
Krankenhaus
Hospital
Hôpital
建築, 公共建築
Bebaute Fläche, öffentliches Gebäude
Built-up area, public building
Zones bâties, edifice public
工業區
Industriegelände
Industrial area
Zone industrielle
公園, 森林
Park, Wald
Park, forest
Parc, bois
马可·波罗，体验之旅一
MARCO POLO Erlebnistour 1
MARCO POLO Discovery Tour 1
MARCO POLO Tour d'aventure 1
马可·波罗，体验之旅
MARCO POLO Erlebnistouren
MARCO POLO Discovery Tours
MARCO POLO Tours d'aventure
MARCO POLO Highlight
1
MARCO POLO Highlight

FOR YOUR NEXT TRIP...

MARCO POLO TRAVEL GUIDES

Algarve
Amsterdam
Andalucia
Athens
Australia
Austria
Bali & Lombok
Bangkok
Barcelona
Berlin
Brazil
Bruges
Brussels
Budapest
Bulgaria
California
Cambodia
Canada East
Canada West / Rockies & Vancouver
Cape Town & Garden Route
Cape Verde
Channel Islands
Chicago & The Lakes
China
Cologne
Copenhagen
Corfu
Costa Blanca & Valencia
Costa Brava
Costa del Sol & Granada
Crete
Cuba
Cyprus (North and South)
Devon & Cornwall
Dresden
Dubai
Dublin
Dubrovnik & Dalmatian Coast
Edinburgh
Egypt
Egypt Red Sea Resorts
Finland
Florence
Florida
French Atlantic Coast
French Riviera (Nice, Cannes & Monaco)
Fuerteventura
Gran Canaria
Greece
Hamburg
Hong Kong & Macau
Iceland
India
India South
Ireland
Israel
Istanbul
Italy
Japan
Jordan
Kos
Krakow
Lake Garda
Lanzarote
Las Vegas
Lisbon
London
Los Angeles
Madeira & Porto Santo
Madrid
Mallorca
Malta & Gozo
Mauritius
Menorca
Milan
Montenegro
Morocco
Munich
Naples & Amalfi Coast
New York
New Zealand
Norway
Oslo
Oxford
Paris
Peru & Bolivia
Phuket
Portugal
Prague
Rhodes
Rome
Salzburg
San Francisco
Santorini
Sardinia
Scotland
Seychelles
Shanghai
Sicily
Singapore
South Africa
Sri Lanka
Stockholm
Switzerland
Tenerife
Thailand
Turkey
Turkey South Coast
Tuscany
United Arab Emirates
USA Southwest (Las Vegas, Colorado, New Mexico, Arizona & Utah)
Venice
Vienna
Vietnam
Zakynthos & Ithaca, Kefalonia, Lefkas

INDEX

This index lists all sights, museums, and destinations in this guide. Numbers in bold indicate a main entry. Destinations in Macau are marked (MA).

WRITE TO US

e-mail: info@marcopologuides.co.uk

Did you have a great holiday?
Is there something on your mind?
Whatever it is, let us know!
Whether you want to praise, alert us to errors or give us a personal tip – MARCO POLO would be pleased to hear from you.
We do everything we can to provide the very latest information for your trip.

Nevertheless, despite all of our authors' thorough research, errors can creep in. MARCO POLO does not accept any liability for this. Please contact us by e-mail or post.

MARCO POLO Travel Publishing Ltd
Pinewood, Chineham Business Park
Crockford Lane, Chineham
Basingstoke, Hampshire RG24 8AL
United Kingdom

PICTURE CREDITS
Cover photo: Nathan Road, tram and buses (Look/Nordic Photos)
Photos: DuMont Bildarchiv: Riehle (114); R. Freyer (11, 30, 32, 36, 38, 53, 100/101, 102, 112, 117), T. Hallnei (4 top, 26/27, 44, 46); huber-images: Cozzi (8, 14/15), Eisele-Hein (7), Gräfenhain (flap right, 12/13, 130/131), J. Lawrence (2); Laif: Celentano (60 left), Riehle (112/113); Look/Nordic Photos (1); mauritius images: Vidler (flap left), S. Vidler (20/21, 40, 66, 114/115), J. Waarburton-Lee (18 bottom); mauritius images/age (61); mauritius images/age fotostock: L. Vallecillos (110); mauritius images/Alamy (3, 4 bottom, 6, 9, 17, 19 bottom, 34, 42, 48, 54/55, 56, 59, 60 right, 63, 64/65, 71, 88/89, 93, 97, 116 top, 116 bottom), S. Hamblin (18 top), P. Horree (24), P. Jonsson (108), L. Lilac (78), S. Vidler (76); mauritius images/Alamy/ Zoonar AG (115); mauritius images/Alamy/Osb70 (85); mauritius images/Alamy/robertharding (22/23); mauritius images/Alamy/RosalreneBetancourt 3 (69); mauritius images/imagebroker: Tack (10, 80/81, 82); Mountain Yam: Timothy Leung (18 centre); C. Nowak (105, 107, 113); Para/Site Art Space: Joo Choon-Lin (19 top); T. Stankiewicz (51); White Star: M. Gumm (5, 74/75)

2nd Edition 2018 – fully revised and updated
Worldwide Distribution: Marco Polo Travel Publishing Ltd, Pinewood, Chineham Business Park, Crockford Lane, Basingstoke, Hampshire RG24 8AL, United Kingdom. Email: sales@marcopolouk.com

Chief editor: Marion Zorn
Author: Dr. Hans-Wilm Schütte; editor: Franziska Kahl
Programme supervision: Stephan Dürr, Lucas Forst-Gill, Susanne Heimburger, Nikolai Michaelis, Martin Silbermann, Kristin Wittemann; Picture editor: Gabriele Forst; What's hot: Dr. Hans-Wilm Schütte; wunder media, Munich
Cartography street atlas & pull-out map: © MAIRDUMONT, Ostfildern
Design cover, p. 1, cover pull-out map: Karl Anders – Büro für Visual Stories, Hamburg; interior design: milchhof:atelier, Berlin; p. 2/3, Discovery Tours: Susan Chaaban Dipl.-Des. (FH)
Translated from German by Robert Scott McInnes; Susan Jones
Prepress: writehouse, Cologne; Intermedia, Ratingen
Phrase book: Dr. Hans-Wilm Schütte, in cooperation with Ernst Klett Sprachen GmbH, Stuttgart, Editorial by Pons Wörterbücher

Printed in China

DOS & DON'TS 

A few things you should bear in mind in Hong Kong

DO BE CAREFUL BUYING ELECTRONIC EQUIPMENT

You want to buy a camera, compare prices and then decide on the really special deal only to notice later that the guarantee is just valid in Hong Kong or that, instead of the quality lens, a cheaper one was palmed off on you. The best thing is not to even consider buying goods that seem amazingly cheap. Nobody sells anything below cost. Being sceptical is not enough because it is very difficult to see through the tricks a dealer works with. That is also why you should never do your expensive shopping on the last day in Hong Kong.

DON'T GO ON A ONE-DAY TRIP ACROSS THE BORDER

Short trips across the border to Shenzhen, Canton and Macau are usually more stress than pleasure. There is no relation between the result and the costs and effort involved. Canton is definitely worth a visit but only if you stay for at least one night. This also applies to Macau; it is often underestimated as a destination but you will need longer than just the normal day trip if you really want to soak up the atmosphere.

DON'T FOLLOW TOUTS

This only applies to men, especially if they are alone. Ladies stand outside dubious bars in Wan Chai on the lookout for clients. A poster promises cheap beer. And the beer actually is cheap; but the short chat with the scantily clad barmaid, or the drink for the hostess who sits down at your table, is much more expensive and can put quite a dent in your budget. And, protesting won't help. There is always a price list hanging in an out-of-the-way place and the fleeced man has to cough up.

DO USE THE SLOWER FERRIES

The fast ferries to Cheung Chau and Mui Wo are perfect for commuters but completely unattractive for tourists. They don't have a sundeck and are expensive. You can't even really look out of the windows. If at all possible, take one of the big, old, slow ferries. That way, you will be able to take in the photogenic panorama of Hong Kong from the open top deck at the stern.

DON'T GO ON EXCURSIONS AT WEEKENDS

If the weather is fine, half of Hong Kong pours into any available means of transport on Saturday afternoon and heads for the great outdoors. If you do the same, you will have to queue up wherever you go, will probably have just as little space at the beach as in town, and have to pay expensive weekend surcharges. Take a walk in the parks on Hong Kong Island instead. The same applies to trips to Macau and then you will even have the additional problem of getting back on Sunday evening.